Women Who Can Dish It Out

Acknowledgements & Index

JLS Committee List

1 9 9 3 - 1 9 9 7

Women Who Can Dish It Out was truly created from a labor of love. After countless hours and great determination, we now see the outcome of our efforts. This book, however, is not the final product of our work but rather the means to the end. The final product will be the help given to the Springfield community as a result of the sales proceeds from this book.

With more than 1.5 million dollars and one million hours of service already donated to charitable causes by the Junior League of Springfield, Missouri, we thank you for your additional support. We hope to see the true rewards of our efforts for many years to come.

1996-97 Healthy Cookbook

Chair - Judith Payton*
Assistant Chair - Sue McCoy*
Sustaining Advisor - Nancy Southworth
Committee Members:
Susy Barr
Sandy Buckner
Sherry Bureman
Lisa Clary
Sherry Cook*
Martha Gaither
Liz Godwin*
CeCe Haden
Janie Harris
Nila Hayes*
Jill Headley
Leslie Heard
Ginger Jones
Karen Lang Johnson
Kathy McWilliams
Darla Morrison
Cynthia Nixon
Bev Roberts
Karen Shannon*
Crista Shuler*
Kathy Smith
Tina Stillwell
Lisa Tanner
Ann Vincel
Anita Young

* Ad Hoc Marketing Committee

1995-96 Healthy Cookbook

Chair - Susy Barr
Assistant Chair - Judith Payton
Sustaining Advisor - Susan Mihalevich
Committee Members:
Neva Belkham-Gomez
Sandy Buckner
Emily Fox
Sherry Grillot
CeCe Haden
Kim Heard
Leslie Heard
Ginger Jones
Abby Kropp
Kathy Kruse-Reecht
Molly Ledger
Sue McCoy
Cynthia Nixon
Dianna Parker
Angela Priest
Jill Reynolds
Bev Roberts
Kristin Schneider
Yoko Shimoda-Williams
Nancy Southworth
Tina Stillwell
Jill Struttman
Ann Vincel

1994-95 Healthy Cookbook

Chair - Tina Stillwell
Assistant Chair - Susy Barr
Sustaining Advisor - Susan Mihalevich
Committee Members:
Joni Bishop
Lisa Clary
Michelle Clifton
Penni Crumpley
Debbie Edwards
Cathy Fredrick
Margaret Grubb
Ginger Jones
Sue McCoy
Stacy Mummert
Kathy Nunn
Donna Smith
April Vincel
Charlene Whitlock
Wendy Wright

1993-1994 Ad Hoc Committee

Chair - Lisa Clary
Penni Crumpley
Cindy Kendall
Susan Mihalevich
April Vincel
Charlene Whitlock

JLS Membership List

Kim Acuff
Pat Adams
Jennifer Ailor
Elaine Alford
Janet Altiery
Janet Anderson
Susan Armstrong
Margie Arnold
Hava Ashkenasi
Debbie Atkinson
Beverly Aton
Nancy Aton
Becky Bach
Nancy Back
Connie Bagby
Paula Baird
Ann Marie Baker
Holly Baker
Jo Baker
Jenny Baldwin
Susan Baldwin
Suzanne Ball
Cheryl Banister
Margaret Banta
Jan Barclay
Joni Barcomb
Susy Barr
Paula Bart
Harriet Bates
Mary S. Bauer
Jan M. Baumgartner
JoNell C. Beall
Barbara Becker
Carla Beezley
Susan J. Beine
Neva Belkham-Gomez
Bonnie Bell
Karen Bell
Holly Benedict
Cynthia Bennett
Roseann Bentley
Cynthia Bernskoetter
Debbie Edwards Bingham

Joni Bishop
Joyce T. Blades
Roseann Blunt
Kerry Bodenhausen
Kristy Bowenschulte
Shanna Boyle
Anise Brasher
Nancy Breaux
RoAnne Brell
Judy Brierly
Nancy Broaddus
Sherry Brock
Patty Brooks
Linda Broshears
Gloria Brown
Monica Browne
Patty Bruer
Pammie Bryce
Rochelle Buckner
Sandy Buckner
Marilyn Bueker
Andee Bullock
Karen Bult
Sherry Bureman
Lynn Burk
Shelly Burri
Elizabeth Burton
Cyndi M. Bussen
Jill M. Campbell
Emily Canlas
Debbie Cantwell
Nancy Caplinger
Marie Carmichael
Susan A. Carnahan
Peg Carolla
Brenda Carrell
Julie Carter
Shara Cash
Carla A. Cates
Phyl Chalender
Nancy Chalfant
Caryl Chaney
Carol Chappell

Kay Charles
Tami Cheek
Sue Ann Childers
Alexis Childs
Kathy Christy
Jerry E. Clark
Lisa Clary
Marty Close
Kaye Clothiaux
Meon Cloud
Linda Clouse
Cyndy Cobb
Barbara A. Collins
Bernie Compton
Virginia Compton
Deborah Comstock
Elaine M. Cook
Maralee Cook
Paula Cook
Rosalie Cook
Sherry Cook
Cynthia Cooper-Hollander
Rebecca Corson
Valerie Corwin
Angela Cotner
Jennifer Cotner
Mary Coulter
Saundra Covey
Anne Craigmyle
Donalda Crane
Mary Craven
Marilyn K. Creek
Andrea Croley
Penni Crumpley
Cynthia Cunningham
Helen J. Curtis
Virginia Dailey
Sue Dalton
Barbie Davis
Janette M. DeGood
Jill Denton
Linda Dickinson
Jennifer Dixson

Cara Domann
Joretta Lynn Donald
Judy Doran
Barbara Dorr
Rebecca Dowler
Rona Downs
Kathryn Driscoll
Kimberly Ann Dunaway
Sheri Duncan
Patti Dwyer
Linda Eccher
LaShae A. Eck
Susie Edel
Jeanna Edwards
Judy Eiffert
Janet Ellison
Voncille Elmer
Gina Engleman
Diane Etheridge
Kathy Evans
Sarah Evans
Julie Evenson
Sandra Everett
Leslie Fankhauser
Elizabeth Farris
Nancy Farthing
Sharon S. Faulkner
Carolyn Fay
Kathy Fer
Nancy Ferguson
Lindy Fielder
Jackie Findley
Kristie Fischer
Jan Fisk
Georgeanne Folkins
Susie Forsythe
Lisa Fortner
Mary Lou Foss
Linda Fowler
Emily Fox
Bev Francis
Marge Francis
Cynthia Frank

Mary Kay Frazier
Cathy Fredrick
Anna Freeman
Susan Froelich
Mary Quinn Fry
Tammy Fulk
Martha Gaither
Mary Gallagher
Diana Galli
Raylene Galloway
Susan Gamber
Ruth Gammon
Kris Garcia
Stacy Garner
Stephanie Garrison
Martha Gaska
Lisa Geier
Susan H. Gelner
Audrey Gentry
Susan Gentry
Donna J. Gibson
Susan Gilkerson
Billie Gillespie
Linda Gipson
Liz Godwin
Stacey Gold
Betty Golik
Janet Tracy Gore
Jennifer Gourley
Ann Grace
Nancy Graff
Paula Green
Cindy Gregston
Sherry Grillot
Sherri Grove
Margaret Grubb
Evelyn H'Doubler
Carol Ann Haake
Teri L. Hacker
CeCe Haden
Mary Martha Hagale
Lee Haik
Lisa Hains

Annette E. Hall
Barbara J. Hall
Melissa Hall
Robin Hall
Beth Halsell
Carla Halverson
Lu Ann Hancock
Sally Hargis
Jean Harmison
Darla Harmon
Judy Harrill
Janie Harris
Kim Harrison
Carolyn Hart
Elena Hastings
Ann Hawkins
Nila Hayes
Jill Headley
Kimberly Heard
Leslie Heard
Liz Hedges
Cindy Heider
Susie Henry
Mary Ann Herfkens
Victoria Herman
Ann Hicks
Helen Hills
Nancy S. Hoeman
Paula Hoffman
Becky Hogan
Nikki Holden
Susie Holliday
Carla Holloway
Elizabeth Hopkins
Jan Horton
Jane J. Horton
Robyn Horton
Myra Houge
Dee Houser
Barbara A. Hover
Denise Howard
Sandy Howard
Debbie Howell

Trellis C. Howell
Janet Hudson
Jacque Huff
Mary Jane Huning
Jana Hutchens
Jeanette Hutcheson
Mary A. Hutton
Heather Ince
Beverly Roberts Jackson
Ellen Jackson
Kim Jacobi
Terri James
Kathy Jester
Connie L. Jobe
Celeste Johns
Abby Johnson
Jane Johnson
Judy C. Johnson
Karen Lang Johnson
Laura J. Johnson
Marcia Sublett Johnson
Marcia Williams Johnson
Michelle Johnson
Eileen Jones
Ginger Jones
Hannah Jones
Jana Jones
Kathy Jones
Marianne Jones
Vicky Jones
Rita Joyner
Jo Ann Junge
Marci Justice
Kimberly Karnes
Beverly Kelley
Gail Kelling
Marie E. Kelly
Judy Kennedy
Nancy Kessler
Laura Kinne
Rhonda King
Lesa M. Kinney
Elizabeth S. Kinser

Barbara Kipfer
Sharan Klingner
Nancy Knauer
Sara Knauer
Ann Koppers
Karen E. Kramer
Sherrie Kratz
Abby Kropp
Kathy Kruse-Reecht
Dana Kuntz
Randy LaFerriere
Patti Langston
Jeanne Lasley
Molly Ledger
Lynne Lee
Marguerite Lee
Suzanne Lennard
Judith Lenzini
Rosemary Lewis
Terri Libel
Felicia Liebman
Peggy C. Lindsey
Cathy B. Lindstrom
Julia Linn
Kitty Lipscomb
Tracy L. Lipscomb
Julia Lister
Brenda R. Logsdon
Pat Lohmeyer
Sharon Long
Kathy Loomer
Robin Looney
Buffy Lovett
Lyndsay Lowe
Melissa Lowe
Ann Ludeke
Barbie Lyons
Beverly Mace
Melissa K. Mace
Fredna Mahaffey
Jennifer G. Mahaffey
Virginia Maher
Suzy Major

Evelyn Mangan
Brigitte Marrs
Mary Martin
Tara Martz
Becky Mathenia
Lori Matthews
Barbara Mauck
Michelle Maxfield
Sheila Ann Mayse
Michelle Maxfield
Linda R. McAllister
Mona McCann
Barb McCarty
Joanne McCluer
Sue McCoy
Darlene McCracken
Vicki McCurry
Janice McDonald
Jane McElvaine
Cindy McGinnis
Cinda McKenzie
Jane McKinney
Susan McNeal
Kathryn McPhail
Mary H. McQueary
Kathy McWilliams
Morey Mechlin
Mary Kay Meek
Susan Melton
Spencer Meyer
Susan Mihalevich
Jan Millington
Susan Milne
Karen S. Mitchell
Faith Moeller
Pauline Moeller
Connie Montgomery
Melissa Montgomery
Vanessa Montileone
Patti Moore
Kathy J. Morelock
Marcia Morgan
Darla Morrison

Women Who Can Dish It Out

The Lighter Side Of the Ozarks

The Junior League of
Springfield, Missouri, Inc.

The Junior League of Springfield is an organization committed to promoting volunteerism and to improving the welfare of children and older adults, women and families, education, the environment, the arts, health issues and victims of abuse and violence.

Proceeds from the sale of this book shall be returned to the community through projects approved or sponsored by the Junior League of Springfield, Missouri, Inc.

To order additional copies of
Women Who Can Dish It Out,
The Lighter Side Of The Ozarks,
fill out the order form provided
in the back of the book.

First Printing: 15,000 copies, May 1997

Library of Congress Catalog Number: 97-70486
ISBN: 0-9613307-5-9
UPC Number: 051 5332 1217

Concept & Copywriting: Melissa Burnett
Art Directors: Matt Graif & Matthew Rose
Illustration: Matt Graif
Editors: Rhonda Glaser & Marilyn Glaser

Contents printed

on recycled paper

Printed in the USA by
WIMMER
The Wimmer Companies, Inc.
Memphis

We're dishing it out again with the perfect complement to our successful cookbook, *Sassafras! The Ozarks Cookbook*.

Women Who Can Dish It Out says it all, as the women of The Junior League of Springfield, Missouri, are doing just that. Dishing up deliciously-light recipes while dishing out age-old myths about Ozarks' foods and lifestyles. For instance, no matter what you might have heard, a seven-course meal in the Ozarks does not consist of a pork fritter and a six-pack.

Let our comical retort about exaggerated stereotypes of unrefined etiquette and dietary habits enlighten and entertain you while our great tasting recipes tempt you. The fact is, healthy recipes can taste sinful. And Ozarkians do not believe that pie a la mode is best when served with ice cream.

This is truly a unique book. Our novel approach to Ozarks' humor and whimsical illustrations makes for easy reading. Eight great sections feature more than 300 triple-tested recipes, and helpful nutritional information is provided for each.

So if you're expecting hog jowls and red-eye gravy from this book, go ahead–we dare you to look further. Because from here on, it's your turn to dish it out.

Table of Contents

BREADS & BRUNCH

Myth No. 23:
"People from the Ozarks wear belts with their names on the back."

Fact:
"While this can prove an effective way to identify guests, the Junior League of Springfield suggests placing name cards at the table."

BREADS

BRUNCH

Cool-Rise French Bread

Prep Time: 30 minutes
Cooking Time: 25 minutes

- 6 cups flour
- 2 Tablespoons sugar
- 1 Tablespoon salt
- 2 packages dry yeast (2 Tablespoons)
- 3 Tablespoons margarine, softened
- 2 1/4 cups hot water (120-130 degrees)
- 1 teaspoon vegetable oil
- 2 Tablespoons cornmeal
- 1 egg white
- 1 Tablespoon cold water

Preheat oven to 450 degrees. In a large mixing bowl, thoroughly combine 2 cups flour, sugar, salt and yeast. Add softened margarine and gradually add hot water. Beat at medium speed of an electric mixer equipped with dough hooks for 2 minutes. Stir in more flour to make soft dough. Turn onto lightly-floured surface and knead 10 minutes. Cover and let rest for 20 minutes. Punch dough and divide into halves. Shape each portion into a 10 x 15-inch rectangle. Beginning at a long side, roll up tightly, pinching edges to seal. Taper ends by rolling loaf back and forth. Sprinkle cornmeal over a large baking sheet greased with vegetable oil and place loaves on the sheet. Cover loosely with plastic wrap and refrigerate 2 to 24 hours. When ready to bake, remove from refrigerator and let sit at room temperature for 10 minutes. Puncture any air bubbles with a greased toothpick. Make four diagonal cuts along the top of the loaves with a sharp knife. Bake for 20-25 minutes. Remove from oven and brush with egg white and cold water. Bake 5 minutes longer. Makes 2 loaves. Serves 32. Serving size: 1 (1-inch) slice

Amount Per Serving:

Calories 103	Saturated Fat 0 g	Sodium 216 mg
Total Fat 1 g	Cholesterol 0 mg	

Ozark Wheat Bread

- 3 3/4 cups all-purpose flour
- 1 cup whole wheat flour
- 1/2 cup oat bran
- 2 teaspoons salt
- 1 package yeast (1 Tablespoon)

- 1 cup skim milk
- 1 cup water
- 3 Tablespoons reduced calorie margarine
- 2 Tablespoons white cornmeal

In a large mixing bowl, combine 1 1/2 cups all-purpose flour, whole wheat flour, oat bran, salt and yeast. Set aside. In a 4-cup measuring cup, combine milk, water and margarine. Microwave on high for 2 minutes. Pour over flour mixture. Beat mixture at medium speed with an electric mixer equipped with dough hooks for 2 minutes. Gradually stir in 2 cups of all-purpose flour. Turn dough onto a lightly-floured surface. If dough is sticky, knead in remaining 1/4 cup of flour. Cover dough with a large bowl. Let stand for 10 minutes. Coat 2 (8 1/2 x 4 1/2 x 3-inch) pans with non-stick cooking spray and sprinkle with cornmeal. Divide dough and place in pans. Cover pans and let dough rise in a warm place for 1 hour or until doubled in bulk. Preheat oven to 400 degrees. Bake for 25 minutes. Remove loaves from pans and cool on a wire rack. Makes 2 loaves. Serves 34.
Serving size: 1 (3/4-inch) slice

Amount Per Serving:

Calories 74	Saturated Fat 0 g	Sodium 143 mg
Total Fat 1 g	Cholesterol 0 mg	

Buttermilk Cheese Bread
(Recipe for use with bread maker.)

- 1 package dry yeast (1 Tablespoon)
- 3 cups flour
- 1 teaspoon baking powder
- 1 teaspoon salt

- 1 Tablespoon sugar
- 1 cup buttermilk (at room temperature)
- 1/4 cup warm water
- 1 cup extra-sharp cheddar cheese,grated

Pour all ingredients into bread maker in order listed. Bake on white bread setting. Makes 1 loaf. Serves 16. Serving size: 1 slice

Amount Per Serving:

Calories 106	Saturated Fat 0 g	Sodium 231 mg
Total Fat 0 g	Cholesterol 2 mg	

Cheese Bread

- 1 pint fat-free mayonnaise
- 8 ounces fat-free cheddar cheese, grated
- 1/4 cup green onion, chopped
- 1/8 teaspoon garlic powder
- 1/4 teaspoon dill (optional)
- 1/4 teaspoon oregano (optional)
- 1/4 teaspoon parsley (optional)
- 1 loaf French bread

Preheat oven to 350 degrees. Mix together mayonnaise, cheddar cheese, green onion, garlic powder, dill, oregano and parsley. Spread over French bread slices. Bake about 20 minutes until bubbly. Serves 16. Serving size: 1 (1-inch) slice

Amount Per Serving:

Calories 45	Saturated Fat 0 g	Sodium 481 mg
Total Fat 0 g	Cholesterol 3 mg	

Lemon Loaf

- 1/2 cup sugar
- 1/4 cup margarine
- peel of 1 lemon, grated
- 1 cup whole wheat flour
- 1 cup all-purpose flour
- 1/4 teaspoon salt
- 2 teaspoons baking powder

- 1 teaspoon baking soda
- 1/4 cup lemon juice
- 3/4 cup buttermilk
- 1/3 cup walnuts, chopped
- 2 Tablespoons lemon juice
- 3 Tablespoons sugar

Preheat oven to 375 degrees. Cream 1/2 cup sugar and margarine. Add grated lemon peel and mix until smooth. Mix together flours, salt, baking powder and soda; set aside. Mix buttermilk and 1/4 cup lemon juice and set aside. Add flour mixture to creamed mixture alternately with buttermilk mixture. Do not over mix. Stir in walnuts. Pour into a loaf pan coated with non-stick cooking spray. Bake for 30 to 45 minutes. In a small saucepan, combine 2 Tablespoons lemon juice with remaining sugar. Stir over low heat until sugar dissolves. Pierce top of loaf with fork. Spoon lemon sugar mixture over top. Let cool for slicing. Serves 10. Serving size: 1 slice

Amount Per Serving;

Calories 212	Saturated Fat 1 g	Sodium 342 mg
Total Fat 7 g	Cholesterol 1 mg	

Blueberry-Lemon Bread

- 3/4 cup sugar
- 2 Tablespoons margarine
- 1/2 cup plain fat-free yogurt
- 1/2 cup egg substitute
- 1 teaspoon lemon juice
- 2 cups flour

- 1 Tablespoon baking powder
- 1/4 teaspoon baking soda
- 1/4 teaspoon salt
- 3/4 cup skim milk
- 1 cup blueberries
- 4 teaspoons lemon peel, finely shredded

Preheat oven to 350 degrees. Cream sugar and margarine. Mix in yogurt, egg substitute and lemon juice. Add flour, baking powder, baking soda and salt. Add milk and mix until just combined. Fold in blueberries and lemon peel. Pour into a loaf pan coated with non-stick cooking spray. Bake for 40-45 minutes. Serves 16. Serving size: 1 slice

Amount Per Serving:

Calories 126	Saturated Fat 0 g	Sodium 173 mg
Total Fat 2 g	Cholesterol 0 g	

Contributed by St. John's Nutrition Center, Springfield, Missouri.

Pineapple-Carrot Bread

Prep Time: 20 minutes
Cooking Time: 60 minutes

- 3 cups flour, sifted
- 1 teaspoon baking soda
- 1 teaspoon salt
- 1 teaspoon cinnamon
- 3/4 cup egg substitute
- 3 cups sugar
- 1 cup vegetable oil
- 2 cups carrots, finely grated
- 1 (9-ounce) can crushed pineapple, drained
- 2 teaspoons vanilla

Preheat oven to 350 degrees. In a large mixing bowl, sift flour, baking soda, salt and cinnamon together. Add egg substitute and sugar. Beat at medium speed of electric mixer until well blended. Beat in oil, a small amount at a time. Stir into flour mixture, carrots, pineapple and vanilla. Place in 2 loaf pans coated with non-stick cooking spray. Bake 60 minutes. Makes 2 loaves. Serves 36. Serving size: 1 slice

Amount Per Serving:

Calories 169	Saturated Fat 1 g	Sodium 108 mg
Total Fat 6 g	Cholesterol 0 mg	

8

Pineapple Crunch Bread

Batter:

- 2 1/4 cups flour
- 2 teaspoons baking powder
- 1 teaspoon baking soda
- 1/2 cup brown sugar
- 3 egg whites
- 2 Tablespoons canola oil
- 1 teaspoon vanilla
- 1 (8-ounce) can unsweetened crushed pineapple, undrained
- 1/4 cup skim milk

Topping:

- 2 Tablespoons brown sugar
- 2 Tablespoons flour
- 1 teaspoon cinnamon
- 1 Tablespoon canola margarine

Preheat oven to 375 degrees. Coat a loaf pan with non-stick cooking spray. In a large bowl, thoroughly mix flour, baking powder, baking soda and brown sugar. In a medium bowl, beat egg whites until frothy. Mix in oil, vanilla, pineapple and milk. Combine wet and dry ingredients. Stir until completely moist. Do not overstir. To make topping, mix together brown sugar, flour and cinnamon. Cut in margarine with pastry cutter or fork until mixture forms crumbs. Spoon batter into prepared loaf pan. Sprinkle topping evenly over top and press very lightly into batter. Bake 45-50 minutes or until top is brown and firm. Cool 5 minutes. Remove from pan. Cool on rack 10-15 minutes before slicing. Serves 12. Serving Size: 1 (3/4-inch) slice

Amount Per Serving:

Calories 178	Saturated Fat 0 g	Sodium 138 mg
Total Fat 4 g	Cholesterol 0 mg	

Myth No. 5:

"The pastry of choice in the Ozarks is the pop tart.
Frosted of course."

Sweet Potato Rolls

- 2 packages dry yeast (2 Tablespoons)
- 1 1/2 cups warm water (105-115 degrees)
- 3 cups whole wheat flour
- 3 cups all-purpose flour
- 1/3 cup brown sugar

- 1 1/4 teaspoons salt
- 1/4 cup fat-free plain yogurt
- 4 Tablespoons extra-light margarine
- 1/2 cup egg substitute
- 1 (16-ounce) can cut sweet potatoes, drained

Combine yeast and water in a food processor or blender. Process for 30 seconds. Let stand for 5 minutes. In a large bowl, combine flours. Add 1 cup of flour mixture, brown sugar, salt, yogurt, margarine, egg substitute and sweet potatoes to yeast mixture. Process until smooth. Stir yeast mixture into remaining flour mixture. Knead dough 5 minutes. Place in bowl coated with non-stick cooking spray. Cover and let rise until doubled. Punch dough down and divide in half. Roll each half into a 16-inch circle and cut each into 16 wedges. Roll up wedges. Place on a baking sheet coated with non-stick cooking spray. Cover and let rise until doubled. Bake at 350 degrees for 15 minutes. Serves 32. Serving size: 1 roll

Amount Per Serving:

Calories 115	Saturated Fat 0 g	Sodium 101 mg
Total Fat 1 g	Cholesterol 0 mg	

Branberry Muffins

- 3/4 cup bran
- 3/4 cup whole wheat flour
- 1/2 cup quick oats
- 3/4 cup dark brown sugar
- 1/2 teaspoon salt
- 1 teaspoon baking soda
- 1/4 teaspoon nutmeg
- 1 cup blueberries, fresh or frozen
  grated zest of 1 lemon, grated

- 1/2 cup raisins (optional)
- 1/4 cup vegetable oil
- 2/3 cup yogurt
- 1/4 cup egg substitute
- 1/4 teaspoon rum extract or
  1/2 teaspoon rum

Preheat oven to 400 degrees. In a large bowl, combine bran, flour, oats, brown sugar, salt, baking soda and nutmeg. Be sure to break up brown sugar with a fork. Add berries, lemon zest and raisins. In a small bowl, whisk together oil, yogurt, egg substitute and rum. Combine this mixture with the flour and fruit mixture. Mix well. Do not overbeat. Coat muffin cups with non-stick cooking spray and fill about 3/4 full with mixture. Place on a cookie sheet and bake 25 minutes or until edges begin to brown. Serves 12. Serving size: 1 muffin

Amount Per Serving:

Calories 180	Saturated Fat 0 g	Sodium 279 mg
Total Fat 5 g	Cholesterol 0 mg	

Banana Raisin Bran Muffins

Prep Time: 20 minutes
Cooking Time: 20-25 minutes

- 1 cup ripe bananas, mashed
  (2-3 large bananas)
- 2 egg whites
- 1/2 cup skim milk
- 3 Tablespoons canola oil
- 1 1/2 cups raisin bran cereal

- 1 cup flour
- 1/4 cup sugar
- 2 teaspoons baking powder
- 1/4 teaspoon salt
- 1/8 teaspoon nutmeg or cinnamon

Preheat oven to 400 degrees. Line 12 muffin tins with paper baking cups. In a medium bowl, combine bananas, egg whites, milk, oil and cereal. Let stand 10 minutes. Stir to break up cereal. In a large bowl, combine flour, sugar, baking powder, salt and nutmeg. Add cereal mixture to the dry mixture all at once, stirring just until moistened. Divide evenly among muffin cups. Bake 20-25 minutes or until tester inserted in center comes out clean. Remove from pan to cool. Serves 12. Serving size: 1 muffin

Amount Per Serving:

Calories 133	Saturated Fat 0 g	Sodium 96 mg
Total Fat 4 g	Cholesterol 0 mg	

French Toast

Prep Time: 10 minutes
Cooking Time: 8 minutes

- 1 Tablespoon sugar
- 1/4 teaspoon cinnamon
- 4 egg whites or egg substitute
  equal to 2 eggs

- 1/2 cup skim milk
- 8 slices light, whole wheat bread

Coat griddle with non-stick cooking spray. In a small bowl, combine sugar and cinnamon and set aside. Mix egg whites or egg substitute and milk. Dip bread slices into egg mixture and cook on griddle until golden brown on each side (approximately 4 minutes each side). Sprinkle cinnamon and sugar mixture over the top. Serve with low-calorie or fat-free syrup or fresh fruit. Serves 4. Serving size: 2 slices

Amount Per Serving:

Calories 132	Saturated Fat 1 g	Sodium 305 mg
Total Fat 1 g	Cholesterol 1 mg	

12

Carrot Patch Muffins

Prep Time: 20 minutes
Cooking Time: 20 minutes

- 2 1/4 cups all-purpose flour
- 2/3 cup sugar
- 1/2 cup coconut, shredded or flaked
- 1/2 cup walnuts, chopped
- 1/2 cup dark seedless or golden raisins
- 1 Tablespoon baking powder
- 1 1/2 teaspoons salt

- 1 teaspoon ground cinnamon
- 1 1/2 cups carrots, shredded
- 2/3 cup skim milk
- 1/4 cup applesauce
- 1 teaspoon vanilla extract
- 1 egg
- 7 teaspoons corn syrup

Preheat oven to 375 degrees. In a large bowl, mix first 8 ingredients. Stir in carrots. In a small bowl, beat milk, applesauce, vanilla and egg until blended. Stir into flour mixture until moistened. Fill mini-muffin tins 1/3 full. Bake 4 minutes. Open oven, pull out rack and squeeze a little corn syrup in center of muffins. Return to oven for 5 more minutes. Serves 28. Serving size: 2 mini-muffins

Amount Per Serving:

Calories 97	Saturated Fat 1 g	Sodium 129 mg
Total Fat 2 g	Cholesterol 8 mg	

Contributed by Laura Scheer-McCune, Partyworks Catering, Inc.

Made-at-Home Bagels

- 2 packages yeast
- 6 Tablespoons sugar
- 2 cups warm water
- 5-6 cups flour

- 1/2 cup liquid oil
- 2 teaspoons salt
- 2 quarts boiling water
- 1/3 cup sugar

Mix first 3 ingredients with wire whisk. Note that water should be warm but not hot. Add 2 cups of flour. Mix, cover, and let rise in a warm place. Add oil, salt and remainder of flour to yeast mixture. (If using a food processor, add the yeast mixture to the flour.) Knead mixture until it won't take any more flour. This can be done by hand or in a mixer with a dough hook. Cover, and let rise in a warm place until doubled. Divide dough into 24 balls. Push one finger through the middle of the balls, and form into bagel shapes. Place each bagel on a floured surface, and let rise until doubled. Bring water and sugar to a boil. Preheat oven to 325 degrees. Coat cookie sheet with non-stick cooking spray. Drop one bagel as a test bagel into the boiling water. The bagel must float when put in the water. If it does not float, remove and allow the bagels to stand longer. When the bagels are ready per the test bagel, drop them into the boiling water, and boil for 10 seconds, turning them over midway during the boiling. Remove the bagels with a strainer-spoon, and place them on the cookie sheet. Bake for 25 to 30 minutes. Bagels should be light golden brown. Yields 24 bagels. Serves 24. Serving size: 1 bagel

Amount Per Serving:

Calories 172	Saturated Fat 1 g	Sodium 179 mg
Total Fat 5 g	Cholesterol 0 mg	

Contributed by Tony Tarrasch, Tony's Bagel Bin.

Lemon-Poppy Seed Hotcakes

Prep Time: 15 minutes
Cooking Time: 10 minutes

- 1/2 lemon, thinly sliced
- 1 cup honey
- 1 1/2 cups flour
- 1/4 cup sugar
- 1 Tablespoon poppy seeds
- 1 teaspoon baking soda
- 1/4 teaspoon salt

- 3/4 cup skim milk
- 1/2 cup low-fat sour cream
- 2 teaspoons lemon rind, grated
- 2 teaspoons fresh lemon juice
- 1 teaspoon almond extract
- 1 egg
- 1 egg white

Coat griddle with non-stick cooking spray, repeat as necessary when cooking hotcakes. In small bowl, combine lemon and honey. Warm thoroughly over medium heat and set aside. In a large bowl, combine flour, sugar, poppy seeds, baking soda and salt. In a medium bowl, combine milk, sour cream, lemon rind, lemon juice, almond extract, egg and egg white. Stir well. Add to flour mixture, stirring until smooth. Spoon 1/3 cup batter for each pancake onto hot griddle. Turn over when edges begin to brown. Place on serving platter. Pour lemon-honey mixture over the top. Serves 8. Serving size: 1 hotcake

Amount Per Serving:

Calories 268	Saturated Fat 1 g	Sodium 254 mg
Total Fat 2 g	Cholesterol 28 mg	

Egg Brunch Casserole

Prep Time: 20 minutes
Cooking Time: 40 minutes

- 2 cups egg substitute
- 6 slices bread, cut into cubes
- 1 pound light pork sausage, cooked and crumbled
- 2 cups skim milk

- 1 pound low-fat cheddar cheese, shredded
- 1 teaspoon salt
- 1 teaspoon dry mustard

Preheat oven to 350 degrees. Combine all ingredients. Bake for 40 minutes in a 9 x 13-inch baking dish coated with non-stick cooking spray. Serves 8. Serving size: 1 (4 x 3-inch) section

Amount Per Serving:

Calories 424	Saturated Fat 7 g	Sodium 1667 mg
Total Fat 24 g	Cholesterol 65 mg	

Breakfast Pizza

- 1 (10-ounce) package pizza dough
- 1 cup low-fat cheddar cheese, shredded
- 1 cup mozzarella cheese, shredded
- 1 1/2 cups egg substitute
- 1/2 cup skim milk
- 3/4 teaspoon oregano
- 1/8 teaspoon pepper
- 1/2 cup green pepper, chopped
- 1/2 cup red pepper, chopped
- 1/2 cup green onion, chopped
- 1/2 cup mushrooms, chopped
- 1/2 cup tomato, chopped

Preheat oven to 375 degrees. Coat a rectangular pan with non-stick cooking spray. Place pizza dough in pan and press to edges of pan. Bake for 5 minutes. Reduce oven to 350 degrees. Sprinkle crust with cheese. In a mixing bowl, combine egg substitute, milk, oregano and pepper. Pour over cheese. Sprinkle vegetables on top. Bake for 30-35 minutes or until egg mixture is set. Serves 6. Serving size: 1 slice

Amount Per Serving:

Calories 409	Saturated Fat 5 g	Sodium 817 mg
Total Fat 12 g	Cholesterol 28 mg	

Myth No. 47:
"Mixing bowls are used for haircuts as often
as they're used for pancake batter."

APPETIZERS & BEVERAGES

Myth No. 17:

"All Ozark beverages come from stills."

Fact:

"Stories about moonshine and Granny's recipe are simply legends of days gone by. Besides, why would we want to drink from jugs when you can now buy fine wine in a box?"

APPETIZERS

BEVERAGES

Dreamy, Creamy Fruit Dip

- 1 small jar marshmallow cream
- 1 (8-ounce) package fat-free cream cheese, softened
- 1 cup light whipped topping
- 1/2 cup fresh fruit, chopped (may use strawberries, pineapple, banana, kiwi, etc.)

Blend first three ingredients well. Fold in chopped fruit. Serve as a dip for fresh fruit or crackers. Serves 12. Serving size: 5 Tablespoons

Amount Per Serving:

Calories 82	Saturated Fat 0 g	Sodium 125 mg
Total Fat 1 g	Cholesterol 3 mg	

Dill Dip

Prep Time: 10 minutes
Chill Time: 24 hours

- 1 (8-ounce) package fat-free cream cheese
- 1 cup fat-free mayonnaise
- 1/2 cup fat-free sour cream
- 3 teaspoons dill weed
- 2 teaspoons Beau Monde seasoning
- 2 Tablespoons parsley flakes
- 2 Tablespoons onion flakes
- round loaf of rye bread

Mix cream cheese, mayonnaise, and sour cream until well blended and smooth. Stir in remaining ingredients. Chill for 24 hours. Hollow out the loaf of rye bread and fill with dip. Cut the bread from center of loaf into chunks for dipping. Also good with fresh vegetables. Serves 12. Serving size: 4 Tablespoons

Amount Per Serving:

Calories 42	Saturated 0 g	Sodium 640 mg
Total Fat 0 g	Cholesterol 3 mg	

Artichoke-Chili Dip

- 1 (8-ounce) package low-fat cream cheese, softened
- 1 (8-ounce) can artichoke hearts, drained
- 1 cup fat-free Parmesan cheese
- 1 (4-ounce) can green chilies, chopped
- 1 1/2 cups fat-free mayonnaise

Preheat oven to 350 degrees. Mash artichokes and combine with other ingredients. Put in shallow baking dish. Bake for 25 minutes until heated throughout. Serve with fat-free crackers or low-fat tortilla chips. Serves 40. Serving size: 2 Tablespoons

Amount Per Serving:

Calories 22	Saturated Fat 0 g	Sodium 172 mg
Total Fat 0 g	Cholesterol 3 mg	

Myth No. 76:

"People from the Ozarks think artichoke dip is an exotic flavor of chewing tobacco."

Creamy Spinach Dip

Prep Time: 20 minutes
Chill Time: 12 hours

- 2 (10-ounce) boxes frozen chopped spinach, thawed
- 1 bunch green onions including stems, chopped
- 1 cup low-fat mayonnaise
- 1 1/2 cups fat-free sour cream
- 1 package ranch salad dressing mix, dry
- 3 Tablespoons dry parsley

Squeeze spinach to drain excess liquid. Add green onions, mayonnaise, sour cream, ranch salad dressing mix and parsley. Mix and refrigerate for up to 12 hours or overnight. Serves 28. Serving size: 3 Tablespoons

Amount Per Serving:

Calories 39	Saturated Fat 0 g	Sodium 102 mg
Total Fat 2 g	Cholesterol 3 mg	

Chunky Chili Dip

Prep Time: 15 minutes
Chill Time: 2 hours

- 3/4 cup fat-free plain yogurt
- 1/3 cup fat-free mayonnaise
- 1/3 cup green pepper, finely chopped
- 1/4 cup chili sauce
- 1 1/2 Tablespoons green onion, finely chopped
- 1/3 cup red bell pepper, finely chopped
- 1 Tablespoon prepared horseradish
- fat-free tortilla chips

In a mixing bowl, stir together first seven ingredients. Cover and chill before serving. Serve with fat-free tortilla chips. Yields 2 cups. Serves 32.
Serving size: 1 1/2 Tablespoons

Amount Per Serving:

Calories 23	Saturated Fat 0 g	Sodium 174 mg
Total Fat 0 g	Cholesterol 0 mg	

Water Chestnut Dip

Prep Time: 10 minutes
Chill Time: 4 hours

- 1 (8-ounce) can whole water chestnuts, drained and diced
- 1 (8-ounce) carton light sour cream
- 1 cup fat-free mayonnaise

- 1 garlic clove, minced
- 1/4 cup fresh parsley, minced
- 2 Tablespoons onion, minced
- 1 teaspoon light soy sauce

Combine all ingredients and mix well. Chill 4 hours. Serve with fresh vegetables. Serves 16. Serving size: 3 Tablespoons

Amount Per Serving:

Calories 34	Saturated Fat 0 g	Sodium 214 mg
Total Fat 1 g	Cholesterol 5 mg	

Seven Layer Dip

Prep Time: 15 minutes

- 1 (8-ounce) can fat-free bean dip
- 1 (8 ounce) carton guacamole dip
- 1 (16-ounce) carton fat-free sour cream
- 2 tomatoes, diced

- 1 bunch green onions, chopped
- 2 ounces ripe olives, chopped (optional)
- 3 cups fat-free cheddar cheese, grated
- Fat-free chips

Layer each item in order given. Place fat-free chips around dip and serve. Serves 20. Serving size: 6 Tablespoons

Amount Per Serving:

Calories 112	Saturated Fat 0 g	Sodium 311 mg
Total Fat 3 g	Cholesterol 3 mg	

Creamy Salmon-Cucumber Spread

- 1 (8-ounce) Neufchatel cheese, softened
- 3 green onions, finely chopped
- 1 (6 1/8-ounce) can pink salmon in water, drained and flaked
  skinless and boneless
- 1/3 cup cucumber, seeded and finely chopped
- 2 Tablespoons red bell pepper, chopped
- pumpernickel or rye crackers

In a bowl, combine first five ingredients and blend well. Cover and refrigerate for 1-2 hours to blend flavors. Serve with pumpernickel or rye crackers. Serves 32.
Serving size: 1 Tablespoon

Amount Per Serving:

Calories 53	Saturated Fat 2 g	Sodium 86 mg
Total Fat 4 g	Cholesterol 13 mg	

Fruit 'n Nut Cheese Ball

- 3 (8-ounce) packages fat-free cream cheese
- 1 (4-ounce) package blue cheese
- 1 cup low-fat cheddar cheese, shredded
- 1 (8-ounce) package dates, chopped
- 1 cup golden raisins
- 1/2 cup pecans, chopped and toasted

Combine first 5 ingredients and divide in half. Shape each portion into a ball, and roll in pecans. Makes 2 (4- inch) balls. Cover and chill. Serve with reduced-salt and low-fat crackers or with apple and pear slices. Serves 40. Serving Size: 3 Tablespoons

Amount Per Serving:

Calories 69	Saturated Fat 1 g	Sodium 147 mg
Total Fat 2 g	Cholesterol 6 mg	

Pepper Cheese Ball

- 1 package zesty Italian dressing mix
- 1 Tablespoon skim milk
- 1 (8-ounce) package fat-free cream cheese
- 1 Tablespoon seasoned pepper

Mix dressing, milk and cheese. Shape into ball and roll in pepper. Chill for 30 minutes. Serves 8. Serving size: 2 Tablespoons

Amount Per Serving:

Calories 33	Saturated Fat 0 g	Sodium 404 mg
Total Fat 0 g	Cholesterol 5 mg	

Mushroom Pita Pizzas

- 2 pita breads (6-inch diameter)
- 1 (4-ounce) can mushroom stems and pieces
- 1 small red onion, thinly sliced and separated into rings
- 1/4 cup green, red or yellow bell pepper, chopped
- 2 teaspoons dried basil
- 1 cup low-fat mozzarella cheese, finely-shredded
- 1 Tablespoon Parmesan cheese, grated

Preheat oven to 425 degrees. Split each bread into halves to make 4 rounds. Place rounds, cut side up, on ungreased cookie sheet. Arrange mushrooms on bread rounds. Top with onion rings and bell pepper. Sprinkle with basil and cheeses. Bake until cheese is melted, about 8-10 minutes. Cut each round into 8 pieces for appetizers, or serve whole as an entree. Serves 8. Serving size: 4 pieces

Amount Per Serving:

Calories 90	Saturated Fat 2 g	Sodium 221 mg
Total Fat 3 g	Cholesterol 9 mg	

Spinach Balls

Prep Time: 15 minutes
Cooking Time: 15 minutes

- 1 (20-ounce) package spinach, chopped and cooked
- 2 cups Italian bread crumbs
- 1/4 cup margarine
- 3/4 cup egg substitute
- garlic to taste
- Italian seasoning to taste

Preheat oven to 350 degrees. In a small bowl, mix all ingredients together. Form into balls (1 dozen). Bake for 10-15 minutes. Serves 12. Serving size: 1 piece

Amount Per Serving:

Calories 131	Saturated Fat 1 g	Sodium 645 mg
Total Fat 5 g	Cholesterol 0 mg	

Contributed by St. John's Nutrition Center, Springfield, Missouri.

Turkey Meatballs

Prep Time: 20 minutes
Cooking Time: 45 minutes

- 1 pound ground turkey
- 1/2 cup dry bread crumbs
- 1/4 cup skim milk
- 1/2 teaspoon salt
- 1/2 teaspoon Worcestershire sauce
- 1/4 teaspoon pepper
- 1 small onion, chopped (about 1/4 cup)
- 1 egg
- 1 Tablespoon fresh parsley, chopped
- 1 (12-ounce) bottle chili sauce
- 1 (10-ounce) jar grape jelly

Mix together ground turkey, bread crumbs, milk, salt, Worcestershire sauce, pepper, onion, egg and parsley. Shape mixture into 1-inch balls. Cook meatballs in a 12-inch skillet over medium heat about 15 minutes. Remove meatballs from skillet. Drain skillet. Heat chili sauce and jelly in skillet, stirring constantly until jelly is melted. Add meatballs, and stir until coated. Simmer uncovered for 30 minutes. Serve hot. Serves 15. Serving size: 4 meatballs

Amount Per Serving:

Calories 155	Saturated Fat 1 g	Sodium 449 mg
Total Fat 4 g	Cholesterol 39 mg	

Vegetable Nachos

- 1/2 cup fat-free sour cream
- 2 Tablespoons cilantro, finely-snipped
- 1 small zucchini, quartered lengthwise and thinly sliced (1 cup)
- 1/2 cup carrot, shredded
- 1/3 cup green onion, sliced
- 1 1/2 teaspoons ground cumin
- 4 teaspoons vegetable oil
- 1 (15-ounce) can pinto beans, drained and rinsed
- 4 cups baked tortilla chips
- 1 (4-ounce) can green chilies, chopped
- 4 ounces cheddar cheese, shredded
- 1/2 cup tomato, seeded and chopped
- Salsa (optional)

Preheat oven to 350 degrees. In a small bowl, mix sour cream and cilantro. Cover and set aside. In a large skillet, cook zucchini, carrot, onion and cumin in hot vegetable oil for 3-4 minutes until vegetables are tender but crisp. Stir in pinto beans. Spread chips about 1 inch deep on a baking sheet. Spoon bean mixture over chips. Sprinkle with chilies and cheese. Bake for 5-7 minutes or until cheese melts. Carefully move chips to serving platter. Top chips with the cilantro cream mixture, and sprinkle with tomatoes. Salsa can be served on the side. Serves 8. Serving size: 8 ounces

Amount Per Serving:

Calories 238	Saturated Fat 3 g	Sodium 347 mg
Total Fat 8 g	Cholesterol 20 mg	

Zesty Tortilla Pinwheels

- 1 (8-ounce) package fat-free cream cheese
- 1 small can green chilies, do not drain
- 1 (8-ounce) carton fat-free sour cream
- 1 packet ranch salad dressing mix
- A few dashes hot sauce
- 1 package flour tortillas (8-inch diameter)

Mix together first 5 ingredients. Spread a thin layer of the mixture over each tortilla. Roll each tortilla. Place rolled tortillas in zip-lock bag and store in refrigerator until ready to serve. (Prepare no more than 24 hours in advance.) To serve, cut rolled tortillas diagonally into 1-inch thick slices. Serves 24. Serving size: 3 pinwheels

Amount Per Serving:

Calories 93	Saturated Fat 0 g	Sodium 224 mg
Total Fat 2 g	Cholesterol 2 mg	

Black Bean Quesadillas

- 1 can black beans
  (thoroughly rinsed and drained)
- 1 small can tomato sauce
- 1 (4-ounce) can
  mild green chilies, diced
- 1 teaspoon dried onion flakes
- 1 teaspoon cumin
- 1 teaspoon coriander
- 1 teaspoon dried cilantro
- 1 cup low-fat cheese, grated
  (cheddar/Monterey Jack combination)
- 8 flour tortillas (8-inch diameter)
- garnish with chopped lettuce, tomato,
  salsa and fat-free sour cream

Mix all of the ingredients except tortillas in a large saucepan. Cook over medium heat approximately 20-25 minutes until hot. Warm tortillas in non-stick skillet over medium heat. Remove from pan. Place one tortilla in skillet, sprinkle with 1/4 cup grated cheese, and spread 1/4 of the bean mixture over the tortilla. Cover with another tortilla. Heat on both sides for about two minutes. Cut into quarters. Serve with chopped lettuce, tomato, salsa and fat-free sour cream as a garnish. Serves 4.

Serving size: 4 quarters

Amount Per Serving:

Calories 426	Saturated Fat 2 g	Sodium 1085 mg
Total Fat 8 g	Cholesterol 10 mg	

Chicken Medallions

- 6 (8-ounce) chicken breast halves, skinless and boneless
- 12 ounces fresh spinach
- 1 (15-ounce) carton part-skim ricotta cheese
- 9 Tablespoons Parmesan cheese, grated
- 2 Tablespoons Dijon mustard
- 2 1/4 teaspoons dried basil
- 1 1/2 teaspoons garlic, minced
- 1 1/2 teaspoons salt
- 1 teaspoon pepper
- 1 (4-ounce) jar pimentos, drained well
- paprika

Preheat oven to 375 degrees. Pound chicken breasts between 2 pieces of wax paper to about 1/4-inch thickness. Clean and remove stems from spinach. Steam spinach in a covered skillet with small amount of water until wilted. Drain, rinse under cold water, and drain again. Dry well, patting flat with paper towels. Set aside. Mix remaining ingredients together, except paprika, until well blended to make filling. Place an even layer of spinach on breasts. Spread an even layer of filling on top of spinach to within 1/2 inch of the edges. Roll up in jelly-roll fashion, starting with the long side. Line a cooking sheet with aluminum foil and place rolls seam-side down, tucking ends under. Sprinkle with paprika. Cover with foil, and bake for 20-25 minutes until chicken is opaque and juices run clear when meat is pierced. About 15 minutes into baking time, drain off excess juice, and loosely recover. Cool to room temperature. Refrigerate several hours or overnight. Cut each roll into 1/2-inch slices. Serves 36. Serving size: 2 medallions

Amount Per Serving:

Calories 75	Saturated Fat 1 g	Sodium 182 mg
Total Fat 3 g	Cholesterol 29 mg	

Contributed by Laura Scheer-McCune, Partyworks Catering, Inc.

Zucchini Appetizers

- 3 cups thinly-sliced zucchini with peel (4 small)
- 1 cup biscuit mix
- 1/2 cup onion, finely-chopped
- 2/3 cup Parmesan cheese
- 3 Tablespoons parsley, chopped

- 1/2 teaspoon seasoned salt
- 1/2 teaspoon dried marjoram
- 1/2 teaspoon oregano
- 1 teaspoon salt-free spicy pepper
- 2 cloves garlic, minced
- 2 Tablespoons olive oil
- 1 cup egg substitute

Preheat oven to 350 degrees. Coat a 13 x 9-inch pan with non-stick cooking spray. In a mixing bowl, combine all ingredients except oil and egg substitute. Beat oil and egg substitute together in a separate bowl. Add dry ingredients, and mix well. Pour into pan. Bake 25 minutes until golden brown. Cut into squares. Serve warm.
Serves 16. Serving size: 2 x 2-inch square

Amount Per Serving:

Calories 58	Saturated Fat 1 g	Sodium 212 mg
Total Fat 3 g	Cholesterol 2 mg	

Stuffed Mushrooms

- 1 (10-ounce) package frozen chopped spinach, thawed
- 1 1/2 pounds large fresh mushrooms (about 20)
- 1/4 cup onion, chopped
- 2 cloves garlic, minced
- 1 Tablespoon margarine

- 1/4 cup grated fat-free Parmesan cheese
- 1/4 cup fine, dry bread crumbs
- 1/4 cup pimento, finely-chopped
- 1/2 teaspoon dried, crushed basil
- 1/2 teaspoon dried, crushed oregano
- 1/4 teaspoon salt
- dash of pepper

Preheat oven to 425 degrees. Squeeze spinach to drain excess liquid. Coat a 15 x 10 x 1-inch non-stick baking pan with non-stick cooking spray. Remove stems from mushrooms, and set tops aside. Chop enough stems to make 2 cups. In a 10-inch skillet, cook chopped mushroom stems, onion and garlic in margarine until onion is tender but not browned. Add thawed spinach. Cook over low heat until most of the liquid is evaporated. Stir Parmesan cheese, bread crumbs, pimento, basil, oregano, salt and pepper into spinach mixture. Spoon mixture into mushroom tops. Place stuffed mushroom tops in the prepared pan. Bake until mushrooms are tender, approximately 15 minutes. Serves 20. Serving size: 1 mushroom top

Amount Per Serving:

Calories 42	Saturated Fat 0 g	Sodium 83 mg
Total Fat 1 g	Cholesterol 1 mg	

Deli-Wrapped Pickles

Prep Time: 10 minutes
Chill Time: 2 hours

- 8 whole dill pickles, medium size
- 1 (4-ounce) package wafer-sliced, low-fat meat (chicken, beef, ham or turkey)
- 1 (8-ounce) package fat-free cream cheese, softened

Drain pickles, trim ends. Dry on paper towels. Separate meat slices and place on cutting board. Spread each slice carefully with cream cheese. Lay pickle at the edge of meat slice and roll, covering pickle. Repeat process rolling each pickle with 3 slices of meat. Crimp ends shut. Roll each finished pickle in waxed paper. Chill. Slice in 1/3-inch slices to serve. Serves 8. Serving size: 5-6 slices

Amount Per Serving:

Calories 52	Saturated Fat 0 g	Sodium 1172 mg
Total Fat 0 g	Cholesterol 16 mg	

Frisco Shrimp Cocktail Sauce

Prep Time: 10 minutes
Chill Time: 2 hours

- 1 cup chili sauce
- 1 cup ketchup
- 2 teaspoons Worcestershire sauce
- 4 drops hot sauce
- 1 teaspoon prepared horseradish
- 1/2 teaspoon chives, chopped
- juice of 1/2 lemon

Mix in order listed above. Chill. Yields about 2 cups. Serves 16. Serving size: 1/8 cup

Amount Per Serving:

Calories 35	Saturated Fat 1 g	Sodium 415 mg
Total Fat 1 g	Cholesterol 0 mg	

*As served at the Harvey House in the Old Frisco Station. Contributed by the History Museum for Springfield-Greene County from their cookbook, **Secrets**.*

Vegetable Bars

- 2 packages crescent rolls (8 count each)
- 3/4 cup fat-free mayonnaise
- 1/2 cup fat-free sour cream
- 2 (8-ounce) packages low-fat cream cheese, softened
- 1 envelope ranch salad dressing mix
- 3/4 cup green pepper, chopped
- 3/4 cup green onion, chopped
- 3/4 cup tomatoes, seeded and chopped
- 3/4 cup broccoli, chopped
- 3/4 cup carrots, shredded
- 3/4 cup cauliflower, chopped
- 3/4 cup low-fat cheddar cheese, shredded

Preheat oven to 350 degrees. Cover bottom of 11 x 17-inch cookie sheet with crescent rolls. Bake for 7-8 minutes. Set crust aside to cool. Combine mayonnaise, sour cream, cream cheese and ranch salad dressing mix. Spread over cooled crust. Combine vegetables and distribute over cream cheese mixture. Sprinkle with cheese. Cover with plastic wrap and refrigerate 3-4 hours before serving. Cut into 24 bars. Serves 24. Serving size: 1 (2-inch square)

Amount Per Serving:

Calories 124	Saturated Fat 1 g	Sodium 538 mg
Total Fat 4 g	Cholesterol 7 mg	

Almond Tea

- 4 cups strong tea
- 1 cup sugar
- 1 teaspoon almond extract
- 1 (6-ounce) can frozen lemonade, thawed
- 4 cups water

Mix together all ingredients in a pitcher or punch bowl. Add orange slices and maraschino cherries. Serve hot or over ice. Serves 8. Serving size: 1 cup

Amount Per Serving:

Calories 141	Saturated Fat 0 g	Sodium 4 mg
Total Fat 0 g	Cholesterol 0 mg	

Smoothie

- 1 cup fruit
- 1 cup fat-free yogurt
- 1 cup fat-free ice cream
- 1 Tablespoon honey
- 1/2 cup ice cubes

Mix in blender until smooth. Serves 3. Serving size: 1 cup

Amount Per Serving:

Calories 137	Saturated Fat 0 g	Sodium 101 mg
Total Fat 1 g	Cholesterol 2 mg	

Red Velvet Punch

Prep Time: 15 minutes

- 80 ounces Cranberry Juice Cocktail
- 1 (6-ounce) can each of:
    - frozen pineapple juice, thawed
    - frozen lemon juice or lemonade, thawed
    - frozen orange juice, thawed
- 64 ounces ginger ale (May use diet lemon-lime carbonated drink.)

Mix juices together in a large container. Add ginger ale (or diet lemon-lime carbonated drink) just before serving. Garnish with slices of lemon or lime. Serves 25.
Serving size: 8 ounces

Amount Per Serving:

Calories 116	Saturated Fat 0 g	Sodium 10 mg
Total Fat 0 g	Cholesterol 0 mg	

Hot Cinnamon Punch

Prep Time: 10 minutes

- 3 quarts apple cider
- 1/3 cup red cinnamon candies
- 1 Tablespoon whole allspice
- 3 Tablespoons honey

Heat cider, cinnamon candies and allspice to boiling. Reduce heat, cover and simmer 5 minutes. Remove allspice. Stir in honey. Serve hot. Serves 24. Serving size: 4 ounces

Amount Per Serving:

Calories 82	Saturated Fat 0 g	Sodium 5 mg
Total Fat 0 g	Cholesterol 0 mg	

Myth No. 51:
"Ozarkians know that a good red wine must breathe from a wide-mouthed glass to acquire a full-bodied flavor. That's why Cabernet Sauvignon is *always* served in a mason jar."

Ozark Mountain Mulled Cider

- 2 quarts (8 cups) apple cider
- 1/4 cup brown sugar, firmly-packed
- 1/2 teaspoon cardamom
- 1/2 teaspoon ground nutmeg
- 1/2 teaspoon allspice

- 2 teaspoons whole cloves
- 4 cinnamon sticks
- juice of 1 orange
- peel of 1 orange

In a large saucepan, combine all ingredients. Bring to a boil. Reduce heat. Simmer 30 minutes. Remove cinnamon sticks and orange peel. Serve warm. Serves 8.
Serving size: 8 ounces

Amount Per Serving:

Calories 170	Saturated Fat 0 g	Sodium 12 mg
Total Fat 1 g	Cholesterol 0 mg	

"In the Ozarks it is believed that caviar is best
found on the end of a ten-pound fishing line as opposed to melba toast."

SOUPS AND SALADS

Myth No. 35:
"People from the Ozarks go around barefoot all the time."

Fact:
"Going out in public without shoes is not condoned and would certainly not be acceptable behavior for a dinner party. In fact, we polled the women of the Junior League and found that the average league member owns 67.3 pairs of shoes in approximately 17.9 different colors."

Black Bean Soup

Prep Time: 30 minutes
Cooking time: 2 hours

- 2 pounds black beans
- 1 bunch green onions, diced
- 2 yellow onions, diced
- 2 tomatoes, diced
- 1 bell pepper, diced
- 1 bunch carrots, diced
- 1/2 cup olive oil
- 1 (4-ounce) can green chilies, chopped
- 1 Tablespoon garlic, minced
- 1/2 Tablespoon ground cumin
- 1 Tablespoon chili powder
- 2 teaspoons ground oregano
- 1/2 cup fresh cilantro, chopped
- 2 Tablespoons salt
- 1 Tablespoon black pepper

Wash and sort black beans. Sauté onions, tomatoes, bell pepper and carrots in olive oil until tender. Place beans and vegetable mixture in large, heavy-gauge pot. Add green chilies, garlic, cumin, chili powder, oregano, cilantro, salt and pepper. Fill pot with cold water 2-3 inches over beans. Bring to a boil. Reduce heat, and simmer on low until beans are tender and liquid is absorbed (approximately 2 hours). If necessary, add more water during the cooking process. When beans are tender, remove and puree one half of the beans. Return the pureed beans to the pot. Stir in to obtain a rich consistency. Serve with cornbread. Serves 10. Serving size: 1 1/2 cups

Amount Per Serving:

Calories 329	Saturated Fat 2 g	Sodium 1433 mg
Total Fat 11 g	Cholesterol 0 mg	

Contributed by James Clary, Clary's American Grill in Springfield, Missouri.

Cabbage Soup

Prep Time: 25 minutes
Cooking Time: 1 hour

- 1 medium head of cabbage, cleaned, cored and sliced
- 4 cups celery with leaves, sliced
- 1 (46-ounce) can tomato juice
- 46 ounces water
- 4 packets instant vegetable broth
- 1/4 cup dried onion
- salt and pepper to taste
- hot sauce (optional)

Combine all ingredients in a Dutch oven. Bring to a boil. Reduce heat. Cover and simmer for 1 hour. Serves 20. Serving size: 1 cup

Amount Per Serving:

Calories 32	Saturated Fat 0 g	Sodium 296 mg
Total Fat 0 g	Cholesterol 0 mg	

Andy's Chicken Soup

Prep Time: 15 minutes
Cooking Time: 2 hours and 15 minutes

* water
* 1 roasting chicken or
  2 frying chickens
* 16 carrots, chopped
* 4 celery stalks, chopped
* 2 yellow onions, chopped
* 12 ounces barley
* 1 package dried
  vegetable soup mix
* 1 (2-ounce) jar instant
  chicken flavor bouillon

In a Dutch oven, boil chicken for 1 hour. Remove chicken from water and reserve the water. Remove skin and remove meat from bones. Combine carrots, celery, onions, barley, soup mix and bouillon with the chicken broth and cook for about 1 hour, stirring frequently. Broth will be done when barley is cooked. The broth will cook down, so add water when necessary. Cut chicken into bite-size pieces and add to the mixture. Simmer for another 15 minutes. Serves 12. Serving size: 1 cup

Amount Per Serving:

Calories 263	Saturated Fat 1 g	Sodium 1334 mg
Total Fat 4 g	Cholesterol 41 mg	

Contributed by Andy Williams, Moon River Theatre in Branson, Missouri.

Chili-Chicken Soup

- 3 large fresh tomatoes
- 1 Tablespoon vegetable oil
- 2/3 cup onion, chopped
- 1 (4-ounce) can mild green chilies, chopped
- 1-2 garlic cloves, minced
- 1 teaspoon ground cumin
- 1 teaspoon oregano leaves, crushed
- 1 teaspoon sugar
- 1/8 teaspoon ground cloves
- 1/8 teaspoon white pepper
- 1 (14 1/2-ounce) can chicken broth
- 1 (15-ounce) can white great northern beans, rinsed and drained
- 2 cups chicken, cooked and cubed
- fat-free sour cream (optional garnish)
- low-fat cheddar cheese (optional garnish)
- chopped cilantro (optional garnish)

Core and coarsely chop tomatoes (about 4 cups). Set aside. In a large saucepan, heat oil until hot. Add onion and cook until tender, stirring occasionally. Stir in tomatoes, chilies, garlic, cumin, oregano, sugar, cloves, and pepper. Reduce heat and simmer, stirring occasionally until tomatoes are softened (5-10 minutes). Add chicken broth and bring to a boil. Reduce heat. Cover and simmer to blend flavors (about 20 minutes), stirring occasionally. Add beans and chicken; cook for 5-8 minutes or until hot. Garnish, if desired. Serves 4. Serving size: 1 cup

Amount Per Serving:

| Calories 380 | Saturated Fat 2 g | Sodium 521 mg |
| Total Fat 9 g | Cholesterol 87 mg | |

Gazpacho

Prep Time: 40 minutes
Chill time: 4 hours

Soup Base:

- 3 1/2 cups tomato juice
- 1 Tablespoon wine vinegar
- 1/2 teaspoon Worcestershire sauce
- 3 Tablespoons vegetable or olive oil
- 1 teaspoon minced garlic
- 2 teaspoons snipped parsley
- 1/2 teaspoon hot sauce
- 1/4 teaspoon white pepper
- 1 Tablespoon fresh lemon juice

Vegetables:

- 1 1/2 cups tomatoes, finely chopped
- 1/2 cup celery, finely chopped
- 1/2 cup green pepper, finely chopped
- 1/2 cup red bell pepper, finely chopped
- 1/2 cup onion, finely chopped
- 1 small cucumber, peeled, seeded and finely-chopped

- Croutons (optional garnish)

Combine soup base ingredients and mix well. Stir in vegetables, and refrigerate at least 4 hours or overnight. Garnish with croutons. Serves 5. Serving size: 1 1/2 cups

Amount Per Serving:

Calories 97	Saturated Fat 0 g	Sodium 624 mg
Total Fat 3 g	Cholesterol 0 mg	

Vegetable Beef Soup

Prep Time: 15 minutes
Cooking Time: 60 minutes

- 1 pound lean ground beef
- 1-2 Tablespoons dried onion, minced
- 4 cups hot water
- 1 (16-ounce) can tomatoes, chopped
- 1 Tablespoon celery salt
- 2 beef bouillon cubes
- 1 Tablespoon Worcestershire sauce
- 1/2 teaspoon pepper
- 1 (10-ounce) package frozen mixed vegetables
- 1 cup noodles

In a Dutch oven, brown beef and drain. Add onions, water, tomatoes, celery salt, bouillon, Worcestershire sauce and pepper. Bring to a boil. Cover and simmer for 30 minutes. Add mixed vegetables and noodles. Bring to a boil. Cover and simmer for 15 minutes. Serves 10. Serving size: 1 cup

Amount Per Serving:

Calories 166	Saturated Fat 2 g	Sodium 945 mg
Total Fat 6 g	Cholesterol 36 mg	

Curried Tomato Soup with Pasta

- 2 Tablespoons olive oil
- 1 large onion, finely chopped
- 2 garlic cloves, finely minced
- 3 teaspoons curry powder
- 2 (28-ounce) cans Italian plum tomatoes
- 4 cups fat-free chicken broth
- 1/4 teaspoon ground cinnamon
- 1/4 teaspoon salt
- 4 cups cooked angel hair pasta

Place oil in a Dutch oven. Add onion. Cook over low heat for 5 minutes. Add garlic and curry powder. Cook for 5 minutes, stirring frequently. Chop tomatoes, and add to pot with their liquid. Add 2 cups chicken broth, cinnamon and salt. Simmer partially covered over medium-low heat for 25 minutes. Remove from heat, and cool slightly. Puree soup in small batches, and return to pot. Add remaining 2 cups chicken broth. Taste and correct seasonings if necessary. Heat until very hot. Divide the cooked pasta among 8 bowls. Ladle hot soup over the pasta. Serves 8. Serving size: 1 cup

Amount Per Serving:

Calories 170	Saturated Fat 1 g	Sodium 559 mg
Total Fat 4 g	Cholesterol 0 mg	

Clam Chowder

- 1 (14 1/2-ounce) can clear chicken broth
- 2 cups water
- 3 medium potatoes, chopped
- 1 stalk celery, chopped
- 1 small onion, chopped
- 1 (6 1/2-ounce) can minced clams, drained
- 2 Tablespoons pimento, chopped
- 1/4 teaspoon cumin
- salt and pepper to taste
- red pepper to taste
- butter buds to taste
- 1/4 cup flour
- 1/4 cup water

Combine broth, water, potatoes, celery and onion in saucepan, and cook until potatoes are tender. Add minced clams and pimento. Cook on low heat for 15 minutes. Add cumin and season to taste with salt, pepper, red pepper and butter buds. Mix flour and water. With heat still on low, gradually add to chowder until desired consistency is achieved. Serves 4. Serving size: 1 1/2 cups

Amount Per Serving:

Calories 392	Saturated Fat 0g	Sodium 888 mg
Total Fat 2 g	Cholesterol 31 mg	

Minestrone Soup

- 1/4 cup olive oil
- 2 garlic cloves, minced
- 1 large onion, diced
- 5 carrots, sliced
- 2 stalks celery, diced
- 1/2 head cabbage, cut coarse
- 1/2 cup fresh parsley, chopped
- 4 (14 1/2-ounce) cans fat-free beef broth
- 3 cups stewed tomatoes
- 1 teaspoon salt
- 1 teaspoon pepper
- 1 teaspoon oregano
- 1 (16-ounce) can navy beans
- 1 cup potatoes, diced
- 1 cup frozen peas
- 1/4 pound vermicelli, broken

Heat oil, and sauté onions and garlic. Add carrots, celery, cabbage, parsley, tomatoes and broth. Simmer 1 1/2 hours. Add remaining ingredients, adding pasta last, and simmer until tender. Serves 16. Serving size: 1 cup

Amount Per Serving:

Calories 156	Saturated Fat 1 g	Sodium 417 mg
Total Fat 4 g	Cholesterol 0 mg	

Southwest Bean Soup

- 1 Tablespoon olive oil
- 1 1/2 cups onion, chopped
- 2 large tomatoes, chopped
  (approximately 4 cups)
- 1 (4-ounce) can green chilies, chopped
- 1 1/2 Tablespoons chili powder
- 1 teaspoon ground cumin
- 1 Tablespoon garlic powder

- 1 (15-ounce) can
  red kidney beans, undrained
- 1 (15-ounce) can great northern
  beans, undrained
- salt to taste
- 1/4 cup cilantro leaves,
  chopped (optional)

Heat oil in Dutch oven over medium heat. Add onion and cook until tender, stirring occasionally. Stir in tomatoes, chilies with liquid, chili powder, cumin and garlic powder. Add beans with liquid. Bring to a boil. Reduce heat to low, cover and simmer for 15 minutes, stirring occasionally. Salt to taste. Sprinkle individual servings with cilantro. Serves 4. Serving size: 2 cups

Amount Per Serving:

Calories 303	Saturated Fat 1 g	Sodium 546 mg
Total Fat 5 g	Cholesterol 0 mg	

French Onion Soup

- 2 Tablespoons butter
- 6 large onions,
  thinly sliced (3 pounds)
- 2 (10 1/2-ounce) cans
  beef consommé, undiluted
- 1 (13 3/4-ounce) can
  low-sodium, fat-free beef broth

- 1 1/3 cups water
- 1/4 cup Chablis or
  other dry white wine
- 1/4 teaspoon
  freshly-ground pepper
- 7 (1-inch thick) slices French bread
- 1/4 cup grated Parmesan cheese

Melt butter in a Dutch oven coated with non-stick cooking spray. Add onion and cook over medium heat 10 minutes, stirring often. Add 1 can of beef consommé and cook over low heat for 30 minutes. Gradually add remaining beef consommé and next 4 ingredients. Bring to a boil, reduce heat, and simmer for 10 minutes. Place bread slices on a baking sheet. Sprinkle with Parmesan cheese. Broil, until cheese is golden brown. Ladle soup into serving bowls and top each with a toasted bread slice. Serves 7. Serving size: 1 cup

Amount Per Serving:

Calories 261	Saturated Fat 3 g	Sodium 9270 mg
Total Fat 6 g	Cholesterol 12 mg	

Old Fashioned Potato Soup

- 3 Tablespoons low-fat margarine
- 1/4 cup all-purpose flour
- 4 cups skim milk
- 2 cups diced potatoes

- 1/2 cup chopped onion
- 1/2 teaspoon salt
- 1/2 teaspoon pepper

Melt margarine in large saucepan over low heat. Add flour, stirring constantly. Gradually add milk. Stir in potatoes, onion, salt and pepper. Cook over medium heat, stirring frequently, until mixture is thickened and potatoes are done. Serves 5. Serving size: 1 cup

Amount Per Serving:

Calories 208	Saturated Fat 1 g	Sodium 397 mg
Total Fat 4 g	Cholesterol 3 mg	

Hearty Potato Soup

Prep Time: 25 minutes
Cooking Time: 40 minutes

- 2 pounds baking potatoes
- 1/4 cup margarine
- 2 leeks, thinly sliced
  (Use only white portion of leek.)
- 2 ribs celery, thinly sliced
- 2 (14 1/2-ounce) cans
  fat-free chicken broth
- 1 carrot, grated
- 1 (13-ounce) can
  evaporated skim milk
- 2 Tablespoons fresh parsley, minced
- 1/2 teaspoon dried
  thyme leaves, crushed
- salt and pepper to taste
- shredded cheddar cheese (optional)
- crumbled bacon (optional)

Peel potatoes and cut into 1/2-inch cubes. In large saucepan, melt margarine over medium heat. Add leeks and celery. Cook until tender, about 5 minutes, stirring occasionally. Add chicken broth and bring to a boil. Stir in potatoes and carrots. Reduce heat, cover and simmer until potatoes are tender, about 15 minutes. Mash potatoes slightly to thicken soup. Stir in evaporated milk, parsley and thyme. Cook until heated through. Do not boil. Season with salt and pepper to taste. Garnish with shredded cheddar cheese or crumbled bacon, if desired. Serves 8. Serving size: 1 cup

Amount Per Serving:

| Calories 238 | Saturated Fat 4 g | Sodium 537 mg |
| Total Fat 7 g | Cholesterol 18 mg | |

Chicken Tortilla Soup

- 1/2 cup onion, chopped
- 1/2 cup green pepper, chopped
- 2 garlic cloves, pressed
- 1 (14 1/2-ounce) can tomatoes
- 1 (4-ounce) can chopped green chilies
- 1/2 cup picante sauce
- 3 (6-ounce) chicken breast halves, cooked and chopped*
- 1 (10 1/2-ounce) can fat-free beef bouillon
- 1 (10 3/4-ounce) can fat-free chicken bouillon
- 1 (10 1/2-ounce) can tomato juice
- 1 1/2 cups water
- 1 teaspoon ground cumin
- 1 cup sliced zucchini
- 6 corn tortillas, cut into 1/2-inch slices
- 1/2 cup shredded, low-fat cheddar cheese

Coat a large Dutch oven with non-stick cooking spray. Sauté onions, green pepper, and garlic until tender. Add the next 10 ingredients. Bring to a boil. Cover, reduce heat, and simmer about 1 hour. Add tortillas, and simmer for 5 minutes. Top each serving with cheese. Serves 8. Serving size: 1 1/2 cup

Amount Per Serving:

Calories 210	Saturated Fat 1 g	Sodium 648 mg
Total Fat 4 g	Cholesterol 57 mg	

* 1 (15-ounce) can light kidney beans, rinsed and drained, may be substituted for the chicken.

Myth No. 80:
"In the Ozarks the practice of tipping is more commonly associated with cows than waiters."

Red Bean Soup

- 1 1/2 pounds dry red beans
  (soaked overnight)
- 1/2 stick margarine
- 1 cup onion, chopped
- 1 cup celery, chopped
- 1 1/2 cups tomatoes,
  diced (2 medium)
- 1 1/2 ounces lean
  cooked ham, diced
- 2-2 1/2 cups potatoes, diced (4 small)

- 1/2 teaspoon black pepper
- 1/2 teaspoon crushed or fresh thyme
- 1 bay leaf
- 10 (14 1/4-ounce) cans fat-free,
  low-sodium beef broth
  (approximately 1 gallon of broth)
- 2 Tablespoons fresh parsley, chopped
- 4 Tablespoons flour
- 1/2 cup cold water

Soak red beans overnight. Melt margarine in heavy skillet. Add onions and celery. Sauté for 5 minutes. Add tomatoes and ham. Sauté 2 minutes longer. Put ingredients in Dutch oven. Add red beans and next 5 ingredients. Bring to a boil. Simmer 3 hours on low heat, stirring occasionally. Bring soup to a boil. Mix flour and water and add to soup stirring constantly until thickened. Serves 25. Serving size: 1 cup

Amount Per Serving:

Calories 159	Saturated Fat 0 g	Sodium 99 mg
Total Fat 2 g	Cholesterol 1 mg	

Autumn Vegetable Soup

- 6 cups water
- 6 chicken bouillon cubes
- 2 medium carrots,
  pared and cut into 1-inch pieces
- 1 cup cabbage, shredded
- 2 medium celery stalks,
  cut into 1-inch pieces

- 1 medium onion, chopped
- 2 medium potatoes,
  peeled and cut into 1-inch pieces
- 1/8 teaspoon nutmeg
- 1/8 teaspoon pepper

Bring water and bouillon cubes to a boil in a 3-quart saucepan. Add remaining ingredients, and bring to a boil again. Cover and boil gently until vegetables are very tender (approximately 25 minutes). Let cool, then process in a food processor until smooth. Soup can be refrigerated at this point or served immediately. Reheat as necessary. Stir well, and ladle from the bottom when serving. Serves 8.
Serving size: 1 cup

Amount Per Serving:

Calories 104	Cholesterol 1 mg	Sodium 604 mg
Total Fat 1 g	Saturated Fat 0 g	

Myth No. 280:
"Ozarkians believe that cleansing the palate has something to do with the use of an automatic dishwasher."

Beef Stew

- 1 pound lean beef chuck,
  all fat trimmed, cut into 1-inch cubes
- 3 Tablespoons flour
- 2 teaspoons oil
- 2 cups onions, sliced
- 2 cups mushrooms, sliced
- 3 garlic cloves, minced
- 3 Tablespoons tomato paste
- 2 cups beef broth
- 1 cup and 1 Tablespoon water

- 3 cups carrots, sliced
- 3 cups unpeeled, red potatoes, sliced
- 1 cup fresh green beans,
  snapped into 1-inch pieces
- 1/2 teaspoon red pepper flakes
  (optional)
- 1 teaspoon oregano
- 1 teaspoon thyme
- 1 Tablespoon cornstarch
- fresh parsley (optional)

Coat beef with flour and brown in a Dutch oven coated with non-stick cooking spray. Remove from pan. Add oil to pot and heat. Add onions, mushrooms and garlic. Sauté for 10 minutes. Return beef to pot and add tomato paste, broth and 1 cup water. Bring to a boil, reduce heat and simmer 2 hours, adding more water as needed. Add carrots, potatoes, green beans and spices. Simmer for 1 more hour. Combine cornstarch and 1 Tablespoon water. Stir into stew. Boil for 1 minute until thickened. Garnish with parsley, if desired. Serves 6. Serving size: 2 cups

Amount Per Serving:

Calories 413	Saturated Fat 2 g	Sodium 496 mg
Total Fat 7 g	Cholesterol 76 mg	

Boxcar Willie's Hobo Stew

- 1 1/2 pounds stew meat, cut into 1-inch pieces (beef, pork, lamb or veal)
- 2 Tablespoons vegetable oil (cooking spray may be substituted)
- 1 garlic clove, minced
- 1 bay leaf
- 1 teaspoon salt
- 1 teaspoon prepared mustard or horseradish
- 1/2 teaspoon dried, crushed herbs (basil, oregano, marjoram or thyme)

- 1/4 teaspoon pepper
- 1 (10 1/2 or 10 3/4-ounce) can condensed broth (beef or chicken)
- 5 cups fresh vegetables, chopped (any combination of peeled potatoes, carrots, celery, rutabagas, turnips, onions, parsnips or green peppers)
- 1/4 cup cold water
- 2 Tablespoons all-purpose flour

In a large saucepan, brown meat, half at a time, in hot oil. Return all meat to the pan. Stir in garlic, bay leaf, salt, mustard or horseradish, herbs and pepper. Add the condensed beef or chicken broth. Bring to a boil. Reduce heat. Cover, and simmer until meat is tender (about 30 minutes for pork, lamb or veal and about 1 1/4 hours for beef). Add vegetables. Cover, and simmer for 30 minutes or until vegetables are tender. Blend water and flour in a separate bowl. Stir into stew. Cook, and stir until thickened and bubbly. Remove bay leaf. Great served with hot bread or rolls! Serves 6.
Serving size: 1 cup

Amount Per Serving:

Calories 272	Saturated Fat 3 g	Sodium 855 mg
Total Fat 8 g	Cholesterol 73 mg	

Contributed by Boxcar Willie and the Boxcar Willie Theater, Motel in Branson, Missouri.

Myth No. 82:

"People from the Ozarks think opossum is a major food group."

Vegetable Stew for Two

Prep Time: 5 minutes
Cooking Time: 1 hour

- 1-pound package
  frozen stew vegetables
  (e.g., potatoes, carrots,
  celery and onions)
- 3 cups water
- 1 vegetable bouillon cube
- 2 Tablespoons whole wheat flour
- 1/2 teaspoon salt
- 1/4 teaspoon pepper
- 2 teaspoons parsley
- 1/4 teaspoon sage
- 1/4 teaspoon thyme
- 2 Tablespoons instant mashed potatoes

Using a large saucepan, boil frozen vegetables in 2 cups of water. Bring to a boil, then turn down heat and simmer for 10 minutes. While boiling vegetables, use a medium saucepan to bring 1 cup water to a boil. Lower heat, add bouillon cube, and stir until dissolved. Gradually add flour, blending with wire whisk. Add salt, pepper, parsley, sage and thyme. Simmer 2-3 minutes until mixture thickens. Add sauce to vegetables, and simmer 30-45 minutes on stove or slow cook 4 or more hours in a crockpot. When ready to serve, add instant potatoes to thicken sauce. Serves 2. Serving size: 1 1/2 cups

Amount Per Serving:

Calories 218	Saturated Fat 0 g	Sodium 684 mg
Total Fat 1 g	Cholesterol 0 mg	

Chicken-Chili Stew

- 2 (8-ounce) chicken breasts, boneless and skinless
- 1 1/4 cups onion, chopped
- 1 medium green pepper, chopped
- 2 garlic cloves, minced
- 2 Tablespoons vegetable oil
- 2 (14 1/2-ounce) cans stewed tomatoes
- 1 (15-ounce) can pinto beans, drained
- 2/3-3/4 cup chunky picante sauce
- 1 teaspoon chili powder
- 1 teaspoon ground cumin
- 1/2 teaspoon salt (optional)
- brown rice, cooked according to package directions
- low-fat cheddar cheese (optional topping)
- green onion, diced (optional topping)
- fat-free sour cream (optional topping)

Cut chicken into 1-inch pieces. Cook chicken, onion, green pepper and garlic in oil in Dutch oven until chicken loses its pink color. Add next six ingredients. Simmer 20 minutes. Ladle into bowls over brown rice. Add toppings, if desired. Serves 8.
Serving size: 1 cup

Amount Per Serving:

Calories 287	Saturated Fat 1 g	Sodium 1264 mg
Total Fat 6 g	Cholesterol 38 mg	

Chili Supreme

- 1 cup brown rice, uncooked
- 2 (15-ounce) cans kidney and/or red beans
- 1 (46-ounce) can peeled or stewed tomatoes
- 1 green pepper, chopped
- 1 cup fresh mushrooms, sliced
- 1 garlic clove
- 1/4 cup ketchup
- 3 Tablespoons chili powder (more if desired)
- salt and pepper to taste
- 1/2 -1 cup water

Mix all ingredients together in a crockpot. Add more water if you prefer a soup-like chili. Set on low, and cook until rice is tender and liquid is absorbed (approximately 2 hours). Serves 12. Serving size: 1 cup

Amount Per Serving:

Calories 147	Saturated Fat 0 g	Sodium 486 mg
Total Fat 1 g	Cholesterol 0 mg	

Turkey Chili

- 2 pounds lean ground turkey
- 1 large onion, chopped
- 2 1/2 Tablespoons chili powder
- 1 Tablespoon cumin
- 2 teaspoons paprika
- 1/4 teaspoon garlic powder
- 1 (46-ounce) can low-sodium tomato juice
- 2 (15-ounce) cans chili beans

Brown turkey and onion in large Dutch oven. Drain off any liquid. Stir in chili powder, cumin, paprika and garlic powder. Continue cooking for 3 minutes, stirring occasionally. Add tomato juice. Cover and simmer over low heat at least 2 hours, stirring occasionally. Add chili beans, and continue cooking an additional 45 minutes. Serves 12. Serving size: 1 cup

Amount Per Serving:

Calories 329	Saturated Fat 2 g	Sodium 553 mg
Total Fat 11 g	Cholesterol 58 mg	

Vegetarian Chili

- 1 Tablespoon canola oil
- 3 garlic cloves, minced
- 1 large onion, chopped
- 2 stalks celery, chopped
- 1/2 pound mushrooms, sliced
- 2 (16-ounce) cans unsalted tomatoes, cut up with juice
- 1 (16-ounce) can kidney beans, drained
- 1 (16-ounce) can great northern beans, drained
- 2 Tablespoons chili powder
- 1/4 teaspoon hot sauce (optional)

Heat oil in a Dutch oven. Lightly sauté garlic, onions, celery and mushrooms in oil. Add tomatoes, beans and spices. Cook covered for 1 hour on low heat. Serves 10. Serving size: 3/4 cup

Amount Per Serving:

Calories 143	Saturated Fat 0 g	Sodium 182 mg
Total Fat 2 g	Cholesterol 0 mg	

Turkey Sausage Stew

- 1 pound turkey sausage, 85% fat-free
- 1 cup celery, sliced
- 1/2 cup onion, chopped
- 2 garlic cloves, minced
- 1/2 teaspoon thyme
- 1/2 teaspoon rosemary
- 2 (16-ounce) cans great
  northern beans, drained and crushed
- 1 (28-ounce) can diced,
  peeled tomatoes, undrained
- 1 teaspoon brown sugar
- red pepper as desired
- 1/2 cup green onions, sliced
- fat-free sour cream

Brown sausage in non-stick Dutch oven. Remove sausage, and set aside. Reserve 1/2 teaspoon drippings. Add celery, onions and garlic. Cook until crisp and tender. Add cooked sausage and other ingredients except green onions and fat-free sour cream. Bring to a boil. Reduce heat. Cover and simmer 10 minutes or until thoroughly heated. Top each serving with sliced green onions and 1 teaspoon fat-free sour cream.
Serves 8. Serving size: 1 cup

Amount Per Serving:

| Calories 280 | Saturated Fat 2 g | Sodium 576 mg |
| Total Fat 9 g | Cholesterol 32 mg | |

Creamy Coleslaw

- 1/3 cup plain, fat-free yogurt
- 2 Tablespoons Dijon mustard
- 1 Tablespoon fat-free salad dressing
- 2 teaspoons sugar
- freshly-ground pepper, to taste
- 3 cups cabbage, finely shredded
- 1/2 cup carrots, shredded
- 3 Tablespoons red onion, chopped

Mix yogurt, mustard, salad dressing, sugar and pepper in a medium-size bowl. Stir in remaining ingredients until evenly coated. Cover and chill for 1 hour before serving. Serves 4. Serving size: 6 ounces

Amount Per Serving:

Calories 54	Saturated Fat 0 g	Sodium 265 mg
Total Fat 1 g	Cholesterol 0 mg	

Black Bean Salad

- 1 (15-ounce) can corn, drained, or 3 ears freshly-cut corn from the cob
- 1 (15-ounce) can black beans, drained and rinsed
- 1 red bell pepper, minced
- 3 green onions, thinly sliced
- 1 large tomato, chopped
- 3 Tablespoons olive oil
- 1 1/2 Tablespoons cider vinegar
- 1/4 teaspoon dry mustard
- 1/2 teaspoon sugar
- 1-2 teaspoons chili powder
- 1-3 Tablespoons fresh cilantro, chopped
- 1 jalapeno pepper, chopped
- lettuce leaves

Combine all ingredients and chill. Serve on crisp lettuce leaves. Serves 6. Serving size: 6 ounces

Amount Per Serving:

Calories 109	Saturated Fat 1 g	Sodium 235 mg
Total Fat 4 g	Cholesterol 0 mg	

(Serves 12, 3-ounce servings when served as an appetizer.)

Cucumber Dressing Salad

Croutons:

- 4 slices sourdough bread, cubed
- 1/2 cup vegetable broth
- 1/4 teaspoon oregano
- 1/4 teaspoon garlic salt
- 1/4 teaspoon basil
- 1 teaspoon dried parsley

Salad and Dressing:

- 1/2 head romaine lettuce
- 1/2 head red leaf lettuce
- 2 cucumbers, peeled and sliced
- 1/3 cup onion, sliced
- 1 clove garlic
- 1 cup fat-free yogurt
- salt and pepper to taste

To make croutons, dip bread cubes into vegetable broth. Place on baking sheet, and sprinkle with oregano, garlic salt, basil and parsley. Bake in preheated oven at 350 degrees until crunchy (about 10-20 minutes). Watch carefully. Toss together torn romaine and red leaf lettuce leaves. Add one sliced cucumber and sliced onion. Coarsely chop the remaining cucumber for the dressing. Add cucumber, garlic and yogurt to blender, and puree. Toss over salad, and serve. Serve 4. Serving size: 16 ounces

Amount Per Serving:

Calories 146	Saturated Fat 0 g	Sodium 343 mg
Total Fat 1 g	Cholesterol 1 mg	

Pickled Coleslaw

- 4 cups grated cabbage
- 1/2 medium green pepper, minced
- 1 small red bell pepper, minced
- 1 teaspoon salt
- 1 cup water
- 1/2 cup apple cider vinegar
- 1/2 cup sugar
- 1/2 teaspoon celery seed
- 1/2 teaspoon mustard seed

In large bowl, combine cabbage and peppers. In small saucepan, heat salt, water, vinegar and sugar enough to dissolve sugar. Add celery seed and mustard seed. Pour over cabbage and pepper mixture. Mix well. Chill for 24 hours before serving. Will keep several days in refrigerator. Serves 12. Serving size: 4 ounces

Amount Per Serving:

Calories 49	Saturated Fat 0 g	Sodium 184 mg
Total Fat 0 g	Cholesterol 0 mg	

Surprise Salad

Prep Time: 15 minutes

- 1 cup apples, chopped
- 1 teaspoon lemon juice
- 1/2 cup fat-free mayonnaise
- 1/4 cup fat-free sour cream
- 1/4 teaspoon salt

- 1/8 teaspoon black pepper
- 3/4 cup canned beets, drained and diced
- 1/4 cup green onion, chopped
- 1 head iceberg lettuce, shredded
- 1 yellow or red pepper, sliced into 6 rings

Toss lemon juice with the chopped apple. Set aside. Mix together the mayonnaise, sour cream, salt and pepper. Add apple mixture to mayonnaise mixture. Fold beets and onion into mixture. Place shredded lettuce onto six salad plates. Spoon apple, beet and onion mixture onto lettuce. Top with pepper ring. Serves 6. Serving size: 1 salad

Amount Per Serving:

Calories 59	Saturated Fat 0 g	Sodium 324 mg
Total Fat 0 g	Cholesterol 0 mg	

Layered Summer Salad

Prep Time: 20 minutes
Chill Time: 4 hours or overnight

- 1/4 pound turkey bacon
- 1 head lettuce
- 1 1/2 cups cauliflower, sliced
- 1 medium onion, chopped

- 1 cup shredded, fat-free cheddar cheese
- 1 1/2 cups fat-free salad dressing
- 2 tablespoons sugar

Fry or microwave turkey bacon. Drain. Layer lettuce, cauliflower, onion, bacon and cheddar cheese in order listed in a large bowl. Spread salad dressing over top of ingredients, sealing to the edges. Sprinkle with sugar. Refrigerate overnight or several hours. Toss and serve. Serves 10. Serving size: 8 ounces

Amount Per Serving:

Calories 116	Saturated Fat 1 g	Sodium 805 mg
Total Fat 4 g	Cholesterol 11 mg	

Creamy Broccoli & Cauliflower Salad

- 1 head cauliflower
- 1 head broccoli
- 1 carton cherry tomatoes, halved
- 1 cup fat-free mayonnaise
- 1/2 cup fat-free sour cream
- 1 medium onion, chopped
- 1 Tablespoon cider vinegar
- 2 Tablespoons sugar
- Salt and pepper to taste

Prepare broccoli and cauliflower in bite-size flowerets. Stir broccoli, cauliflower and tomato halves in large bowl. In small bowl, combine fat-free mayonnaise, sour cream, onion, vinegar, sugar, salt and pepper. Add mayonnaise mixture to vegetable mixture and toss. Serves 12. Serving size: 4 ounces

Amount Per Serving:

Calories 58	Saturated Fat 0 g	Sodium 320 mg
Total Fat 0 g	Cholesterol 0 mg	

Dilled Broccoli-Potato Salad

- 2 pounds red potatoes
  (approximately 6 cups)
- 3/4 cup red onion, chopped
- 1/2 cup chicken broth
- 1/2 cup cider vinegar
- 2 Tablespoons vegetable oil

- 1/4 cup Parmesan cheese,
  grated
- 1 teaspoon dill
- 1 teaspoon sugar
- 1/2 teaspoon white pepper
- 3 cups small broccoli flowerets

Scrub potatoes, and cut into half-inch cubes. In a 4-quart Dutch oven, cook potatoes in 1/2 inch of boiling water until just tender (about 8 minutes). Drain well, and pour into large bowl. Add onion. Set aside. In separate bowl, whisk together the chicken broth, vinegar, vegetable oil, Parmesan cheese, dill, sugar and pepper. Pour over potato mixture, and toss lightly to coat. Let stand 20 minutes. Cover and refrigerate to chill. In same Dutch oven, cook broccoli in 2 inches of boiling water until crisp and tender (about 2 minutes). Be careful not to overcook broccoli. Drain and rinse in cold water to retain bright green color of broccoli. Just before serving, toss broccoli into potato mixture. Serves 8. Serving size: 8 ounces

Amount Per Serving:

Calories 259	Saturated Fat 1 g	Sodium 130 mg
Total Fat 5 g	Cholesterol 3 mg	

Confetti Crunch Salad

- 2 cups broccoli flowerets
- 2 cups cauliflower flowerets
- 1 cup celery, sliced
- 1 cup cherry tomatoes, halved
- 1 cup zucchini, sliced
- 3/4 cup green onion, sliced
- 1/3 cup pitted ripe olives, sliced
- 1/2 cup carrots, sliced
- 1 cup fat-free Italian salad dressing

In a large bowl, combine all ingredients. Cover and marinate in refrigerator, turning occasionally. Let chill for at least 4 hours or overnight. Serves 8. Serving size: 8 ounces

Amount Per Serving:

Calories 60	Saturated Fat 0 g	Sodium 517 mg
Total Fat 2 g	Cholesterol 0 mg	

69

Mostaccioli Pizza Salad

Prep Time: 30 minutes
Cooking Time: 12 minutes

- 1 1/2 cups uncooked mostaccioli pasta
- 3 Tablespoons white vinegar
- 2 Tablespoons water
- 1 Tablespoon olive oil
- 3/4 teaspoon dried Italian seasoning
- 1/4 teaspoon salt (optional)
- 1/4 teaspoon pepper

- 2 garlic cloves, crushed
- 1 cup sliced mushrooms
- 3/4 cup cherry tomato halves
- 1/2 cup green pepper, chopped
- 1/2 cup (2 ounces) shredded, part-skim, mozzarella cheese

Cook pasta according to package directions, omitting salt and fat. Rinse with cool water. Drain and set aside to cool. Combine vinegar, water, olive oil, seasonings and garlic in a medium-size bowl. Whisk until blended. Add cooled pasta, mushrooms, tomatoes, pepper and cheese. Toss gently to coat. Serve at room temperature, or chill if desired. Serves 5. Serving size: 8 ounces

Amount Per Serving:

Calories 190	Saturated Fat 2 g	Sodium 61 mg
Total Fat 5 g	Cholesterol 6 mg	

Mandarin Spinach Salad

Prep: 20 minutes

- 1/3 cup fat-free mayonnaise
- 1/4 cup unsweetened orange juice
- 1 teaspoon sugar
- 1 teaspoon poppy seeds
- 1/2 pound fresh spinach, washed and torn
- 2 cups fresh strawberries, sliced, or red pears, cored and sliced
- 1 (11-ounce) can mandarin oranges, drained

Combine mayonnaise, orange juice, sugar and poppy seeds in a small bowl. Set aside. Gently toss spinach, strawberries (or pears) and oranges in large bowl. Arrange salad on individual serving plates. Drizzle 1 Tablespoon poppy seed mixture over each salad. Serves 8. Serving size: 8 ounces

Amount Per Serving:

Calories 49	Saturated Fat 0 g	Sodium 138 mg
Total Fat 1 g	Cholesterol 0 mg	

Wild Rice Salad

Prep Time: 1 1/2 hour
Cooking Time: 1 hour

- 1 cup wild rice
- 2 cups chicken broth
- 1 (6-ounce) package long grain and wild rice
- 1/2 cup green onions, chopped
- 1/2 cup pecans, chopped
- 1 (8-ounce) can mandarin oranges, drained
- 1 cup golden raisins, plumped
- 2 Tablespoons fresh parsley, chopped
- 1 cup fat-free salad dressing
- 1/2 cup orange juice

Simmer wild rice in chicken broth until tender, 45 minutes to 1 hour. Meanwhile, cook package of long grain and wild rice according to package directions. Set aside. Combine rices, green onions, pecans, mandarin oranges and raisins in large bowl. (To plump raisins, drop in boiling water for 30 seconds, then drain.) In a small bowl, combine salad dressing and orange juice until blended and of liquid consistency. Add more orange juice if needed. Toss dressing with rice mixture and refrigerate. Serves 6. Serving size: 10 ounces

Amount Per Serving:

Calories 372	Saturated Fat 1 g	Sodium 772 mg
Total Fat 7 g	Cholesterol 0 mg	

Kidney Beans Monterey

Prep Time: 15 minutes
Chill Time: 30 minutes

- 2 (16-ounce) cans dark red kidney beans, drained
- 1/4 cup cider vinegar
- 2 Tablespoons vegetable oil
- 1/8 teaspoon chili powder
- 1 cup green onion, chopped
- 2 Tablespoons cilantro, chopped
- 1 garlic clove, minced
- 1 (4-ounce) can green chilies, chopped

Combine all ingredients, and toss gently. Chill 30 minutes before serving. Serves 8. Serving size: 4 ounces

Amount Per Serving:

Calories 160	Saturated Fat 1 g	Sodium 251 mg
Total Fat 4 g	Cholesterol 0 mg	

Fire & Ice

Prep Time: 20 minutes
Chill Time: 1 hour

- 1 large tomato, chopped
- 1 cucumber, peeled and chopped
- 1/4 cup red onion, diced
- 1 Tablespoon red wine vinegar
- 1 Tablespoon parsley, chopped
- 1 garlic clove, minced
- 1/8 teaspoon salt
- 1/4 teaspoon pepper

Gently mix tomato, cucumber and onion in medium bowl. In separate bowl, combine vinegar, parsley, garlic, salt and pepper. Stir vinegar mixture into cucumber mixture. Chill. Serves 6. Serving size: 4 ounces

Amount Per Serving:

Calories 14	Saturated Fat 0 g	Sodium 48 mg
Total Fat 0 g	Cholesterol 0 mg	

Apple Salad

- 1 /4 cup sugar
- 1/2 cup raisins
- 1 cup fat-free mayonnaise
  or salad dressing
- 1 cup red apple, diced
- 1 cup green apple, diced

- 1 cup broccoli, chopped
- 1 cup celery, chopped
- 1/4 cup onion, chopped
- 1/4 cup almonds, slivered
  (optional)
- 1 Tablespoon white vinegar

In a small mixing bowl, mix sugar, raisins and mayonnaise. Place apples, broccoli, celery, onion, almonds and vinegar into a large bowl, and toss. Add dressing mixture, and mix well. Chill and serve. Serves 6. Serving size: 8 ounce

Amount Per Serving:

Calories 190	Saturated Fat 0 g	Sodium 591 mg
Total Fat 3 g	Cholesterol 0 mg	

Contributed by Leonard Neese, Lambert's Cafe,
"Home of the Throwed Rolls", Ozark, Missouri, and Sikeston, Missouri.

Fiesta Lime Fruit Cup

- 1/2 cup banana, sliced
- 1 Tablespoon fresh lime juice
- 1 cup melon, peeled and cubed
  (cantaloupe, honeydew or watermelon)

- 1 cup fresh blueberries, stemmed
- 1/2 cup fresh pineapple chunks
- 1/2 teaspoon ground cinnamon
- 1 teaspoon sugar

Toss banana slices in lime juice. In medium bowl combine melon, blueberries, banana and pineapple chunks. Combine cinnamon and sugar. Add cinnamon and sugar mixture to combined fruit, and gently toss. Chill for 30 minutes. Serves 4. Serving size: 6 ounces

Amount Per Serving:

Calories 72	Saturated Fat 1 g	Sodium 6 mg
Total Fat 1 g	Cholesterol 0 mg	

Moroccan Fruit Salad

- 3 cups cooked couscous, cooled
- 1 large banana, peeled and sliced
- 3/4 cup red apples,
  unpeeled and chopped
- 1/3 cup celery, sliced

- 1/3 cup walnut pieces, toasted
- 2/3 cup orange juice
- 1 1/2 Tablespoons lemon juice
- 1/4 teaspoon ground cinnamon

Combine couscous, banana, apples, celery and walnuts. In a separate bowl, whisk together orange juice, lemon juice and cinnamon. Pour juice mixture over fruit mixture and gently toss. Serves 4. Serving size: 10 ounces

Amount Per Serving:

Calories 276	Saturated Fat 1 g	Sodium 16 mg
Total Fat 6 g	Cholesterol 0 mg	

Italian Ambrosia

- 1 medium cantaloupe,
  peeled and cut into chunks
- 2 navel oranges, peeled and sectioned
- 2 cups fresh pineapple chunks
- 2 plums, pitted and sliced

- 1 cup seedless green grapes
- 3/4 cup peach nectar
- 1/4 cup honey
- 2 Tablespoons balsamic vinegar
- 1-2 Tablespoons lemon juice

Combine cantaloupe, oranges, pineapple, plums and grapes in a large bowl. Whisk together nectar, honey, vinegar and lemon juice. Pour over fruit, and toss to mix. Chill for 1 hour, stirring occasionally. Serves 8. Serving size: 8 ounces

Amount Per Serving:

Calories 142	Saturated Fat 0 g	Sodium 34 mg
Total Fat 0 g	Cholesterol 0 mg	

Tropical Fruit Salad

- 2 ripe bananas, peeled and sliced
- 2 oranges, peeled and sectioned
- 1 cup fresh pineapple, peeled and diced
- 1 mango, peeled and sliced

- 1/2 teaspoon cinnamon
- 1 teaspoon honey
- 1/4 cup coconut, grated

Mix all ingredients together, using coconut as a garnish. Chill slightly. Serves 4.
Serving size: 4 ounces

Amount Per Serving:

| Calories 188 | Saturated Fat 2 g | Sodium 19 mg |
| Total Fat 4 g | Cholesterol 0 mg | |

Myth No. 162:

"People from the Ozarks believe a discussion on hog-calling techniques is interesting and appropriate dinner party conversation."

Fruit 'n Cream Layered Salad

- 2 Tablespoons almonds, sliced
- 1 (3-ounce) package
  low-fat cream cheese
- 1 (8-ounce) carton
  fat-free strawberry yogurt
- 1 Tablespoon sugar
- 2 teaspoons lemon juice
- 2 cups light whipped topping
- 1/4 teaspoon almond extract
- 8-10 cups assorted fresh
  and/or canned fruits (5 varieties)

Lightly toast almonds in dry skillet, stirring to prevent scorching. Set aside. Combine cream cheese, yogurt, sugar and lemon juice. Stir in whipped topping and almond extract. Beat until smooth. Refrigerate topping while preparing fruit. If canned fruit is used, drain off juices. Chop or slice fresh fruit, peeling if necessary. In a large bowl, layer three fruits. Spoon on half of topping mixture, spreading to edges of bowl. Layer remaining fruit. Spoon on remaining topping mixture. Top with toasted almonds. Serves 24. Serving size: 4 ounces

Amount Per Serving:

Calories 71	Saturated Fat 0 g	Sodium 38 mg
Total Fat 2 g	Cholesterol 2 mg	

Georgia's Fruit Salad

- 1 (15-ounce) can pineapple chunks
- 1 (15-ounce) can chunky pears
- 1 (15-ounce) can chunky peaches
- 1 (10-ounce) can mandarin oranges
- water
- 1 small package lemon pudding
  (not instant)
- sweetener to taste
- maraschino cherries

Drain juice from fruit and save. If needed add water to juice to make 2 cups. Cook juice with lemon pudding until thick. Add sweetener to taste, if too tart. Mix with fruit and refrigerate. Top with maraschino cherries. Serves 8. Serving size: 1 cup

Amount Per Serving:

Calories 137	Saturated Fat 0 g	Sodium 54 mg
Total Fat 0 g	Cholesterol 0 mg	

Strawberry Gelatin Salad

1st layer:

- 2 1/2 cups pretzels, crushed
- 1/2 cup margarine, melted
- 3 Tablespoons sugar

Preheat oven to 375 degrees. Mix ingredients and spread in 9 x 13-inch pan. Bake for 10 minutes. Cool.

2nd layer:

- 1 cup sugar
- 2 (8-ounce) packages fat-free cream cheese
- 1 (8-ounce) carton light whipped topping

Cream sugar with cream cheese. Fold in whipped topping. Spread on top of crust. Refrigerate for 1 hour.

3rd layer:

- 2 (6-ounce) packages strawberry gelatin
- 2 1/4 cups boiling water
- 2 (10-ounce) packages frozen strawberries

Prepare gelatin with boiling water. Add strawberries. Cool. Pour over cream cheese layer. Refrigerate overnight and serve. Serves 24. Serving size: 1 (2 x 2-inch) square

Amount Per Serving:

Calories 180	Saturated Fat 1 g	Sodium 573 mg
Total Fat 5 g	Cholesterol 0 mg	

Tortellini and Fruit Salad

Prep Time: 30 minutes
Cooking Time: 10 minutes

- 1/3 cup skim milk
- 1/4 cup plain fat-free yogurt
- 1 Tablespoon sugar
- 2 teaspoons orange peel, grated
- 1 (9-ounce) package refrigerated, cheese tortellini
- 1 cup cantaloupe, cubed
- 1/2 cup blueberries
- 1/2 cup seedless, green grapes
- 1/4 cup almonds, slivered
- salt and pepper to taste

In a small bowl, combine milk, yogurt, sugar and orange peel. Blend until smooth, and set aside. Cook tortellini according to package directions. Drain and rinse with cold water. In a large bowl, gently combine cooled tortellini, fruits and almonds. Pour dressing mixture over salad. Stir gently and serve. Serves 6. Serving size: 4 ounces

Amount Per Serving:

Calories 205	Saturated Fat 0 g	Sodium 236 mg
Total Fat 7 g	Cholesterol 24 mg	

Sunny Day Pasta Salad

Prep Time: 20 minutes
Cooking Time: 10 minutes

- 1 (16-ounce) package rotini pasta, cooked
- 1 cup zucchini, sliced
- 1 cup cherry or Roma tomatoes, quartered
- 1 cup green peppers, diced
- 1 cup orange peppers, diced
- 1 cup broccoli flowerets
- 1 (2.25-ounce) can sliced black olives
- 1 cup cucumbers, sliced
- 1 (8-ounce) bottle Italian salad dressing

Cook pasta according to package directions. Drain, rinse and chill cooked pasta. Gently mix the pasta, vegetables and salad dressing in a large bowl. Serves 12. Serving size: 8 ounces

Amount Per Serving:

Calories 141	Saturated Fat 1 g	Sodium 188 mg
Total Fat 4 g	Cholesterol 2 mg	

Cottage Pasta Salad

Prep Time: 8 to 12 hours to marinate
Cooking Time: 10 minutes
Marinade Time: 8 to 12 hours

- 1 large garlic clove, pressed
- 3 Tablespoons olive oil
- 1/2 cup red wine vinegar
- 1 dash Worcestershire sauce
- 1/2 teaspoon ground pepper
- 1/4 teaspoon salt

- 1 teaspoon oregano
- 2 Tablespoons fresh parsley, minced
- 1 pound linguini, cooked al dente
- 6 ounces cheddar cheese, shredded
- 12 sundried tomatoes, cut into pieces
- 1/2 cup pine nuts

Combine garlic, olive oil, vinegar, Worcestershire sauce, pepper, salt, oregano and parsley in a jar and shake well. Pour over cooked pasta. Toss and marinate 8 to 12 hours. In a large bowl, layer pasta, cheese, tomatoes and nuts three times. Serve at room temperature. Serves 8. Serving size: 8 ounces

Amount Per Serving:

Calories 494	Saturated Fat 5 g	Sodium 437 mg
Total Fat 19 g	Cholesterol 22 mg	

Tip: Soften sundried tomato pieces by pouring boiling water over them and covering. Let set until cool. Drain. Rinse. Pat dry.

Contributed by Jimmy Osmond, Osmond Family Theater, Branson, Missouri.

Crabby Pasta Salad

Prep Time: 30 minutes
Cooking Time: 12 minutes

- 1 (8-ounce) package curly
  tri-color or small shell pasta
- 1 (8-ounce) package imitation crab
- 1 (8-ounce) jar marinated artichokes,
  drained

- 1 cup frozen peas
- 1/3 cup bottled pesto dressing
- 1/3 cup carrots, grated
- 6 canned ripe olives, sliced

Cook pasta according to package directions. Drain and set aside. Heat crab in skillet coated with non-stick cooking spray. Add artichokes and peas. Heat until warmed and peas are no longer frozen. Stir crab mixture into pasta, and toss with pesto dressing. Stir in carrots and olives. Serves 6. Serving size: 8 ounces

Amount Per Serving:

Calories 277	Saturated Fat 1 g	Sodium 474 mg
Total Fat 7 g	Cholesterol 9 mg	

Aloha Chicken Salad

- 4 cups chicken, cooked, cooled and cubed
- 1 cup green grapes, sliced or 1 cup pineapple tidbits
- 3/4 cup celery, chopped
- 1/3 cup pecans, chopped
- 1 cup fat-free mayonnaise
- 1/2 teaspoon curry powder
- 1/8 cup orange juice
- 1 teaspoon tarragon (optional)

In large bowl, combine chicken, grapes or pineapple, celery and pecans. In separate bowl, combine fat-free mayonnaise, curry powder, and orange juice. Add mayonnaise mixture to chicken mixture, and toss gently. Serve on a bed of lettuce or as a sandwich filling. Serves 10. Serving size: 6 ounces

Amount Per Serving:

Calories 147	Saturated Fat 1 g	Sodium 355 mg
Total Fat 5 g	Cholesterol 47 mg	

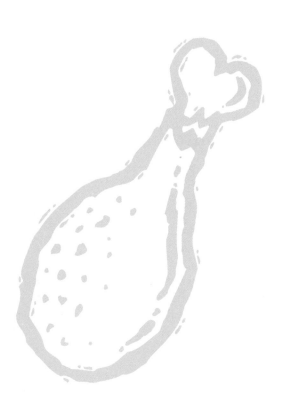

Chicken Salad

- 7 cups chicken,
  cooked and cubed
- 3 cups green or
  red seedless grapes, halved
- 1 cup tidbit-sized pineapple,
  drained, reserving juice
- 1/2 cup green olives,
  rinsed and sliced
- 1/4 cup fat-free mayonnaise
- 2 Tablespoons almonds,
  sliced/slivered and toasted

Mix all ingredients except almonds. For added moisture use 1-2 Tablespoons pineapple juice. Vary proportions according to taste. Chill before serving. To serve, top with toasted almonds. Flavor improves overnight. Serves 10. Serving size: 8 ounces

Amount Per Serving:

Calories 199	Saturated Fat 1 g	Sodium 268 mg
Total Fat 6 g	Cholesterol 75 mg	

Contributed by St. John's Nutrition Center, Springfield, Missouri.

Caribbean Chicken Salad

- 1/2 pound chicken breast,
  boneless and skinless, cooked
- 2-4 lettuce leaves
- 1/4 pound asparagus
  (or green beans), steamed
- 1 (8-ounce) can pineapple slices
  in juice, undrained
- 1 cup assorted fresh fruit, sliced
- 1/2 cup vanilla yogurt
- 2-3 Tablespoons chutney, chopped
- 1 teaspoon lemon peel, grated

Slice chicken diagonally into 1/2-inch slices and set aside. Line salad plates with lettuce. Arrange chicken and asparagus on top of lettuce. Drain pineapple, reserving 3 Tablespoons of juice for use in dressing. Arrange pineapple and fresh fruit on salad plates. For dressing, combine reserved pineapple juice, yogurt, chutney and lemon peel in a small bowl. Serve with salad. Serves 2. (As a main dish salad.)
Serving size: 12 ounces

Amount Per Serving:

Calories 391	Saturated Fat 1 g	Sodium 139 mg
Total Fat 5 g	Cholesterol 98 mg	

Herbed Chicken Salad

Prep Time: 1 hour
(includes cooking time for chicken)
Chill Time: 1 hour

- 3 cups cooked chicken breast, cubed
- 1/4 cup plain, fat-free yogurt
- 1/4 cup fat-free mayonnaise
- 1/4 cup fat-free sour cream
- 4 green onions with tops, chopped
- 1 small carrot, grated
- 4 radishes, grated
- 4 Tablespoons celery, chopped
- 2 Tablespoons green pepper, chopped

- 2 Tablespoons red pepper, chopped
- 3 Tablespoons parsley, chopped
- 1 teaspoon Worcestershire sauce
- 1 teaspoon Herb Seasoning
  (see following recipe)
- 1/4 teaspoon white pepper
- 2 Tablespoons tarragon vinegar
- lettuce leaves (garnish)
- 3 sliced tomatoes (garnish)

Combine all ingredients except lettuce and tomatoes. Mix well. Cover and refrigerate at least 1 hour. To serve, place a scoop of salad on lettuce leaf, and garnish with tomato slices. Serves 8. Serving size: 6 ounces

Amount Per Serving:

Calories 129	Saturated Fat 1 g	Sodium 166 mg
Total Fat 2 g	Cholesterol 48 mg	

Herb Seasoning

Prep Time: 10 minutes

- 1/2 teaspoon cayenne pepper
- 1 Tablespoon garlic powder
- 1 teaspoon dried basil
- 1 teaspoon freshly-ground black pepper
- 1 teaspoon dried thyme
- 1 teaspoon dried parsley

- 1 teaspoon dried savory seasoning
- 1 teaspoon dried mace
- 1 teaspoon onion powder
- 1 teaspoon dried marjoram
- 1 teaspoon ground sage

Combine all ingredients in medium bowl. Toss gently with spoon until well blended. Store in an airtight container in cool, dry, dark place for up to 6 months. Use your imagination in using this wonderful seasoning blend. It is used in the previous recipe (Herbed Chicken Salad). You might try tossing it into a pasta salad or sprinkling it over a favorite garden salad. Yields 1/3 cup seasoning.

Ziti Salmon Salad

Prep Time: 30 minutes
Cooking Time: 10 minutes
Chill Time: 1 hour

- 8 ounces ziti pasta, uncooked
- 1 (16 ounce) can salmon, drained, skin and bones removed
- 1 (6 ounce) package frozen snow peas, thawed
- 1 medium red bell pepper, chopped
- 1 medium yellow bell pepper, chopped
- 1/2 cup green onions, sliced
- 1/2 cup bottled, fat-free Italian dressing
- 1/2 teaspoon salt-free herb seasoning

Prepare ziti according to package directions. Drain. In a large bowl, combine ziti and remaining ingredients. Mix well. Cover and chill thoroughly. Toss gently before serving. Serves 8. Serving size: 6 ounces

Amount Per Serving:

Calories 206	Saturated Fat 1 g	Sodium 490 mg
Total Fat 4 g	Cholesterol 22 mg	

Shrimp and Rice Salad

Prep Time: 30 minutes
Cooking Time: 20 minutes
Chill Time: 1 hour

- 3 cups cooked converted rice
- 1 pound jumbo shrimp, cooked and diced
- 2/3 cup celery, finely-diced
- 1/4 cup green onion, finely-chopped
- 1/4 cup green pepper, finely-chopped
- 1 (8-ounce) can water chestnuts, sliced
- 1 (10-ounce) package small frozen peas
- 1 cup low-fat mayonnaise
- 4 teaspoons soy sauce
- 1/2 teaspoon curry powder (optional)

Cook rice according to package directions. Combine rice, shrimp, celery, green onion, green pepper, water chestnuts and peas in large bowl. In a smaller bowl, mix the mayonnaise, soy sauce and curry powder to make the dressing. Stir the dressing into the other ingredients. Cover and chill. Serve on green leafy lettuce. Salad may be served as an entree or side dish. Serves 8. Serving size: 8 ounces

Amount Per Serving:

Calories 262	Saturated Fat 1 g	Sodium 717 mg
Total Fat 9 g	Cholesterol 85 mg	

Contributed by retired Chef Ernest G. Joseph.

Citrus Salad Dressing

- 3 teaspoons orange peel
- 3/4 cup orange juice
- 1 teaspoon lemon peel
- 2 Tablespoons white wine vinegar
- 3 Tablespoons fresh basil, minced
- 2 dashes hot sauce

- 2 teaspoons Dijon mustard
- 1 teaspoon brown sugar
- 1 teaspoon ground cumin
- 2 garlic cloves, minced
- salt (optional)

Combine all ingredients and chill at least 4 hours before serving. Serves 10.
Serving size: 2 Tablespoons

Amount Per Serving:

Calories 14	Saturated 0 g	Sodium 80 mg
Total Fat 0 g	Cholesterol 0 mg	

Myth No. 261:

"Molasses is considered an Ozarkian household staple.
Not only is it useful in the kitchen, but it also serves as a
great fly strip refurbisher, denture adhesive and caulking compound."

Cran-Raspberry Ring

1st layer:
- 1/4 cup sugar
- 1 (1-ounce) package sugar-free raspberry gelatin
- 1 1/4 cups cranberry juice cocktail
- 1 cup fresh or frozen cranberries, finely chopped
- 1 cup fresh or frozen raspberries, finely chopped

2nd layer:
- 1 (1-ounce) package sugar-free raspberry gelatin
- 1 cup cranberry juice cocktail
- 1 cup fat-free sour cream
- 1 1/4 pounds seedless green grapes, halved
- 3/4 cup whole, seedless green grapes (for garnish)

To make first layer, combine sugar and gelatin in medium-sized bowl. Stir to mix well. Place juice in small saucepan, and heat to boiling. Pour juice over gelatin mixture. Stir until dissolved. Cool to room temperature. Stir in chopped cranberries and raspberries. Pour mixture into a 6-cup ring mold. Chill for several hours or until firm. For second layer, place second package of gelatin in medium bowl. In small saucepan, bring remaining cranberry juice to a boil. Pour hot juice over gelatin, and stir until dissolved. Cool to room temperature. Stir in sour cream and grape halves. Pour second mixture over first layer in mold. Chill several hours until firm. To unmold the ring, dip the mold in warm (not hot) water for 5-10 seconds. (Beware of too hot water or leaving mold in water too long as gelatin will start to melt.) Loosen edges of mold with knife and invert onto lettuce lined serving platter. Garnish with whole grapes. Serves 10.
Serving size: 6 ounces (approximately)

Amount Per Serving:

Calories 119	Saturated Fat 0 g	Sodium 40 mg
Total Fat 0 g	Cholesterol 0 mg	

Poke Salad Mary's Barbecue Brisket of Beef Salad

- 6 ounces cut iceberg and romaine lettuce mix
- 5 ounces cooked beef brisket, diced into 1/2-inch pieces
- 1 ounce cheddar cheese, shredded
- 1 cherry tomato
- 1/4 cup barbecue sauce
- 3 red onion rings
- 1/4 cup croutons

Marinate and heat beef in 1 Tablespoon barbecue sauce. In a salad bowl, layer the mixed lettuce with the beef in two layers. Top with cheese, tomato, red onion and croutons. Top it off with the remaining barbecue sauce, served hot as the dressing. Serves 1. Serving size: 1 salad

Amount Per Serving:

Calories 526	Saturated Fat 3 g	Sodium 878 mg
Total Fat 17 g	Cholesterol 150 mg	

Contributed by Chef Moose Zader, Silver Dollar City in Branson, Missouri.

Myth No. 22:

"Ozarkians believe the only need for more than one spoon
is for musical purposes."

ENTRÉES

Myth No. 4:
"All Ozark dinners begin with the words 'Chicken Fried.'"

Fact:
"This is not true. Nor do we believe that light cooking means using white gravy instead of brown."

Boat Beans

- 1/2 pound extra-lean, ground round
- 1 small onion, chopped
- 1 (15-ounce) can red kidney beans
- 1 (15-ounce) can pork and beans
- 1 (15-ounce) can large butter beans
- 1 (15-ounce) can brown beans
- 1/3 cup brown sugar
- 1/3 cup white sugar
- 1/4 cup ketchup
- 1/4 cup barbecue sauce
- 1 Tablespoon mustard
- 2 Tablespoons molasses
- 1/2 teaspoon chili powder
- 1 teaspoon salt
- 1/2 teaspoon pepper

Preheat oven to 350 degrees. Brown beef and onion in a Dutch oven. Drain well. Add the beans and mix. Add the remaining ingredients, and mix well. Bake for 1 hour. Serves 12. Serving size: 1 cup

Amount Per Serving:

Calories 228	Saturated Fat 1 g	Sodium 934 mg
Total Fat 3 g	Cholesterol 16 mg	

Fiesta Meat Loaf

- 1 pound extra-lean ground beef
- 3/4 cup quick oats, uncooked
- 1/2 cup egg substitute
- 1/2 cup salsa, divided
- 1/2 cup green bell pepper, diced
- 1/4 cup onion, diced
- 1 Tablespoon chili powder
- 1/2 teaspoon salt

Preheat oven to 350 degrees. In a medium bowl, combine beef, oats, egg substitute, 1/4 cup salsa, green pepper, onion, chili powder and salt. Form meat mixture into loaf shape, and place in an 8 x 4 x 3-inch loaf pan coated with non-stick cooking spray. Top with remaining salsa. Bake for 55 minutes. Serves 6. Serving size: 1 slice

Amount Per Serving:

Calories 263	Saturated Fat 4 g	Sodium 353 mg
Total Fat 11 g	Cholesterol 61 mg	

Beef and Cheese with Egg Noodles Casserole

Prep Time: 30 minutes
Cooking Time: 30 minutes

- 1 (8-ounce) package medium egg noodles
- 1 1/2 pounds lean ground beef
- 1 garlic clove, minced
- 1 Tablespoon low-fat margarine, melted
- 3 (8-ounce) cans tomato sauce
- salt and pepper to taste
- 1 Tablespoon sugar
- 1 cup low-fat cottage cheese
- 1 (8-ounce) package low-fat cream cheese
- 1/4 cup fat-free sour cream
- 1/3 cup onion, chopped
- 1/4 cup green pepper, chopped
- 1 cup low-fat cheddar cheese, grated

Preheat oven to 350 degrees. Cook noodles according to package directions. Set aside. Brown ground beef and garlic in margarine in a large skillet. Drain well. Add tomato sauce, salt, pepper and sugar. Cook for 5 minutes. In a medium bowl, blend together the cottage cheese and cream cheese. Add sour cream, onion and green pepper to the cheese mixture. Coat a 9 x 13-inch baking dish with non-stick cooking spray. Place half of the cooked noodles in baking dish, add the cheese mixture, then layer the rest of the noodles on the cheese mixture. Cover with ground beef mixture, and top with cheddar cheese. Bake for 30 minutes. Serves 8. Serving size: 8 ounces

Amount Per Serving:

Calories 410	Saturated Fat 5 g	Sodium 823 mg
Total Fat 14 g	Cholesterol 101 mg	

Green Pepper and Tomato Steak

Prep Time: 30 minutes
Cooking Time: 30 minutes

- 1 Tablespoon olive or vegetable oil
- 1 pound sirloin steak
- 1/2 teaspoon salt
- 1/2 to 3/4 cup onion, diced
- 1(16-ounce) can beef bouillon, broth or consommé
- 1 large garlic clove, finely-minced
- 3 Tablespoons light soy sauce
- 1 or 2 green peppers, cut in 1-inch pieces
- 2 Tablespoons cornstarch
- 1/4 cup cold water
- 2 tomatoes, cut into pieces

Cut meat into 1/2-inch strips and trim off fat. Use oil to grease a wok (or a large skillet). Brown meat on one side. Turn meat, and sprinkle with 1/4 teaspoon salt. Brown other side, and sprinkle with remaining salt. Push meat to the side of the wok. Add onion, and cook until tender. Add bouillon, garlic and soy sauce. Cover and simmer 10 minutes or until meat is tender. Add green pepper. Cover and simmer for 5 minutes. Blend cornstarch with water, and gradually stir into meat mixture. Cook over low heat, stirring, until mixture comes to a boil and thickens. Add tomatoes and heat thoroughly. Serve over hot rice. Serves 4. Serving size: 6 ounces

Amount Per Serving:

Calories 287	Saturated Fat 4 g	Sodium 1210 mg
Total Fat: 12 g	Cholesterol 76 mg	

Beef Tenderloin Au Poivre

Prep Time: 2 minutes
Cooking Time: 45 minutes

- 1 beef tenderloin, trimmed of fat (3 1/2 -4 pounds, after trimming)
- 1/3 cup Dijon mustard
- 4 1/2 teaspoons coarsely-ground black peppercorns
- 4 1/2 teaspoons coarsely-ground white peppercorns

Preheat oven to 425 degrees. Rub tenderloin generously all over with the Dijon mustard. Combine peppercorns, and press them evenly over surface of the meat. Place meat in a roasting pan, and cook to desired doneness (45 minutes for rare meat). Let stand for 5 minutes before slicing. Serves 8. Serving size: 8 ounces

Amount Per Serving:

Calories 361	Saturated Fat 6 g	Sodium 423 mg
Total Fat 16 g	Cholesterol 116 mg	

Beef Stroganoff

- 2 pounds beef sirloin steak
- 2-3 Tablespoons low-fat margarine
- 1 cup onion, chopped
- 1 garlic clove, finely-minced
- 1 pound fresh mushrooms, sliced
- 3 Tablespoons flour
- 2 Tablespoons instant beef bouillon
- 1 Tablespoon ketchup
- 1/2 teaspoon salt
- 1/8 teaspoon pepper
- 1 (10 1/2-ounce) can beef
  or chicken bouillon
- 1/4 cup dry white wine
- 1 Tablespoon fresh dill
  or 1/4 teaspoon dried dill
- 1/2 cups light (or fat-free) sour cream
- cooked wide egg noodles

Trim fat from beef and cut into 1/2 x 2-inch strips. Melt margarine in a large skillet over medium heat. Place beef in skillet, and sear quickly on both sides. Remove meat from skillet, and set aside. In remaining liquid in skillet, sauté onion, garlic and sliced mushrooms until onion is golden (about 5 minutes). Add flour, instant bouillon, ketchup, salt and pepper. Stir until smooth. Gradually add the can of bouillon, and bring to a boil, stirring constantly. Reduce heat, and simmer 5 minutes. Stir in white wine and dill. Mix approximately 1/4 cup of the sauce into sour cream, and stir sour cream into the rest of sauce. Add beef, and reheat just until sauce and beef are heated. Serve over wide egg noodles. Serves 6-8. Serving size: 4 ounces

Amount Per Serving:

Calories 269	Saturated Fat 3 g	Sodium 544 mg
Total Fat 11 g	Cholesterol 90 mg	

Roast Beef with Pesto

Prep Time: 45 minutes
Cooking Time: 60 minutes

- 1 garlic bulb, separated but unpeeled
- 1/2 cup fresh basil, chopped
- dash of salt
- 3 pounds beef eye-of-round roast with all fat removed

Preheat oven to 450 degrees. Fill a medium saucepan half full of water. Add garlic, and cook on medium-high heat for 30 minutes. Drain and cool. Peel garlic. Combine garlic with basil and salt in a food processor or blender, and process until smooth. Spread mixture over the top and sides of roast, covering completely. Insert a meat thermometer, and place on a roasting rack that has been coated with non-stick cooking spray. Cover loosely with foil, and bake for 20 minutes. Uncover, and roast until desired doneness (approximately 25 minutes for medium). Remove from oven, and let rest for 15 minutes before slicing thinly across the grain. Serve with Madeira Sauce (next recipe). Serves 12. Serving size: 4 ounces

Amount Per Serving:

Calories 144	Saturated Fat 2 g	Sodium 75 mg
Total Fat 4 g	Cholesterol 59 mg	

Madeira Sauce

Prep Time: 5 minutes
Cooking Time: 30 minutes

- 4 cups vegetable broth
- 1/2 cup Madeira wine
- 2 Tablespoons cornstarch
- 1-2 Tablespoons water
- salt and pepper, to taste

Boil broth over medium heat until it is reduced by half. Reduce heat, and add wine. Heat for 1 minute, and stir in cornstarch that has been mixed with water. Stir until thickened. Season to taste. Serve warm with meat. Serves 8. Serving size: 1/4 cup

Amount Per Serving:

Calories 26	Saturated Fat 0 g	Sodium 50 mg
Total Fat 0 g	Cholesterol 0 mg	

German Meatballs

- 8 ounces egg noodles
- 1 pound ground round or sirloin
- 1/4 cup dry bread crumbs
- 1 1/2 Tablespoons parsley, chopped
- 1/4 teaspoon salt
- 1 teaspoon prepared mustard
- 1/2 teaspoon Worcestershire sauce

- 1 egg white, lightly beaten
- 2 garlic cloves, minced
- 2 cups mushrooms, sliced
- 1 cup slightly-sweet white wine
- 1/2 cup fat-free sour cream
  (at room temperature)
- 1/4 teaspoon pepper

Cook noodles according to package directions. Set aside. Combine next 7 ingredients in a bowl. Shape into 24, 1-inch meatballs. Coat a large skillet with non-stick cooking spray. Place over medium heat until hot. Add meatballs. Cook 10 minutes or until browned, stirring frequently. Remove from skillet. Set aside. Add garlic and mushrooms to skillet. Sauté for 5 minutes. Add wine, bring to a boil over medium heat, and cook for 1 minute. Return meatballs to skillet, cover, and cook 5-10 minutes or until done. Remove pan from heat. Remove meatballs with slotted spoon. Set aside, and keep warm. Add sour cream and pepper to wine mixture in skillet, and stir well. Spoon meatballs and sauce over noodles. Serves 4. Serving size: 6 meatballs with 1 ounce of noodles

Amount Per Serving:

Calories 483	Saturated Fat 3 g	Sodium 300 mg
Total Fat 12 g	Cholesterol 82 mg	

Barbecued Chicken

Prep Time: 5 minutes
Cooking Time: 30—35 minutes

- 4 (6-ounce) chicken breast halves, boneless and skinless
- 1 stalk celery
- 1 carrot
- 1/2 onion
- 1/2 teaspoon thyme
- 1/2 teaspoon lemon pepper
- 2 cups barbecue sauce

Place all ingredients except barbecue sauce in a Dutch oven. Add water to cover, and bring to a boil. Reduce heat, and simmer for 20 minutes. Remove chicken and cool slightly. Put barbecue sauce in a gallon-size ziplock bag. Add chicken to this, and shake until coated. Put chicken on your grill for 10 to 15 minutes, turning often. Serves 4. Serving size: 1 (6-ounce) chicken breast

Amount Per Serving:

Calories 260	Saturated Fat 1 g	Sodium 618 mg
Total Fat 5 g	Cholesterol 73 mg	

Fiesta Chicken Fajitas

Prep Time: 20 minutes
Chill Time: 1 to 2 hours
Cooking Time: 5 minutes

- 4 (6-ounce) chicken breast halves, boneless and skinless, cut into strips
- 1 to 2 teaspoons fajita seasoning
- 1 each red, green and yellow pepper, sliced into rings
- 1 medium onion, sliced into rings
- 10 flour tortillas
- 5 cups lettuce, shredded
- 4 green onions, chopped
- 2 cups fresh tomatoes, diced
- 5 ounces low-fat cheddar cheese, shredded
- 5 Tablespoons fat-free plain yogurt
- 1 1/2 cups picante sauce

Sprinkle fajita seasoning over chicken breasts, turning to coat. Place chicken in the refrigerator, and chill for 1 to 2 hours, or longer if desired. Coat a large skillet with non-stick cooking spray. Brown chicken over medium heat, cooking thoroughly. Add pepper rings and onion slices, cooking until browned. Set aside. Keep mixture warm. Warm tortillas by briefly microwaving. Place tortillas on serving dish. Top each with lettuce and chicken strips, followed by cooked peppers and onions, green onions, tomatoes and cheese. Garnish with 1/2 Tablespoon yogurt and 2 Tablespoons picante sauce for each tortilla.. Serves 10. Serving size: 1 tortilla

Amount Per Serving:

Calories 262	Saturated Fat 2 g	Sodium 484 mg
Total Fat 6 g	Cholesterol 44 mg	

Chicken with Artichoke Hearts

- 1/4 teaspoon white pepper
- 1/4 teaspoon paprika
- 4 (4-ounce) chicken breast halves, boneless and skinless
- 1 garlic clove, minced
- 1 cup onion, chopped
- 1 large tomato, chopped
- 1/2 teaspoon dried rosemary
- 1/2 teaspoon dried thyme
- 1/4 teaspoon white pepper
- 1/4 cup dry white wine
- 1 (14-ounce) can artichokes, drained and halved
- 1/2 cup plain fat-free yogurt, room temperature
- 1 Tablespoon cornstarch

Combine 1/4 teaspoon white pepper and paprika. Sprinkle on chicken. Coat a nonstick skillet with non-stick cooking spray. Place over medium heat until hot. Cook chicken 5 minutes, turning once. Combine garlic, onion, tomato, rosemary, thyme, white pepper and wine in a medium bowl. Stir well and pour over chicken. Cover and simmer for 10 minutes. Add artichokes, cover and simmer an additional 5 minutes. Remove chicken to serving platter and keep warm. Combine yogurt and cornstarch in small bowl. Spoon a small amount of the hot vegetable mixture into the yogurt mixture and stir gently. Slowly add the yogurt mixture to skillet, stirring constantly. Do not let mixture boil. Pour vegetable sauce over chicken breasts. Serves 4. Serving size: 1 (4-ounce) chicken breast

Amount Per Serving:

| Calories 285 | Saturated Fat 1 g | Sodium 188 mg |
| Total Fat 5 g | Cholesterol 96 mg | |

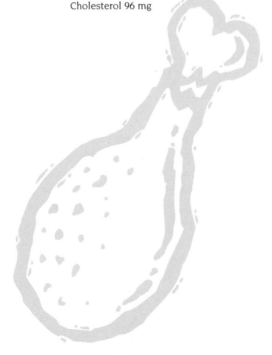

Chicken Enchiladas

- 3 Tablespoons liquid butter substitute
- 1 teaspoon minced garlic
- 1 medium chopped onion
- 1 Tablespoon flour
- 1 Tablespoon cornstarch
- 1 (14- to 15-ounce) can chicken broth
- 1 (4-ounce) can chopped green chilies
- 2 cups white chicken meat, cooked and cubed
- 1 (15-ounce) can corn, drained
- 1 (15-ounce) can tomatoes
- 1/2 cup salsa
- 2 1/2 cups fat-free cheddar cheese, divided
- 2 cups fat-free sour cream
- 12 flour tortillas

Preheat oven to 350 degrees. Combine butter substitute, garlic and onion in a saucepan. Cook until soft. Add flour, cornstarch, chicken broth and green chilies. Stir with a wire whisk until bubbly and smooth. Add cooked chicken and corn. Remove from heat. In a mixing bowl, combine tomatoes, salsa, 1 1/2 cups cheese together and sour cream. Combine both mixtures together. Make enchiladas by spooning mixture onto each tortilla, rolling them up and placing them seam-side down in a casserole dish that has been coated with non-stick cooking spray. Pour the remaining mixture over the rolled-up tortillas, and top with the remaining cheese. Bake for 15 to 20 minutes until bubbly. Serves 12. Serving size: 1 tortilla

Amount Per Serving:

Calories 305	Saturated Fat 1 g	Sodium 880 mg
Total Fat 4 g	Cholesterol 26 mg	

Myth No. 93:
"All five-star restaurants in the Ozarks end with the words 'all you can eat'."

Cha Cha Chicken Chalupas

- 6 ounces low-fat Monterey Jack cheese, grated
- 6 ounces low-fat sharp cheddar cheese, grated
- 2 bunches green onions, tops only, chopped
- 2 (10 3/4-ounce) cans low-fat cream of chicken soup
- 1 (4-ounce) can green chilies, chopped
- 1 (16-ounce) carton fat-free sour cream
- 1 (4-ounce) can black olives, sliced
- 8 (6-ounce) chicken breast halves, boneless and skinless, poached and cut into 1-inch pieces
- 12 (6-inch diameter) flour tortillas

Preheat oven to 350 degrees. Combine cheeses, and reserve 1/2 cup for topping. Divide green onions into 2 equal portions. Combine the rest of the cheese, 1/2 of the onion, soup, chilies, sour cream and black olives. Set aside 1 1/2 cups of this mixture for topping. Add chicken to the remainder, and mix well. Coat a 9 x 13-inch baking dish with non-stick cooking spray. Put 3 heaping Tablespoons of filling on each tortilla, and roll up. Place seam-side down in baking dish. Arrange in a single layer. Spread reserved topping over tortillas. Sprinkle with remaining cheese and onion. May refrigerate overnight if desired. Bake, uncovered for 45 minutes. Let stand for 5 minutes before serving. Serves 12. Serving size: 1 tortilla

Amount Per Serving:

Calories 362	Saturated Fat 4 g	Sodium 606 mg
Total Fat 13 g	Cholesterol 70 mg	

Teriyaki Chicken

Prep Time: 35 minutes
Marinade Time: 30 minutes
Cooking Time: 15 minutes

- 1/4 cup dry sherry
- 1/4 cup light soy sauce
- 2 Tablespoons honey
- 1 medium garlic clove, minced
- 4 (6-ounce) chicken breast halves, skinless and boneless, washed and patted dry
- 1 Tablespoon vegetable oil

In a medium bowl, whisk together the sherry, soy sauce, honey and garlic. Add chicken, turning to coat, and set aside to marinate for at least 30 minutes (or refrigerate and marinate longer if desired). Heat a large, heavy skillet over medium-high heat for about 2 minutes. Remove chicken from marinade, and shake to discard excess liquid. Add oil to skillet, and reduce heat to moderate. Place chicken in pan, and brown on both sides. Cook until done (about 15 minutes). Transfer to a warm platter, and serve. Serves 4.
Serving size: 1 (6-ounce) chicken breast

Amount Per Serving:

Calories 215	Saturated Fat 2 g	Sodium 321 mg
Total Fat 8 g	Cholesterol 73 mg	

Swiss Chicken over Rice

Prep Time: 10 minutes
Cooking Time: 30 minutes

- 2 ounces low-fat Swiss cheese, sliced
- 4 (4-ounce) chicken breast halves, boneless and skinless, pounded to 1/4-inch thick
- 2 Tablespoons flour
- 1/2 teaspoon pepper
- 3/4 cup chicken broth
- 1/2 cup dry white wine
- 1 teaspoon dried parsley leaves
- 1 teaspoon dried oregano leaves

Place half of each slice of cheese on each flattened chicken breast, tightly roll up, and secure with toothpicks. Combine flour and pepper, and gently coat rolled chicken. Brown in a skillet coated with non-stick cooking spray. Add broth, wine and spices. Bring to a boil, reduce heat to simmer and cover. Cook 20 minutes until chicken is cooked and sauce has thickened. (Add more broth, wine or water to sauce as needed.) Place chicken on cooked rice, and pour sauce over chicken and rice. Serves 4.
Serving size: 1 (4-ounce) chicken breast

Amount Per Serving:

Calories 256	Saturated Fat 4 g	Sodium 342 mg
Total Fat 8 g	Cholesterol 106 mg	

Chicken La France

- 4 (6-ounce) chicken breast halves, boneless and skinless
- 1 Tablespoon vegetable oil
- 3 cups fresh mushrooms, sliced
- 1/2 cup shallots, chopped
- 2 Tablespoons capers, drained

- 2 Tablespoons fresh parsley, chopped
- 1/2 teaspoon dried whole tarragon
- 1/2 cup dry white wine
- 2 Tablespoons no-salt-added Dijon mustard
- 1/2 teaspoon white pepper

Place each piece of chicken between 2 sheets of plastic wrap and flatten to 1/4-inch thickness, using a meat mallet or rolling pin. Set aside. Heat oil in large skillet. Sauté mushrooms and shallots in oil for 3 minutes. Add capers, parsley and tarragon, stirring well. Add chicken, and heat over medium heat for 1 to 2 minutes on each side. Combine wine, mustard and pepper, stirring well. Pour over chicken. Simmer uncovered for 6 minutes, turning chicken once. Serves 4.

Serving size: 1 (6-ounce) chicken breast

Amount Per Serving:

Calories 368	Saturated Fat 2 g	Sodium 479 mg
Total Fat 10 g	Cholesterol 146 mg	

Myth No.16:

"In the Ozarks when you really want to impress the dinner guests, you bring out the fancy plates. The ones with food dividers."

Chicken Stroganoff

- 2 (12-ounce) whole chicken breasts, boneless and skinless
- 2 Tablespoons flour
- 1/2 teaspoon salt
- 1/4 teaspoon pepper
- 1 Tablespoon margarine
- 1 Tablespoon shallots, minced
- 3/4 pound fresh mushrooms. sliced

- 1/2 cup dry white wine
- 1 Tablespoon paprika
- 2 cups fat-free sour cream (at room temperature)
- 1 1/2 teaspoons Worcestershire sauce
- 1/2 teaspoon beef bouillon
- salt and pepper to taste

Slice chicken into 3 x 1/4-inch julienne strips. Combine flour, salt and pepper in a bag. Add chicken and shake. In a skillet, sauté chicken in margarine over medium-high heat until just tender and golden. Remove to serving dish, and keep warm. Add shallots, mushrooms and wine to skillet. Cook, stirring until liquid reduces some. Reduce heat to low, and stir in paprika, sour cream, Worcestershire sauce and beef bouillon. Season with salt and pepper. Heat sauce, and pour over chicken. Serve over noodles or rice.
Serves 6. Serving size: 8 ounces

Amount Per Serving:

Calories 191	Saturated Fat 1 g	Sodium 301 mg
Total Fat 4 g	Cholesterol 48 mg	

Indian Chicken

Prep Time: 15 minutes
Cooking Time: 45 minutes

- 2 Tablespoons low-fat margarine
- 1 medium onion, chopped
- 6 (6-ounce) chicken breast halves, boneless and skinless
- 4 to 5 medium apples, peeled and chopped
- 1/2 cup raisins
- 1 teaspoon ginger powder
- 1 1/2 teaspoons curry powder

Preheat oven to 400 degrees. Place margarine in a 9 x 13-inch glass pan. Add the chopped onions and chicken. Cover with chopped apples and raisins. Add seasonings. Cover and bake for 30 to 45 minutes. Serves 6. Serving size: 1 (6-ounce) chicken breast

Amount Per Serving:

| Calories 384 | Saturated Fat 2 g | Sodium 155 mg |
| Total Fat 8 g | Cholesterol 115 mg | |

Chicken Just in Lime

Prep Time: 5 minutes
Cooking Time: 15 minutes

- 6 (6-ounce) chicken breast halves, boneless and skinless
- 1/4 teaspoon salt
- 1/2 teaspoon white pepper
- 1 Tablespoon canola oil
- juice of 1 lime
- 2 Tablespoons low-fat margarine
- 1/2 teaspoon fresh chives, minced or 1 green onion, sliced
- 1/2 teaspoon dried, whole dill weed

Sprinkle chicken with salt and pepper. Sauté in hot oil for 4 minutes or until lightly browned. Turn chicken, cover and reduce heat to low. Cook 10 minutes or until chicken is tender. Remove chicken from skillet, and set aside. Drain pan drippings from skillet. Pour lime juice into skillet, and cook over low heat until it bubbles. Add margarine, and stir until margarine becomes opaque and mixture slightly thickens. Stir in chives or green onions and dill weed. Spoon over chicken. Serves 6.
Serving size: 1 (6-ounce) chicken breast

Amount Per Serving:

| Calories 323 | Saturated Fat 2 g | Sodium 259 mg |
| Total Fat 10 g | Cholesterol 146 mg | |

Orange Curry Chicken

- 1 cup unsweetened orange juice
- 1 cup dry white wine
- 1 Tablespoon onion, minced
- 1 Tablespoon honey
- 1 teaspoon peeled ginger root, minced
  (or 1/2 teaspoon ground ginger)
- 1/2 teaspoon dried tarragon
- 1/4 to 1/2 teaspoon curry powder
  (adjust to taste)

- 1/4 teaspoon ground pepper
- 1 teaspoon Caribbean Jerk seasoning
- 1/4 teaspoon salt
- 6 (6-ounce) chicken breast halves,
  boneless and skinless
- 1/4 teaspoon turmeric (optional)
- 1 Tablespoon cornstarch
- 2 Tablespoons cold water
- hot cooked rice

Combine orange juice, wine, onion, honey and seasonings, and pour over chicken in a non-metal shallow container. Cover and marinate in refrigerator at least 3 hours, turning occasionally. Place chicken and marinade in a large non-stick skillet. Bring to a boil, then reduce heat and simmer 30 minutes until chicken is tender. Sprinkle with turmeric, additional curry powder or Caribbean Jerk seasoning for color. Remove chicken, and keep warm. Mix cornstarch and water, and add to marinade in skillet, stirring occasionally. When thickened, add chicken and heat through. Serve over rice.
Serves 6. Serving size: 1 (6-ounce) chicken breast

Amount Per Serving:

| Calories 332 | Saturated Fat 2 g | Sodium 217 mg |
| Total Fat 6 g | Cholesterol 146 mg | |

Mexican Chicken and Barley

Prep Time: 30 minutes
Cooking Time: 30 minutes

- 1 cup onion, chopped
- 1 garlic clove, minced
- 1 Tablespoon vegetable oil
- 2 1/2 cups water
- 3/4 cup barley
- 1 (16-ounce) can tomatoes, chopped and undrained
- 1 (8-ounce) can tomato sauce
- 1 (14.5-ounce) can reduced-sodium chicken broth (about 1 3/4 cups)
- 1 (11-ounce) can corn, drained
- 1 (4-ounce) can green chilies, chopped
- 1 Tablespoon chili powder
- 1/2 teaspoon ground cumin
- 1/4 teaspoon salt
- 2 cups chicken, cooked and diced
- fat-free sour cream (optional garnish)
- scallions, sliced (optional garnish)

In a Dutch oven, cook onion and garlic in oil until onion is tender. Add remaining ingredients except chicken. Bring to a boil. Reduce heat to low. Cover, and simmer for 10 minutes, stirring occasionally. Add cooked chicken, and continue simmering for 5-10 minutes. Ladle into bowls. Garnish as desired. Serves 9. Serving size: 1 cup

Amount Per Serving:

Calories 234	Saturated Fat 1 g	Sodium 389 mg
Total Fat 5 g	Cholesterol 43 mg	

Oven-Fried Chicken

Prep Time: 20 minutes
Cooking Time: 1 hour

- 4 cups rice cereal
- 1 teaspoon paprika
- 2 egg whites
- 3/4 cup skim milk
- 3/4 cup flour
- 1 teaspoon poultry seasoning
- 1/2 teaspoon salt
- 1/4 teaspoon pepper
- 12 chicken breast halves, boneless and skinless

Preheat oven to 400 degrees. Crush cereal into small crumbs. Add paprika, and mix well. Set aside. Mix egg whites and milk until foamy. Mix in flour, poultry seasoning, salt and pepper. Dip chicken in liquid, and then roll in cereal mixture. Coat chicken well. Place on a cookie sheet coated with non-stick cooking spray. Bake for 1 hour. Serves 12. Serving size: 6 ounces

Amount Per Serving:

Calories 214	Saturated Fat 1 g	Sodium 268 mg
Total Fat 3 g	Cholesterol 73 mg	

Lemon Chicken

Sauce:

- 2 Tablespoons cornstarch
- 2 teaspoons chicken-flavor instant bouillon
- 1 cup water
- 1 teaspoon grated lemon peel
- 3 Tablespoons lemon juice

Other ingredients:

- 1 pound chicken tenderloins
- hot water
- 1 cup carrots, diagonally sliced
- 1 cup celery, diagonally sliced
- 1 cup snow peas
- 1 red bell pepper, cut into thin strips
- 3 cups hot cooked brown minute rice

In a small bowl, combine cornstarch and bouillon and mix well. Stir in remaining sauce ingredients and set aside. Place chicken tenderloins in a large non-stick skillet adding hot water to cover. Cover and poach chicken for 5 minutes (or until chicken is no longer pink in the center). Add carrots and celery. Continue cooking for 2 minutes. Drain. Add sauce mix, snow peas and pepper. Cook until thoroughly heated and slightly thickened, stirring occasionally. Serve over rice. Serves 4. Serving size: 4 ounces

Amount Per Serving:

Calories 370	Saturated Fat 1 g	Sodium 668 mg
Total Fat 4 g	Cholesterol 72 mg	

Champagne Poached Chicken with Creamy Mustard Sauce

- 1 cup champagne
- 1/2 cup chicken broth
- 1 garlic clove, mashed
- 4 (6-ounce) chicken breast halves, boneless and skinless

- 1 cup low-fat milk
  (or 1/2 cup low-fat milk
  and 1/2 cup fat-free yogurt)
- 1 teaspoon Dijon mustard
- 1/4 teaspoon ground red pepper
- 1/4 cup fresh parsley, chopped

Combine champagne and chicken broth with garlic in a heavy skillet. Bring to a boil, and add chicken. Cover, reduce heat, and simmer 15 minutes or until tender. Remove chicken, and set aside. Stir milk (or milk and yogurt), mustard and red pepper into skillet. Cook over medium heat for 8 minutes or until thickened, stirring occasionally. Add chicken to skillet, and cook until thoroughly heated. Sprinkle with fresh parsley to serve. Serves 4. Serving size: 1 (6-ounce) chicken breast

Amount Per Serving:

Calories 196	Saturated Fat 2 g	Sodium 224 mg
Total Fat 5 g	Cholesterol 78 mg	

Stuffed Chicken with Couscous and Mushroom Sauce

Prep Time: 30 minutes
Cooking Time: 45 minutes

- 1 (10-ounce) box couscous, prepared according to package instructions
- 1 Tablespoon extra-virgin olive oil
- 1 (8-ounce) package Portabello mushrooms, 1/2 chopped, 1/2 sliced
- 1 bunch green onions, chopped
- 1 bunch parsley, chopped
- 4 ounces Fontina cheese or low-fat, part-skim mozzarella and Parmesan mix
- 2 Tablespoons bread crumbs
- salt and pepper to taste
- 2 cups fat-free chicken stock
- 2 Tablespoons fresh rosemary, finely minced (or 1 Tablespoon dry rosemary)
- 2 Tablespoons cornstarch
- 4 (6-ounce) chicken breast halves, boneless and skinless, lightly pounded for uniform thickness
- parsley (to garnish)

Preheat oven to 350 degrees. In a non-stick pan, heat olive oil, and saute 1/2 of the mushrooms, green onions and parsley until mushrooms are soft. Remove from heat, and add cheese and bread crumbs. Salt and pepper to taste. Reserve. In a small saucepan, combine remaining chopped green onion and parsley with chicken stock. Add rosemary and remaining mushrooms, and bring to a simmer. Mix cornstarch with 2 Tablespoons of the stock, return to saucepan, and stir until thickened. Reserve and keep warm. Divide filling mixture into 4 equal parts, and form into rope shapes that fit the length of the chicken breasts. Place a rope on the edge of each breast and roll up lengthwise, ending seam side down. Wrap each breast in foil tightly to form cylinder shapes. Bake on a non-stick sheet pan in oven for 25 minutes. Remove and let cool 15 minutes. Reheat couscous, and put a layer on serving plates. Unwrap chicken, slice into 1/2-inch disks, and place on couscous. (Place on end so filling shows.) Cover with sauce, and garnish with parsley. Serves 4. Serving size: 1 rope sliced and served as entree

Amount Per Serving:

Calories 666	Saturated Fat 7 g	Sodium 1030 mg
Total Fat 19 g	Cholesterol 129 mg	

Contributed by Mary Faucett, Nonna's Italian American Café in Springfield, Missouri.

Black Bean Chicken

Prep Time: 30 minutes
Cooking Time: 45 minutes to 1 hour

- 4 (6-ounce) chicken breast halves, boneless and skinless
- 1 Tablespoon olive oil
- 1/2 teaspoon Cajun chicken seasoning (Add more if you like a spicy dish)
- 1 small onion, chopped
- 1 green pepper, chopped
- 2 (15-ounce) cans black beans
- 1 cup mild salsa

Preheat oven to 350 degrees. Brown chicken in olive oil. As chicken is browning, sprinkle with Cajun seasoning. Add onions, green pepper, and cook until soft. Add black beans and salsa. Remove chicken breasts from pan, and place in a 7 x 12-inch baking dish that has been coated with non-stick cooking spray. Spoon bean and salsa mixture over chicken, and bake covered for 45 minutes. Serve over rice. Serves 4. Serving size: 6 ounces

Amount Per Serving:

Calories 629	Saturated Fat 3 g	Sodium 395 mg
Total Fat 11 g	Cholesterol 146 mg	

Pineapple-Apricot Chicken

Prep Time: 10 minutes
Cooking Time: 40 minutes

- 6 (6-ounce) chicken breast halves, boneless and skinless
- 1 (8-ounce) can unsweetened crushed pineapple, undrained
- 1 cup apricot preserves
- 2 teaspoons reduced-sodium soy sauce
- 1 1/2 teaspoons cornstarch
- hot cooked rice

Preheat oven to 375 degrees. Coat a 12 x 8-inch baking dish with non-stick cooking spray. Place chicken in baking dish. Combine pineapple, preserves, soy sauce and cornstarch until thoroughly blended. Pour over chicken, and cover with foil. Bake covered for 30 minutes. Uncover, and bake an additional 5 minutes or until chicken is tender and sauce is thickened and bubbly. Serve over rice. Serves 6. Serving size: 1 (6-ounce) chicken breast

Amount Per Serving:

Calories 313	Saturated Fat 1 g	Sodium 137 mg
Total Fat 3 g	Cholesterol 73 mg	

Grilled Chicken with Corn Salsa

Salsa:

- 1 1/4 cups frozen corn, thawed
- 1/4 cup red onion, chopped
- 1/4 cup red bell pepper, chopped
- 1/4 cup fresh cilantro, chopped
- 1 1/2 Tablespoons fresh lime juice
- 2 teaspoons jalapeno pepper, chopped and seeded

Marinade:

- 1/2 cup light beer
- 1 Tablespoon low-sodium soy sauce
- 2 teaspoons lime juice
- 2 teaspoons jalapeno pepper, seeded
- 1 Tablespoon fresh cilantro, chopped
- 4 chicken breast halves, boneless and skinless
- salt and pepper to taste

Combine salsa ingredients. Cover and refrigerate for 4 hours. Mix marinade ingredients, and pour over chicken. Cover and refrigerate 1 to 4 hours, turning occasionally. Drain chicken. Season with salt and pepper. Grill or broil for 4 to 8 minutes per side until thoroughly cooked. Cut breasts into diagonal slices. Top with salsa. Serves 4.

Serving size: 1 (4-ounce) chicken breast

Amount Per Serving:

Calories 206	Saturated Fat 1 g	Sodium 260 mg
Total Fat 3 g	Cholesterol 73 mg	

Chicken Pot Pie

- 9 cups water
- 1 Tablespoon black peppercorns
- 2 1/2 pounds chicken pieces, skinless (leave bone in)
- 3 stalks celery, cut into 4 pieces
- 1 small onion, sliced
- 1 bay leaf
- 1 1/2 cups potatoes, diced
- 1/2 cup celery, chopped
- 1/2 cup red bell pepper, chopped

- 1 garlic clove
- 3/4 cup carrots, sliced
- 1 cup mushrooms, sliced
- 1/2 cup frozen peas
- 1/3 cup flour
- 1 teaspoon poultry seasoning
- 1/2 teaspoon salt
- 1/2 teaspoon pepper
- 1 cup low-fat milk

Biscuit Topping:

- 2 cups flour
- 2 teaspoons baking powder
- 1/2 teaspoon salt
- 1/4 teaspoon sugar

- 1/8 teaspoon garlic powder
- 1 cup low-fat milk
- 1/2 Tablespoon margarine, melted

Preheat oven to 400 degrees. Combine the first six ingredients in stock pot. Bring to a boil. Reduce heat to medium. Cook uncovered for 1 hour. Remove from heat. Remove chicken from broth, and chill for 15 minutes. Strain broth through a cheesecloth. Set aside 4 1/2 cups broth. Remove chicken from bones. Cut meat into bite-sized pieces. Bring broth to a boil. Add potatoes, celery, pepper, garlic and carrots. Cover and cook for 10 minutes. Add mushrooms and peas. Cook for 5 minutes or until vegetables are tender. Combine flour and next three ingredients in a bowl. Add milk and stir. Add to vegetable mixture. Cook until thickened, stirring constantly. Remove from heat, and add chicken. Coat 13 x 9 x 2-inch baking dish with non-stick cooking spray. Place chicken mixture in dish. To make biscuit topping, combine first 5 ingredients in a bowl, and stir well. Add milk and margarine. Stir until dry ingredients are moistened. Drop biscuit topping onto vegetable mixture to form 16 biscuits. Bake for 30 minutes or until brown. Serves 8. Serving size: one cup chicken mixture with two biscuits

Amount Per Serving:

Calories 396	Saturated Fat 2 g	Sodium 505 mg
Total Fat 6 g	Cholesterol 91 mg	

Easy, Elegant Chicken

Prep Time: 20 minutes
Cooking Time: 45 minutes

- 4 (6-ounce) chicken breast halves, boneless and skinless
- 1/2 to 1 teaspoon paprika
- 1 cup chicken bouillon
- 1/2 cup liquid butter substitute
- 1/2 cup white cooking wine
- 1/2 medium onion, thinly sliced
- dash of white pepper
- 1/4 teaspoon thyme
- 1/4 teaspoon seasoned salt
- 1/2 teaspoon dill weed

Preheat oven to 350 degrees. Thoroughly wash and dry chicken. Sprinkle with paprika. Coat a large skillet with non-stick cooking spray. Brown chicken over medium heat (10 minutes). In a medium bowl, combine bouillon, butter substitute, wine and onion. Microwave on high for 2 minutes. Add pepper, thyme, seasoned salt and dill weed. Mix well. Place chicken in casserole dish, and pour wine mixture over chicken. Cover and bake for 35 minutes. Uncover and bake an additional 5 to 10 minutes. Serves 4. Serving size: 6 ounces

Amount Per Serving:

Calories 319	Saturated Fat 2 g	Sodium 568 mg
Total Fat 7 g	Cholesterol 147 mg	

Marinated Chicken Breasts

Prep Time: 3 minutes
Marinade Time: 1 and 1/2 hours
Cooking Time: 20 minutes

- 1 cup dry white wine
- 1/3 cup light soy sauce
- 1 Tablespoon garlic powder
- 1 teaspoon pepper
- 6 (6-ounce) chicken breast halves, boneless and skinless

Combine wine, soy sauce, garlic powder and pepper. Pour mixture over chicken, and let stand for a minimum of 1 1/2 hours. The longer the chicken marinates, the more flavorful it will be. Remove chicken breasts from marinade, reserving marinade. Grill chicken for approximately 20 minutes or until done, turning frequently, while basting with marinade. Serves 6. Serving size: 1 (6-ounce) chicken breast

Amount Per Serving:

Calories 294	Saturated Fat 2 g	Sodium 470 mg
Total Fat 6 g	Cholesterol 146 mg	

Chicken Cordon Bleu with White Wine Sauce

Prep Time: 30 minutes
Cooking Time: 25 minutes

- 8 (4 ounce) chicken breast fillets, boneless and skinless
- 8 teaspoons fresh parsley, chopped
- 4 ounces part-skim mozzarella cheese, cut into 8 thin and equal pieces
- 4 thin slices boiled ham (4 ounces), cut into halves to yield 8 pieces
- 1 Tablespoon low-calorie, low-fat mayonnaise
- 1 Tablespoon warm water
- 1/4 cup seasoned bread crumbs
- 1 cup fat-free chicken broth
- 3 Tablespoons dry white wine
- 3 Tablespoons sifted flour
- 2/3 cup skim milk
- dash of onion powder
- dash of white pepper
- dash of nutmeg
- 2 Tablespoons fresh parsley, minced

Preheat oven to 425 degrees. Pound chicken breast fillets until very thin. Lay fillets flat, and sprinkle with chopped parsley. Top each fillet with a slice of mozzarella cheese and a half slice of ham. Roll fillet up tightly, and secure with a toothpick if necessary. Combine mayonnaise and warm water in a shallow dish and stir to blend. Dip or roll each fillet in the mayonnaise mixture and then into the bread crumbs. Coat a large baking pan with non-stick cooking spray. Arrange chicken rolls, seamless side down in a single layer in the pan. Bake for 20 to 25 minutes or until fillets are browned, cooked throughout and cheese is melted. Meanwhile, combine chicken broth and wine in a non-stick saucepan. Heat liquid to boiling and then reduce heat. Combine flour and milk, and stir to dissolve completely. Stir flour mixture into the simmering broth. Cook, stirring constantly, until sauce is thick and bubbling. Serve 1/4 cup wine sauce over each baked chicken fillet. Sprinkle with onion powder, white pepper, nutmeg and minced parsley. Serve immediately while still hot. Serves 8. Serving size: 1 (4-ounce) chicken breast with 1/4 cup of sauce

Amount Per Serving:

Calories 235	Saturated Fat 3 g	Sodium 421 mg
Total Fat 7 g	Cholesterol 89 mg	

Cajun Chicken Jambalaya

Prep Time: 20 minutes
Cooking Time: 40 minutes

- 2 ounces bacon, chopped
- 1/2 cup onion, minced
- 1/2 cup celery, minced
- 1/2 cup green pepper, minced
- 1 cup rice, uncooked

- 1/2 Tablespoon chili powder
- 1/2 Tablespoon crushed red pepper
- 2 1/2 cups tomato sauce
- 1 1/2 cups chicken stock
- 1 pound chicken breast, skinless and diced

Sauté bacon in large pot until crisp. Add onion, celery and green pepper, and sauté for 5 minutes. Add rice, chili powder and crushed red pepper, and cook for 5 minutes. Add tomato sauce and chicken stock, and simmer for 15 minutes. Add chicken breast, and simmer for 15 minutes. Serves 8. Serving size: 1 cup

Amount Per Serving:

Calories 232	Saturated Fat 2 g	Sodium 508 mg
Total Fat 5 g	Cholesterol 42 mg	

Contributed by Leonard Neese, Lambert's Café,
"Home of the Throwed Rolls", in Ozark, Missouri and Sikeston, Missouri.

Roasted Chicken with
Herb-Lemon Sauce

Prep Time: 20 minutes
Cooking Time: 2 hours

- 1 (4-pound) whole chicken
- 2 lemons, halved
- 1 medium onion, quartered
- 1 teaspoon rosemary
- 1/2 teaspoon thyme
- 4 garlic cloves
- 1 cup low-sodium chicken broth

- 2 Tablespoons lemon juice
- 1 Tablespoon cornstarch
- 1/4 cup water
- 2 Tablespoons dry white wine
- 1 Tablespoon reduced-sodium soy sauce
- 1/4 teaspoon dried sage leaves

Preheat oven to 400 degrees. Coat a roasting pan with non-stick cooking spray. Remove giblets and neck from cavity of chicken. Rinse and dry chicken well. Arrange lemon halves, onion, rosemary, thyme and garlic in cavity of chicken. Roast chicken 30 minutes. Combine chicken broth and lemon juice. Pour over chicken. Reduce heat to 325 degrees. Roast for 1 1/4 hours, basting frequently. Let stand 15 minutes before carving. Pour pan juices into a medium saucepan. Reserve 1 Tablespoon of liquid. In a small bowl, whisk cornstarch into reserved liquid. Add water, wine, soy sauce and sage to the juices in the saucepan. Bring to a boil, and cook for 5 minutes. Reduce heat to low, and whisk in cornstarch mixture. Cook, stirring constantly, until thick (about 1 minute). Serve sauce on the side with the roasted chicken. Serves 8. Serving size: 8 ounces

Amount Per Serving:

Calories 348	Saturated Fat 4 g	Sodium 223 mg
Total Fat 13 g	Cholesterol 154 mg	

Oriental Chicken & Vegetable Stir-Fry

Prep Time: 10 minutes
Cooking Time: 15 minutes

- 2 teaspoons cornstarch
- 1/2 teaspoon garlic salt
- 1/2 teaspoon pepper
- 2 Tablespoons low-sodium soy sauce
- 1/4 cup water
- 2 Tablespoons vegetable oil

- 1 1/2 teaspoons ground ginger
- 2 1/2 cups frozen stir-fry vegetables, thawed and drained well
- 1 pound chicken breast, cut into bite-sized pieces

In a small bowl, combine cornstarch, garlic salt and pepper. Blend in soy sauce. Add water, and set aside. Add oil to wok or large, non-stick skillet (Dutch oven may also be used). Heat over high heat. Add ginger, vegetables, and stir-fry 2 minutes. Remove vegetables, add chicken pieces, and stir-fry 2 to 3 minutes or until browned. Stir soy sauce mixture, and then mix with chicken in a skillet or wok. Cook and stir until mixture is thickened and bubbly. Stir in cooked vegetables, and keep stirring about 1 minute until thoroughly heated. Serve over rice. Serves 4. Serving size: 8 ounces

Amount Per Serving:

Calories 246	Saturated Fat 1 g	Sodium 684 mg
Total Fat 10 g	Cholesterol 72 mg	

Kung Bao Chicken

Prep Time: 15 minutes
Cooking Time: 15 minutes

- 1/2 teaspoon crushed red (cayenne) pepper
- 6 Tablespoons low-sodium soy sauce
- 2 teaspoons cornstarch
- 2 Tablespoons water
- 2 fresh garlic cloves, minced
- 1 cup fresh mushrooms, sliced
- 2 large green peppers, chopped
- 1 (4-ounce) can water chestnuts, sliced
- 4 tablespoons unsalted peanuts
- 2 large chicken breasts, cubed

Combine red pepper, soy sauce, cornstarch and water in a small bowl. Set aside. Heat an electric skillet to high heat, and coat with non-stick cooking spray. Stir-fry garlic, and add mushrooms, peppers, water chestnuts and peanuts for 2 minutes. Remove from pan. Add chicken to pan, and stir-fry 2 minutes or until cooked. Add soy mixture and vegetables. Cook 2 more minutes. Serve at once over rice. Serves 4.
Serving size: 1 1/2 cups

Amount Per Serving:

Calories 266	Saturated Fat 2 g	Sodium 1042 mg
Total Fat 8g	Cholesterol 73 mg	

Myth No. 281:
"For an authentic Japanese meal in the Ozarks, all family members are encouraged to remove their boots."

Cranberry-Glazed Chicken

Prep Time: 15 minutes
Cooking Time: 1 hour

- 1/2 cup flour
- 1/2 teaspoon salt
- 1/8 teaspoon pepper
- 6 (6-ounce) chicken breast halves, boneless and skinless
- 2 tablespoons oil
- 1 1/2 cup fresh cranberries
- 1 cup brown sugar, firmly-packed
- 3/4 cup water
- 1 Tablespoon flour
- 1/2 teaspoon cinnamon
- 1/4 teaspoon ground cloves
- 1/4 teaspoon ground allspice
- 1 Tablespoon wine vinegar

Combine 1/2 cup flour, salt and pepper. Dredge chicken in flour mixture. Put oil in a large skillet over medium heat. Add chicken and cook until golden brown, about 20 minutes. Remove chicken and drain on paper towels. Add cranberries, brown sugar and water to skillet and cook 10 minutes or until cranberry skins pop. Blend together flour, cinnamon, cloves, allspice and wine vinegar. Add vinegar mixture to cranberries and cook, stirring constantly until thickened. Return chicken to skillet and baste with cranberry mixture. Cover and simmer 30 minutes, turning chicken occasionally.
Serves 6. Serving size: 1 (6-ounce) chicken breast

Amount Per Serving:

Calories 377	Saturated Fat 2 g	Sodium 255 mg
Total Fat 8 g	Cholesterol 73 mg	

Apricot-Glazed Chicken

Prep Time: 10 minutes
Cooking Time: 50 minutes

- 4 (8-ounce) chicken breast halves, boneless and skinless
- water
- 6 ounces apricot preserves
- 2 Tablespoons red wine vinegar
- 1 teaspoon salt
- 1/4 teaspoon pepper

Preheat oven to 400 degrees. Arrange chicken in 9 x 11-inch pan. Add just a small amount of water (for steam). Cover pan with foil and bake for 30 minutes. In a small mixing bowl, mix preserves, vinegar, salt and pepper. Drain excess liquid from chicken. Spoon apricot mixture over chicken and bake 15 minutes, basting occasionally. Serves 4. Serving size: 1 (8-ounce) chicken breast

Amount Per Serving:

Calories 305	Saturated Fat 1 g	Sodium 620 mg
Total Fat 4 g	Cholesterol 96 mg	

Contributed by St. John's Nutrition Center, Springfield, Missouri.

Tomato-Garlic Chicken

Prep Time: 15 minutes
Cooking Time: 50-60 minutes

- 1 cup chicken broth or stock
- 1 medium onion, sliced
- 3 garlic cloves, minced
- 2 Tablespoons white wine
- 4 (3-ounce) chicken breast halves, boneless and skinless each cut into 3 pieces
- 1 (16-ounce) can crushed tomatoes
- 1 Tablespoon balsamic vinegar
- 1 Tablespoon fresh sage leaves
- salt and ground pepper, to taste

In a 4-quart sauté pan, warm the chicken stock over medium heat. Add onion, garlic and wine, and simmer until softened (about 5 minutes). Add chicken pieces, and continue to simmer until the chicken is golden on all sides (about 5-10 minutes). Stir in tomatoes, balsamic vinegar and sage. Cover partially, and simmer over medium heat for 30 minutes, stirring occasionally. Uncover and cook another 5-10 minutes if sauce needs to thicken. Salt and pepper to taste, and mix well. Serves 4. Serving size: 6 ounces

Amount Per Serving:

Calories 217	Saturated Fat 1 g	Sodium 539 mg
Total Fat 4 g	Cholesterol 73 mg	

Chicken Divan

- 2 (10-ounce) packages frozen broccoli
- 2 cups chicken, cooked, cubed, boneless and skinless
- 2 (10-ounce) cans low-fat cream of chicken soup
- 1 cup light mayonnaise
- 1 teaspoon lemon juice
- 1/2 cup soft bread crumbs
- 1 Tablespoon light margarine, melted
- 1/2 cup low-fat American cheese, shredded

Preheat oven to 350 degrees. Cook broccoli until tender and drain. Arrange in 11 1/2 x 7-inch pan coated with non-stick cooking spray. Place chicken on top of broccoli. Combine soup, mayonnaise and lemon juice and pour over chicken. Combine bread crumbs and margarine and sprinkle over top. Top with cheese. Bake for 25-30 minutes. Serves 12. Serving size: 3/4 cup

Amount Per Serving:

Calories 130	Saturated Fat 1 g	Sodium 440 mg
Total Fat 4 g	Cholesterol 29 mg	

Contributed by St. John's Nutrition Center, Springfield, Missouri.

Onion-Bacon Chicken

- 1 (8-ounce) package butter substitute, reconstituted as directed
- 1 envelope (1-ounce) dry, onion-bacon ranch salad dressing mix
- 1 teaspoon lemon juice
- 6 (6-ounce) chicken breast halves, boneless and skinless
- 1 cup seasoned bread crumbs

Preheat oven to 400 degrees. Combine butter substitute, salad dressing mix and lemon juice. Pour over chicken, and marinate at room temperature for 30 minutes. Roll chicken in bread crumbs. Place chicken in a 9 x 13-inch pan that has been coated with non-stick cooking spray. Bake for 30 minutes, turning chicken after 20 minutes. Serves 6. Serving size: 1 (6-ounce) chicken breast

Amount Per Serving:

Calories 379	Saturated Fat 2 g	Sodium 1053 mg
Total Fat 7 g	Cholesterol 146 mg	

Chicken Fajitas

- 1 1/2 pounds chicken breast, boneless and skinless
- 1 garlic clove, minced
- 1 Tablespoon canola oil
- 1 1/2 Tablespoons lemon juice
- 3 Tablespoons Worcestershire sauce
- 1/8 teaspoon pepper
- 1 medium onion, sliced
- 1 medium green pepper, sliced
- 1 Tablespoon canola oil
- 8 flour tortillas

Wash chicken breasts and pat dry. Cut into thin strips. Combine the next 5 ingredients in a medium bowl. Add chicken strips, cover and marinate for 20 minutes. Preheat broiler. Place chicken on broiler pan. Broil chicken 6 inches from heat for 8 minutes or until no longer pink in the center, turning once. Heat 1 Tablespoon oil in large skillet, and sauté onion and green pepper until just tender. Serve on warm flour tortillas with desired toppings. Serves 4. Serving size: 2 fajitas

Amount Per Serving:

Calories 297	Saturated Fat 2 g	Sodium 206 mg
Total Fat 10 g	Cholesterol 108 mg	

South of the Border Chicken & Bean Casserole

- 2 chicken breast halves, cooked and cut into pieces
- 1 envelope taco seasoning mix
- 2 green peppers, chopped
- 1 red pepper, chopped
- 1 (10-ounce) package frozen corn
- 1 1/2 cups mild salsa
- 2 cans black beans, rinsed and drained
- 8 cups cooked rice
- 8 Tablespoons low-fat sour cream
- 8 Tablespoons low-fat cheddar cheese, shredded

Preheat oven to 350 degrees. Toss chicken with taco seasoning mix until well coated. Add peppers, corn, salsa and beans. Toss gently to mix. Pour into 13 x 9-inch or 3-quart baking dish. Bake for 45 minutes. Stir once, halfway through baking. Top with cheese and sour cream, and serve over rice. Serves 8. Serving size: 2 cups

Amount Per Serving:

Calories 514	Saturated Fat 3 g	Sodium 790 mg
Total Fat 6 g	Cholesterol 37 mg	

Country Captain Chicken

- 1 pound, skinless, boneless chicken
- 1/2 teaspoon garlic salt
- 1/2 teaspoon paprika
- 1 cup onion, chopped
- 1 medium green pepper, chopped
- 2 garlic cloves, pressed
- 2 cups canned tomatoes, undrained
- 1 (6-ounce) can tomato paste
- 1 Tablespoon dried parsley flakes
- 1/2 teaspoon thyme
- 1/2 teaspoon curry powder
- 1 Tablespoon red wine vinegar
- 1/4 teaspoon black pepper
- 3 chicken bouillon cubes, dissolved in 1/4 cup boiling water

Sprinkle chicken pieces with garlic salt and paprika. Brown chicken in a large, non-stick skillet over medium heat. Remove chicken and set aside. To the same skillet add onion, green pepper, garlic, and saute until tender (about 4 minutes). Add the next 7 ingredients, and stir until well blended. Add bouillon and reserved chicken. Cover and cook about 40 minutes or until chicken is tender. Serve over steamed rice.

Serves 4. Serving size: 8 ounces

Amount Per Serving:

Calories 284	Saturated Fat 2 g	Sodium 2016 mg
Total Fat 6 g	Cholesterol 74 mg	

Chicken Tequila

- 1 Tablespoon olive oil
- 1/2 cup tequila
- juice of 1 lime
- 1 teaspoon oregano
- 1 garlic clove, flattened
- 3 (6-ounce) chicken breast halves, boneless and skinless
- 1 medium onion, sliced
- 1 teaspoon minced garlic

- 1 Tablespoon chili powder
- 2 teaspoons ground cumin
- 1/2 teaspoon ground coriander
- 1/8 teaspoon cayenne pepper
- 1 (15-ounce) can tomatoes with chilies
- 12 ounces bow-tie pasta
- 1/2 cup feta cheese, crumbled
- 2 Tablespoons fresh cilantro
- 2 Tablespoons scallions, chopped

Mix olive oil, 1/4 cup tequila, lime juice, oregano and flattened garlic in a medium-size bowl. Add chicken breasts. Cover, and refrigerate overnight. Prepare charcoal grill or preheat broiler. Remove chicken from marinade, and reserve marinade. Grill (or broil) chicken until done. Allow to cool slightly, then shred into bite-size pieces. Meanwhile, combine remaining 1/4 cup tequila, onion, minced garlic, spices and reserved marinade. Sauté until onion is softened. Add can of tomatoes with chilies and simmer until thickened (about 15 minutes). In a medium-sized pan, cook pasta according to package directions until al dente. Mix pasta into sauce. Add reserved chicken, and reheat. Serve sprinkled with feta cheese, cilantro and scallions. Serves 4. Serving size: 4 1/2 ounces

Amount Per Serving:

Calories 672	Saturated Fat 6 g	Sodium 661 mg
Total Fat 15 g	Cholesterol 83 mg	

Lemon-Pepper Chicken

- 4 (6-ounce) chicken breast halves, boneless and skinless
- 1/2 cup dry bread crumbs
- 1/2 teaspoon coarsely-ground black pepper
- 1 teaspoon lemon peel, grated
- 1/2 teaspoon salt
- 1/8 teaspoon garlic powder
- 1 egg
- 1 Tablespoon water
- 1/3 cup flour
- 2 Tablespoons olive oil
- 1 cup chicken broth
- 1/2 cup dry white wine
- 3 Tablespoons lemon juice
- lemon slice (garnish)

Rinse and pat dry chicken breast halves. On wax paper, combine bread crumbs, pepper, lemon peel, salt and garlic powder. In a pie plate, beat egg and water until smooth. Coat chicken breasts with flour, dip in egg mixture, and then coat with bread crumb mixture. In a 10- to 12-inch skillet, heat oil over medium heat. Add chicken, and brown 2-3 minutes on each side. Add broth, wine and lemon juice. Cover, and simmer 5-10 minutes or until chicken is tender. Remove chicken to a warm platter and keep warm. To make a sauce, boil liquid remaining in the skillet for 2-3 minutes or until reduced to about 3/4 cup. Cut breasts diagonally into 1/2-inch slices, or serve pieces whole. Arrange on warm dinner plates, top with sauce, and garnish with lemon slices. Serves 4.
Serving size: 1 (6-ounce) chicken breast

Amount Per Serving:

Calories 342	Saturated Fat 2 g	Sodium 657 mg
Total Fat 12 g	Cholesterol 127 mg	

Cashew Chicken

Prep Time: 30 minutes
Cooking Time: 20 minutes

- 1 cup fat-free plain yogurt
- 1 Tablespoon light soy sauce
- 1 pound chicken breasts,
  boneless and skinless,
  cut into bite-size pieces
- 1 package stir-fry seasoning mix
- 1 cup flour
- 1 cup plain, dry bread crumbs

- 2 Tablespoons cornstarch
- 2 cups chicken broth
- 2 Tablespoons oyster sauce
- 1 teaspoon sugar
- pepper, to taste
- 2 ounces cashews
- 1/2 cup green onions, chopped
- hot cooked rice

Preheat oven to 400 degrees. Mix yogurt and soy sauce, and add chicken pieces. Refrigerate for 20 minutes. Mix together seasoning mix, flour and bread crumbs. Dredge chicken in flour mixture, and place on a baking dish or cookie sheet that has been coated with non-stick cooking spray. Coat chicken lightly with cooking spray. Bake 10 minutes on each side or until golden brown. While chicken is cooking, dissolve cornstarch in a small amount of broth in a medium saucepan. Add remaining broth gradually, and stir in oyster sauce, sugar and pepper. Stir over medium heat until sauce boils and begins to thicken. Arrange chicken on platter. Pour sauce over chicken. Sprinkle with cashews and green onions. Serve immediately with soy sauce and rice. Serves 4. Serving size: 8 ounces

Amount Per Serving:

Calories 546	Saturated Fat 3 g	Sodium 1891 mg
Total Fat 12 g	Cholesterol 76 mg	

Tandoori Chicken

Prep Time: 40 minutes
Marinade time: 6 hours
Cooking Time: 30 minutes

- 1 cup plain, fat-free yogurt
- 3 Tablespoons lemon juice, freshly squeezed
- 1 Tablespoon fresh ginger root, peeled and grated
- 3 teaspoons paprika
- 1 teaspoon garlic, finely minced
- 1 1/2 teaspoons ground coriander
- 1 1/2 teaspoons ground cumin
- 1/4 teaspoon ground red pepper
- 6 chicken breast halves (bone in)

In a gallon-size food storage bag, mix yogurt, lemon juice, ginger root, paprika, garlic, coriander, cumin and red pepper. With a small, sharp knife, cut 1/2-inch-deep slits in chicken 1 inch apart. Place chicken in bag with yogurt mixture. Close bag, and shake to coat chicken, rubbing marinade into slits. Refrigerate at least 6 hours or overnight. Coat boiler pan with non-stick cooking spray. Preheat broiler. Broil chicken, bone-side up for 10-15 minutes, 4 to 6 inches from heat. Turn pieces over, and broil 10-15 minutes longer or until juices run clear when meat is pierced. Serves 6.
Serving size: 1 chicken breast half

Amount Per Serving:

Calories 172	Saturated Fat 1 g	Sodium 92 mg
Total Fat 4 g	Cholesterol 74 mg	

Chicken Very Light

Prep Time: 5 minutes
Cooking Time: 1 hour

- 8 (6-ounce) chicken breast halves, boneless and skinless
- 1 (12-ounce) jar red plum jam
- 1 (1-ounce) package dry onion soup mix
- 1 (8-ounce) bottle fat-free red wine vinegar salad dressing

Preheat oven to 350 degrees. Arrange chicken breasts in a 9 x 13-inch baking dish. In a medium-size bowl, combine jam, onion soup mix and salad dressing. Pour over chicken, and bake covered for 1 hour. Serve with rice. Serves 8.
Serving size: 1 (6-ounce) chicken breast

Amount Per Serving:

Calories 304	Saturated Fat 1 g	Sodium 454 mg
Total Fat 4 g	Cholesterol 91 mg	

Chicken & Wild Rice Almondine

Prep Time: 20 minutes
Cooking Time: 1 to 1 1/2 hours

- 6 chicken breast halves, boneless and skinless
- 1/2 cup onion, chopped
- 1 (6-ounce) box wild rice with mushrooms
- 1 (15-ounce) can French-style green beans, drained
- 1/4 cup water
- 1 (10 1/2-ounce) can low-fat cream of mushroom soup, undiluted
- 2 ounces almond slices
- 1 cup cooking sherry

Preheat oven to 350 degrees. Coat a large skillet with non-stick cooking spray. Brown chicken and onions. Remove to a plate. Place wild rice and its seasoning packet in a 2-quart casserole dish, and mix well. Place green beans and water over rice mixture, spreading evenly. Lay chicken breasts and onions over green beans. Cover chicken breasts with soup, and sprinkle with almond slices. Pour 1/2 cup cooking sherry over the top of dish, and bake uncovered for 1-1 1/2 hours until rice is tender. Add additional sherry halfway through cooking time. Serves 6. Serving size: 1 chicken breast with rice

Amount Per Serving:

Calories 393	Saturated fat 2 g	Sodium 664 mg
Total Fat 9 g	Cholesterol 77 mg	

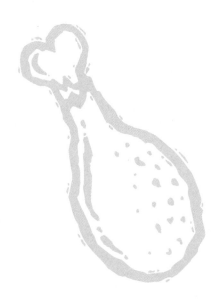

Hot Chicken Salad

- 2 cups low-fat cream of chicken soup, undiluted
- 1 cup fat-free mayonnaise
- 2 cups cooked chicken, cut into pieces
- 1 (8-ounce) can chopped water chestnuts, drained
- 2 cups celery, chopped
- 1 (4-ounce) jar pimentos, drained and chopped
- 2 cups baked potato chips, crushed

Preheat oven to 400 degrees. Coat a 9 x 13-inch pan with non-stick cooking spray. In a large bowl, mix together the soup and mayonnaise. Add the chicken, water chestnuts, celery and pimentos, and mix well. Pour into pan, and top with potato chips. Bake for 30 minutes. Serves 8. Serving size: 1 cup

Amount Per Serving:

Calories 189	Saturated Fat 1 g	Sodium 762 mg
Total Fat 4 g	Cholesterol 35 mg	

Chicken Stock

- 2 pounds chicken pieces, skinless
- 3 quarts water
- 1 large onion, quartered
- 3/4 cup carrots, sliced
- 3/4 cup celery, sliced
- 6 parsley stems
- 10 peppercorns, crushed
- 6 thyme stems
- 1 bay leaf

Place all ingredients into a large stock pot or Dutch oven. Bring to a boil. Reduce heat, and remove foam from top of broth. Partially cover and simmer 2 1/2 hours or until reduced by 1/3. Strain, and refrigerate until fat congeals on surface. Remove fat. Use stock immediately or freeze until needed. Makes 2 quarts. Serves 8. Serving Size: 1 cup

Amount Per Serving:

Calories 30	Saturated Fat 0 g	Sodium 170 mg
Total Fat 0 g	Cholesterol 0 mg	

Tortilla Black Bean Casserole

- 1 pound lean ground turkey
- 1 cup onion, chopped
- 1 cup green pepper, chopped
- 1 (14.5-ounce) can no-salt tomatoes, cut up
- 1 (4.5-ounce) can green chilies, chopped
- 1/4 cup medium to hot picante sauce
- 1 garlic clove, minced
- 2 teaspoons ground cumin

- 2 (15-ounce) cans black beans, drained
- 12 (6-inch diameter) low-fat flour tortillas
- 1 cup low-fat Monterey Jack cheese, shredded
- 1 cup low-fat cheddar cheese, shredded
- 2 cups lettuce, shredded
- 2 green onions, sliced
- 1 (2.25-ounce) can pitted ripe olives, drained and sliced
- 1 tomato, diced
- 1/2 cup fat-free sour cream

Preheat oven to 350 degrees. In a large skillet, brown turkey with onion and green pepper. Drain off any liquid. Add tomatoes with their juice, green chilies, picante sauce, garlic and cumin. Bring to a boil. Reduce heat and simmer uncovered for 10 minutes. Stir in beans. Spread 1/3 of the meat and bean mixture over the bottom of a 9 x 13 x 2-inch baking dish. Top with 6 tortillas and 1/2 of the cheeses. Add another 1/3 of the meat and bean mixture. Top with remaining tortillas. Spread the remaining meat and bean mixture on top of the tortillas. Bake for 30-35 minutes until thoroughly heated. Sprinkle with remaining cheese. Bake 5 minutes longer to melt cheese. Remove from oven, and top with lettuce, green onions, diced tomato and olives. Cut into squares to serve. Garnish with sour cream. Serves 10. Serving size: 8 ounces

Amount Per Serving:

Calories 401	Saturated Fat 3 g	Sodium 705 mg
Total Fat 13 g	Cholesterol 50 mg	

Poppy Seed Turkey Casserole

- 1 1/2 pounds ground raw turkey
- 1/2 cup onion, chopped
- 1/3 cup green pepper, chopped
- 1/3 cup red pepper, chopped
- 1 (15-ounce) can tomato sauce
- 1/2 teaspoon white pepper

- 1 (8-ounce) package wide noodles
- 1 (8-ounce) Neufchatel cheese, cubed
- 1 cup low-fat cottage cheese
- 1/2 cup plain fat-free yogurt
- 1 tablespoon poppy seed

Preheat oven to 375 degrees. In a large skillet, brown ground turkey, onion, green pepper and red pepper. Drain off any liquid. Stir in tomato sauce and pepper. Cook noodles according to package directions (using no salt). Drain. In a small bowl, combine the cheeses, yogurt, and poppy seed. Toss the cheese mixture with the hot noodles. Lay 3/4 of the noodle mixture in a 13 x 9 x 2-inch baking dish. Spoon meat mixture over center of noodles, leaving a 1-inch border of uncovered noodles. Layer remaining noodle mixture over center of meat mixture, leaving a 1-inch meat border. Bake covered for 30 minutes. Uncover, and bake 10 to 15 minutes or until heated through. Serves 8. Serving size: 1 cup

Amount Per Serving:

Calories 334	Saturated Fat 5 g	Sodium 553 mg
Total Fat 9 g	Cholesterol 104 mg	

Myth No. 61

"The concept of using a cooking thermometer when preparing a turkey simply does not register with people from the Ozarks. They'll quickly point out, 'The bird couldn't possibly have a fever, he's already dead'!"

Sage Pork Chops

- 6 (6-ounce) pork chops, trimmed of all visible fat
- 1/3 teaspoon sage
- 1 cup onion, chopped
- 4 potatoes, sliced
- salt and pepper to taste
- 1 (16-ounce) can fat-free chicken broth

Preheat oven to 350 degrees. Place pork chops in a single layer in a 9 x 13-inch pan. Cover chops with sage. Place onions and then potatoes over chops. Sprinkle with salt and pepper to taste. Pour chicken broth over chops to cover. Bake for 1 hour or until chops are tender and no longer pink. Serves 6. Serving size: 1 pork chop

Amount Per Serving:

Calories 288	Saturated Fat 4 g	Sodium 474 mg
Total Fat 11 g	Cholesterol 69 mg	

Pork Chop Casserole

- 4 pork chops, boneless
- 1 serving olive-oil-flavor cooking spray
- 4 cups potatoes, thinly-sliced
- 4 ounces fat-free sour cream
- 1 (10 3/4 -ounce) can low-fat cream of mushroom soup
- 1/4 cup water
- 1/2 teaspoon dill weed
- 2 ounces low-fat cheddar cheese, grated

Preheat oven to 375 degrees. Brown pork chops in a non-stick pan coated with olive-oil-flavor cooking spray. Place pork chops in 9 x 11-inch baking dish. Top with potatoes. In small bowl, combine and mix well the sour cream, soup, water and dill weed. Pour mixture over the potatoes. Bake covered for 1 hour and 30 minutes. Remove from oven, and sprinkle cheese on top. Bake for 5 minutes or until cheese melts. Serves 4. Serving size: 1 pork chop and 1 cup of potatoes with sauce

Amount Per Serving:

Calories 477	Saturated Fat 4 g	Sodium 257 mg
Total Fat 13 g	Cholesterol 70 mg	

Contributed by retired Chef Ernest G. Joseph.

Veggie & Canadian Bacon Pizza

Prep Time: 20 minutes
Cooking Time: 20 minutes

Crust:

- 2 1/2 cups all-purpose flour
- 3 teaspoons baking powder
- 1/2 teaspoon salt
- 1 Tablespoon sugar
- 1/4 cup canola oil
- 1/4 cup oatmeal
- 1 Tablespoon honey or molasses
- 3/4 cup water

Topping:

- 4 ounces spaghetti sauce
- 1 cup broccoli, chopped and sautéed
- 1/2 cup mushrooms, chopped and sauteed
- 1 pepper, chopped and sauteed
- 1/2 cup onion, chopped and sauteed
- 4 ounces Canadian bacon
- 1/2 cup fat-free mozzarella cheese, shredded

Preheat oven to 400 degrees. Sift flour, baking powder, salt and sugar together. Add canola oil, oatmeal, honey or molasses and water. Mix together. Press into pizza pan dusted with flour. Bake for 10 minutes. Top with sauce and toppings, except for cheese. Bake for 5-10 minutes more. Top with cheese and bake until melted. Serves 4.
Serving size: 2 slices

Amount Per Serving:

Calories 586	Saturated Fat 2 g	Sodium 1347 mg
Total Fat 17 g	Cholesterol 17 mg	

Contributed by St. John's Nutrition Center, Springfield, Missouri.

Apricot Pork Medallions

Prep Time: 15 minutes
Cooking Time: 25 minutes

- 1 pound pork tenderloin
- 2 Tablespoons low-fat margarine
- 1/2 cup low-calorie apricot jam
- 2-3 green onions, sliced
- 1/4 teaspoon dry mustard
- 1 Tablespoon cider vinegar

Cut pork into 1-inch slightly-flattened slices. Heat 1 Tablespoon margarine over medium-high heat. Brown pork 2-3 minutes on each side, and remove from pan. To juices in pan, add remaining margarine, apricot jam, onions, mustard and cider vinegar. Cover and simmer 3-4 minutes. Add pork to heat through. Serves 4.
Serving size: 4 ounces

Amount Per Serving

Calories 225	Saturated Fat 2 g	Sodium 178 mg
Total Fat 8 g	Cholesterol 60 mg	

Banana Pork Chops

- 1 Tablespoon margarine
- 4 pork chops, trimmed of fat
- 3 small firm bananas
- salt and pepper, to taste
- pinch of cayenne
- 1 teaspoon flour
- 1/2 cup chicken broth
- 1 lemon, sliced
- sprigs of parsley for garnish

Melt margarine in a large skillet over medium heat. Add pork chops and cook 10-12 minutes on each side, depending on thickness. Five minutes before chops are finished cooking, peel bananas, and cut in half lengthwise. Add to skillet, and sprinkle with salt, pepper and cayenne. Arrange on warm serving dish. Stir flour into pan juices, and gradually add broth. Simmer 2-3 minutes, then pour into small serving pitcher. Serve with hot cooked rice, and garnish with lemon slices and parsley. Serves 4.
Serving size: 1 pork chop

Amount Per Serving:

Calories 283	Saturated Fat 4 g	Sodium 192 mg
Total Fat 14 g	Cholesterol 63 mg	

Apple Orchard Pork Chops

- 4 lean, thick (6-ounce) pork chops
- 3-4 apples, peeled, cored and sliced
- 3-4 Tablespoons brown sugar
- salt and pepper to taste

Brown pork chops on each side in a skillet coated with non-stick cooking spray. Add apple slices. Reduce heat to medium-low. Cover and cook for 20 to 30 minutes or until chops and apples are done. Remove chops, and keep warm. Add brown sugar, salt and pepper to the apples in the skillet. Cook for 2 to 3 minutes until glaze has formed. Serve chops on rice. Top with apple mixture. Serves 4. Serving size: 1 pork chop

Amount Per Serving:

Calories 423	Saturated Fat 6 g	Sodium 157 mg
Total Fat 18 g	Cholesterol 108 mg	

Pork Tenderloins with Pineapple Stuffing

Prep Time: 20 minutes
Cooking Time: 60 minutes

Stuffing:

- 6 slices whole wheat bread (cracked wheat or multigrain)
- 1/2 cup crushed pineapple, drained
- 1/2 cup water chestnuts, chopped
- 1/2 cup onion, finely chopped
- 1/2 cup celery, finely chopped
- 3/4 teaspoon dried sage
- 1/2 teaspoon poultry seasoning
- 1/2 cup egg substitute

Basting Sauce:

- 3 Tablespoons unsweetened pineapple juice
- 3 Tablespoons brown sugar
- 1 Tablespoon spicy mustard

- 3 pork tenderloins, 1 pound each

Preheat oven to 350 degrees. To prepare stuffing, tear 4 slices of bread into pieces. Place pieces in food processor or blender, and process into coarse crumbs. Cut remaining bread into 2-inch cubes. Place crumbs and cubes in a medium-sized bowl. Add crushed pineapple, water chestnuts, onion, celery and seasonings. Toss to mix well. Add egg substitute, and toss to mix well. Set aside. To prepare basting sauce, combine all of the ingredients in a small bowl, and stir to mix well. Set aside. Trim the tenderloins of all visible fat. Rinse with cool water, and pat dry. Split each of tenderloins lengthwise, not quite through. Spread each open like a book. Spread 1/3 stuffing mixture over half of each tenderloin, extending to edges of meat. Fold the facing of each tenderloin over half spread with stuffing. Use a heavy string to tie meat together at 2 1/2-inch intervals. Coat a 13 x 16-inch roasting pan with non-stick cooking spray. Lay tenderloins in the pan about 2 inches apart. Bake 55-60 minutes or until meat is not pink inside, basting occasionally with the prepared sauce. Remove pan from oven, and cover loosely with aluminum foil. Let sit 5-10 minutes before slicing 1/2-inch thick. Serve immediately. Serves 12.
Serving size: 6 slices

Amount Per Serving:

Calories 270	Saturated Fat 3 g	Sodium 207 mg
Total Fat 10 g	Cholesterol 70 mg	

Pork Tenderloin

Marinade:

- 1/4 cup light soy sauce
- 1 Tablespoon onion, grated
- 1 garlic clove, mashed
- 1 Tablespoon vinegar
- 1/4 teaspoon cayenne pepper
- 1/2 teaspoon sugar

Sauce:

- 1/3 cup fat-free mayonnaise
- 1/3 cup fat-free sour cream
- 1 Tablespoon dry mustard
- 1 Tablespoon green onions, chopped
- 1 1/2 teaspoons vinegar
- salt to taste

- 2 pork tenderloins, 1 pound each
- 2 bacon strips

Combine all marinade ingredients and pour over tenderloins. Cover and refrigerate overnight. Preheat oven to 350 degrees. Remove tenderloins, and place in a flat baking dish. Place bacon strips on top of meat. Bake uncovered for 1 1/2 hours. Baste occasionally with marinade. Combine all sauce ingredients until well blended. Slice tenderloins into 1 1/2-inch slices and serve with sauce on the side.
Serves 8. Serving size: 4 ounces

Amount Per Serving:

Calories 173	Saturated 2 g	Sodium 548 mg
Total Fat 5 g	Cholesterol 60 mg	

Myth No. 112:

"Pork rinds are considered an Ozarkian delicacy."

Radical Roughy

- 1 orange roughy fillet
- 1 lemon, thinly-sliced
- 1 scallion, julienne
- Freshly ground black pepper

Preheat oven to 350 degrees. Place roughy fillet in center of aluminum foil. Distribute lemon slices, scallion and black pepper over fillet. Cover with another piece of foil and crimp edges to seal. Bake for 15 minutes. Serve immediately. Serves 1.
Serving size: 1 fillet

Amount Per Serving:

| Calories 129 | Saturated Fat 0 g | Sodium 115 mg |
| Total Fat 1 g | Cholesterol 37 mg | |

Salmon Dijon

Prep Time: 15 minutes
Cooking Time: 30 minutes

- 4 (4 to 6-ounce) salmon steaks
- 1 head broccoli, cut into spears
- 3 Tablespoons olive oil
- 1 cup carrots, grated
- 1 shallot, peeled and chopped
- 1/4 teaspoon salt
- 1/8 teaspoon black pepper

- 1/2 cup dry white wine
- 5 teaspoons Dijon mustard
- 2 Tablespoons flour
- 1/2 cup water
- 1 tomato, diced
- 1 lemon, cut into wedges (garnish)

Preheat oven to 300 degrees. Place salmon in pan coated with non-stick cooking spray. Bake salmon until it starts to flake. Fill saucepan half full with water, and bring to a boil, and add broccoli. Blanche broccoli spears until tender. Sauté carrots and shallots in oil until tender. Add salt, black pepper, white wine and mustard. Bring to a boil. Mix flour and water using enough water to make a paste. Add to boiling mixture, and stir until thickened. Place salmon on plate, add tomatoes to the sauce and pour sauce over the salmon. Serve with 1/4 of the broccoli spears. Decorate with lemon wedges. Serves 4. Serving size: 1 steak, 1/2 cup of sauce and 1/4 cup of broccoli spears.

Amount Per Serving:

Calories 356	Saturated Fat 2 g	Sodium 336 mg
Total Fat 16 g	Cholesterol 76 mg	

Contributed by Roger Evans, J. Parrinos Pasta House and Bar,
Springfield, Missouri.

Ozark Trout Doria

Prep Time: 15 minutes
Cooking Time: 15 minutes

- 1/2 teaspoon soft margarine
- 2 teaspoons canola oil
- 8 ounce boneless trout, uncooked

- flour
- salt and pepper to taste

Sauce:

- 2 Tablespoons dry white wine
- 1/2 teaspoon shallots chopped
- 2 Tablespoons cucumber, peeled, seeded, and cubed
- 1 Tablespoon mushrooms, sliced
- 2 Tablespoons lemon, peeled and diced

- 1 Tablespoon fresh parsley, chopped
- 1/4 cup fish stock, defatted
- 1 teaspoon lemon juice
- 2 Tablespoons tomato, peeled and diced
- 1/2 ounce almonds, sliced (garnish)

Heat margarine and oil in skillet. Lightly flour both sides of trout (salt and pepper to taste) and brown in skillet. Remove trout to platter and discard the skillet grease. Deglaze the pan with white wine. Let wine simmer for a minute, then add shallots, cucumber, mushrooms, diced lemon, chopped parsley. Sauté one minute. Add fish stock and lemon juice and cook until cucumbers are a little soft. Add tomato just before serving. Garnish with almonds and fresh parsley. Serves 2.
Serving size: 1 side of trout

Amount Per Serving:

Calories 469	Saturated Fat 2 g	Sodium 681 mg
Total Fat 17 g	Cholesterol 63 mg	

Contributed by Chef Marcel Bonetti, Hemingway's Café in Springfield, Missouri.

Poached Shrimp and Scallops

- 5 ounces shrimp and scallops
- 1 teaspoon olive oil
- vegetable mix of carrots, broccoli, peppers, and peas, to taste
- 1/8 teaspoon white or black pepper
- 1/8 teaspoon oregano
- 1/8 teaspoon coriander
- 6 ounces water
- few drops of Worcestershire sauce
- salt to taste

Lightly sauté shrimp and scallops in olive oil. Add vegetables and spices. Add water and Worcestershire sauce. Simmer to desired doneness. Serve with couscous and lemon wedges. Serves 1.

Amount Per Serving:

Calories 189	Saturated Fat 1 g	Sodium 2440 mg
Total Fat 6 g	Cholesterol 141 mg	

Contributed by Chef Abraham Karim, Sophia's Cafe in Springfield, Missouri.

Eggplant Parmesan

- 3 Tablespoons balsamic vinegar
- 1 Tablespoon plus 1 teaspoon olive oil
- 1 teaspoon salt, divided
- 3/4 teaspoon sugar, divided
- 1/2 teaspoon oregano
- 1/2 teaspoon pepper
- 1 large eggplant (1 1/2 pounds), cut into 1/2-inch thick slices
- 1 cup onion, chopped
- 1 1/2 teaspoons garlic, minced
- 4 Tablespoons dry white wine, divided
- 1 (16-ounce) can stewed tomatoes
- 1 cup tomatoes, seeded and chopped
- 1/4 cup fresh basil, chopped (or 3 Tablespoons dried basil)
- 4 ounces part-skim mozzarella cheese, shredded, divided
- 1 Tablespoon Parmesan cheese, grated

Preheat oven to 400 degrees. Combine vinegar, 1 Tablespoon olive oil, 1/2 teaspoon salt, 1/2 teaspoon sugar, oregano and pepper in a bowl. Coat a large cookie sheet with non-stick cooking spray. Brush both sides of eggplant slices with vinegar mixture, and arrange in a single layer on cookie sheet. Bake 15 minutes per side or until eggplant is fork tender. Combine 1 teaspoon olive oil, onions, garlic and 2 Tablespoons wine in a large non-stick skillet. Stir while cooking over medium-high heat until onions are soft (5 minutes). Stir in stewed tomatoes with their liquid, chopped tomatoes, basil, remaining 2 Tablespoons of wine, 1/2 teaspoon salt and 1/4 teaspoon sugar. Bring to a boil over high heat. Reduce heat, and simmer uncovered for 10 minutes. Stir occasionally to break up tomatoes. Makes 2 1/2 cups sauce.

Spoon 1/3 of the sauce into a shallow baking dish. Arrange 1/2 of the eggplant slices over sauce. Spoon 1/2 of the remaining sauce over the eggplant. Sprinkle with 2/3 cup mozzarella cheese. Top with remaining eggplant slices, sauce, mozzarella cheese, and top with Parmesan cheese. Cover and bake for 30 minutes. Bake uncovered for 15 to 20 minutes more or until bubbly. Let stand 15 minutes before serving for easier cutting. Garnish with fresh basil. Serves 6. Serving size: 8 ounces

Amount Per Serving:

Calories 227	Saturated Fat 3 g	Sodium 982 mg
Total Fat 7 g	Cholesterol 11 mg	

Mushroom and Garlic Sauce for Lamb

Prep Time: 10 minutes
Cooking Time: 15 minutes

- 1 Tablespoon margarine
- 4 ounces cooking sherry
- 1/4 cup garlic
- 1/4 cup parsley, finely chopped
- 1/2 teaspoon fresh basil
- 1/4 teaspoon onion powder
- 1/2 pound fresh mushrooms, sliced
- 1/2 teaspoon thyme
- 1/2 teaspoon oregano
- 1/2 teaspoon white pepper
- 1/2 teaspoon dry mustard
- 1/4 teaspoon curry powder
- 1/4 teaspoon cumin
- 1/2 teaspoon flour or cornstarch
- 4 ounces evaporated skim milk

Melt margarine in medium saucepan. Sauté and simmer sherry, garlic, parsley, basil and onion powder. Add mushrooms and remaining spices. Add flour or cornstarch for thickening and stir constantly until thickened. Add skim milk, bring to a boil, remove from heat and serve immediately. Serve over lamb chops or rack of lamb. Serves 4. Serving size: 1/3 cup

Amount Per Serving:

Calories 103	Saturated Fat 1 g	Sodium 388 mg
Total Fat 3 g	Cholesterol 1 mg	

Contributed by Chef Abraham Karim, Sophia's Café in Springfield, Missouri.

Myth No. 90:

"Ask Ozarkians what a pork medallion is and they'll proudly show you their ribbons from the feeder pig division at the county fair."

PASTAS

Myth No. 52:
"People from the Ozarks believe Beef Jerky is a main course."

Fact:
"Again, this simply is not true. It also holds false for other varieties
such as Deer Jerky, Sausage Jerky and Turkey Jerky."

Angel Hair Pasta with Tomatoes and Black Beans

Prep Time: 3 minutes
Cooking Time: 3 minutes

- 1 (16-ounce) package angel hair pasta, uncooked
- 2 (15-ounce) cans tomatoes, chopped (no-fat, pizza style)
- 1 (14-ounce) can fat-free black beans
- Asiago cheese, grated (optional)

In a medium saucepan, heat tomatoes and black beans until hot. Do not boil. In a large saucepan, cook pasta in rapidly-boiling water for 2-3 minutes. Drain pasta. Ladle sauce over pasta, and serve. Sprinkle grated Asiago cheese lightly over pasta and sauce (optional). Serves 6. Serving size: 1 cup

Amount Per Serving:

Calories 374	Saturated Fat 1 g	Sodium 494 mg
Total Fat 1 g	Cholesterol 0 mg	

Contributed by Faith Ann Yorty, Springfield Art Museum.

Pommodoro

Prep Time: 5 minutes
Cooking Time: 10 minutes

- 3 ounces fresh tomatoes, chopped
- 2 ounces fat-free chicken stock
- 1 teaspoon garlic, minced
- pinch of salt and white pepper
- 1 ounce pine nuts, toasted
- 1/4 cup fresh basil, chopped
- 1 Tablespoon pure olive oil
- 4 ounces angel hair pasta, cooked to package instructions

In a 10-inch sauté pan, bring tomatoes, chicken stock and garlic to a boil. Reduce heat. Add salt, white pepper, pine nuts, basil and olive oil. Cook for 3 to 5 minutes at a light boil. Add pasta, and toss to mix all ingredients. Serve immediately on warm plate. Serves 1. Serving size: 2 cups

Amount Per Serving:

Calories 761	Saturated Fat 2 g	Sodium 300 mg
Total Fat 30 g	Cholesterol 0 mg	

Contributed by Chef Fred Coco, Metropolitan Grill in Springfield, Missouri.

Chicken Evano

- 4 (4 to 6-ounce) chicken breast halves, boneless and skinless
- 2 (6-ounce) cans pureed tomatoes
- 1 (6-ounce) can tomato paste
- 2 (6-ounce) cans water
- 1/2 cup red wine
- 1/2 small, Bermuda red onion, diced

- 1/4 teaspoon salt
- 1/4 teaspoon garlic, chopped
- 1/4 teaspoon oregano
- 2 bay leaves
- 1 ounce capers, finely chopped
- 1 ounce black olives, finely chopped
- 12 ounces uncooked angel hair pasta

Preheat oven to 350 degrees. In a baking pan coated with non-stick cooking spray, bake chicken breasts for 30 minutes or until done. In a saucepan, combine the tomatoes, tomato paste, water, wine and onions, and heat. Add spices, capers and black olives, and cook until thickened. Cook angel hair pasta according to package directions. Drain. Place pasta on plate with chicken on top. Cover with sauce, and serve. Serves 4. Serving size: 1 chicken breast with 1/2 cup sauce and 1/2 cup pasta

Amount Per Serving:

Calories 622	Saturated Fat 2 g	Sodium 1174 mg
Total Fat 7 g	Cholesterol 96 mg	

Contributed by Roger Evans, J. Parrino's Pasta House and Bar in Springfield, Missouri.

Capellini with Bell Peppers & Snow Peas

- 4 Tablespoons unsalted butter
- 1 small onion, finely chopped
- 1 medium red bell pepper, thinly sliced lengthwise
- 1 medium yellow bell pepper, thinly sliced lengthwise
- 4 ounces snow peas, cut into 1/2-inch diagonal slices
- 3/4 pound dried capellini or angel hair pasta
- 1 Tablespoon fresh parsley, finely chopped
- 1/2 teaspoon salt
- 1/2 teaspoon freshly-ground black pepper
- Parmesan cheese (optional)

Bring large pot of salted water to a boil. Melt butter in a medium skillet. Add onion and cook over moderately high heat until translucent (about 2 minutes), stirring occasionally. Add bell peppers and snow peas and sauté until crisp tender (about 2 minutes), stirring frequently. Set aside. Add capellini to the boiling, salted water, and cook according to package directions, stirring occasionally. Drain well and return to pot. Add sautéed vegetables, parsley, salt and pepper. Toss to combine. Serve with Parmesan cheese if desired. Serves 4. Serving size: 2 cups

Amount Per Serving:

Calories 400	Saturated Fat 4 g	Sodium 277 mg
Total Fat 7 g	Cholesterol 16 mg	

Myth No. 213:

"Formal dining in the Ozarks means everyone gets their own TV tray."

Basil Chicken

- 1 1/2 pounds chicken breast halves, boneless and skinless
- 1 1/2 teaspoons olive oil
- 3 teaspoons garlic, minced
- 1 1/2 Tablespoons fresh basil
- 12 ounces tomatoes
- 12 artichoke hearts, quartered
- 6 ounces dry vermouth
- 2 1/4 cups chicken stock
- cornstarch
- water
- 1 1/8 pounds bowtie or farfalle pasta
- fresh basil sprig (garnish)

Dice chicken into 1-inch squares. Heat a large skillet and add the olive oil. Coat the pan evenly with the oil, then add the garlic, chicken and basil. Stir so the chicken doesn't stick. Once the meat is lightly browned, add the tomatoes and the artichoke hearts. Let simmer for 1 minute, then deglaze with the vermouth, and cook for 1 more minute. Next, add the chicken stock and bring to a boil. Thicken the mixture with a slurry of cornstarch and cold water. Serve over pasta, and garnish with a sprig of fresh basil. Serves 6. Serving size: 8 ounces

Amount Per Serving:

Calories 531	Saturated Fat 1 g	Sodium 398 mg
Total Fat 6 g	Cholesterol 73mg	

Contributed by Chef James Nicholas, Highland Springs Country Club, Springfield, Missouri.

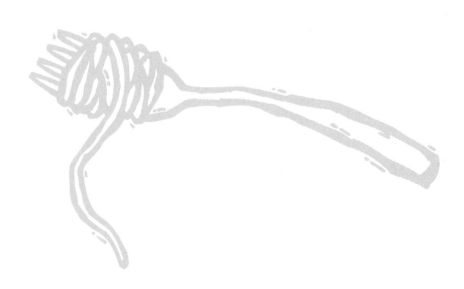

Chicken Marsala Fettuccine

- 3 (6 ounce) chicken breast halves, boneless and skinless
- 2 1/2 cups sliced fresh mushrooms
- 1 1/4 cups marsala wine or any dry wine
- 1/4 cup green onions, chopped
- 1/2 teaspoon salt
- 2 1/2 teaspoons cornstarch
- 1 Tablespoon water
- 8 ounces fettuccine (uncooked)
- 2 Tablespoons fresh parsley, chopped

Coat a large non-stick skillet with non-stick cooking spray and brown chicken breast halves. Set chicken breasts aside and keep warm. Combine mushrooms and next 3 ingredients in the skillet and bring to a boil. Reduce heat and cook uncovered for 5 minutes. Combine cornstarch and water, stir well. Add to mushroom mixture and cook until thickened, stirring constantly. Cook fettuccine according to package directions, omitting salt. Drain. Serve chicken breast halves over fettuccine with sauce spooned over both. Sprinkle with parsley. Serves 6. Serving size: 1 cup

Amount Per Serving:

Calories 271	Saturated Fat 1 g	Sodium 250 mg
Total Fat 5 g	Cholesterol 79 mg	

Fajita Fettuccine

- 1 Tablespoon fajita seasoning
- 1 1/2 pounds chicken breasts, boneless and skinless
- 1 medium onion, cut into thin strips
- 1/2 large red pepper, cut into thin strips
- 1/2 large green pepper, cut into thin strips
- Alfredo Sauce (see following recipe)
- 12 ounces fettuccine, cooked without salt or fat

Sprinkle fajita seasoning on chicken. Coat a large non-stick skillet with non-stick cooking spray. Cook chicken on medium heat until done (15 to 20 minutes). Remove chicken, let cool, and cut into bite-sized pieces. Add vegetables to skillet, and cook over medium heat until tender and crisp (5 to 10 minutes). Stir in chicken, Alfredo sauce and cooked fettuccine. Toss gently and serve. Serves 6. Serving size: 8 ounces

Amount Per Serving:

Calories 475	Saturated Fat 2 g	Sodium 631 mg
Total Fat 4 g	Cholesterol 76 mg	

This analysis includes Fajita Fettuccine and Alfredo Sauce (following recipe).

Alfredo Sauce

- 2 cups fat-free cottage cheese
- 3 Tablespoons Parmesan cheese, grated
- 2 Tablespoons butter-flavored granules
- 1/2 cup evaporated skim milk
- 1/2 teaspoon chicken-flavored bouillon granules
- 1/2 teaspoon dried basil
- 1/4 teaspoon ground black pepper

Combine all ingredients in a blender. Process until smooth. Pour into a saucepan, and heat on low heat until warm. (Do not boil.) Yields 2 3/4 cups. Serves 6.
Serving size: 1/2 cup

Amount Per Serving:

Calories 146	Saturated Fat 1 g	Sodium 843 mg
Total Fat 1 g	Cholesterol 10 mg	

Shrimp Scampi

- 2 pounds unpeeled jumbo shrimp
- 1 medium onion, finely chopped
- 4 garlic cloves, minced
- 1/4 cup margarine, melted
- 1/2 teaspoon dried tarragon
- 1/2 teaspoon salt or salt substitute
- 2 Tablespoons fresh lemon juice
- 1/2 teaspoon steak sauce
- 1/2 teaspoon Worcestershire sauce
- 1/4 teaspoon hot pepper sauce
- 2 Tablespoons fresh parsley, chopped
- Hot, cooked fettuccine

Peel and devein shrimp. Sauté onion, garlic and margarine in a large skillet over medium heat, stirring constantly for 3 to 4 minutes. Add tarragon, salt or salt substitute, lemon juice, steak sauce, Worcestershire sauce and hot pepper sauce. Bring to a boil. Add shrimp and cook for 5 to 6 minutes or until shrimp turns pink, stirring constantly. Sprinkle with parsley. Serve over fettuccine. Serves 4.
Serving size: 4 to 6 shrimp

Amount Per Serving:

Calories 366	Saturated Fat 8 g	Sodium 474 mg
Total Fat 16 g	Cholesterol 375 mg	

Easy Oven Lasagna

Prep Time: 30 minutes
Cooking Time: 1 hour

- 1 pound ground round
- 3/4 cup water
- 1 teaspoon salt
- 1 (32-ounce) jar low-fat
  Marinara Sauce
- 1 (8-ounce) package lasagna noodles ·
- 1 to 1 1/2 cups fat-free cottage cheese
- 12 ounces part-skim mozzarella cheese
- 1/4 cup fat-free Parmesan cheese

Preheat oven to 375 degrees. Brown ground round. Add water, salt and marinara sauce. Bring to a boil. In a 2-quart (11 x 7-inch) baking dish, layer sauce, uncooked noodles and cottage cheese. Repeat layers, ending with sauce. Cover with foil and bake for 1 hour. Let stand 10 minutes before serving. Garnish with Parmesan cheese. Serves 8. Serving size: 1 cup

Amount Per Serving:

| Calories 389 | Saturated Fat 7 g | Sodium 966 mg |
| Total Fat 14 g | Cholesterol 63 mg | |

Vegetable Lasagna

Prep Time: 20 minutes
Cooking Time: 45 minutes

- 1 (8-ounce) box lasagna noodles, uncooked
- 1 (15-ounce) container light ricotta cheese
- 1 (16-ounce) container 1% cottage cheese
- 1 (10-ounce) box frozen, chopped spinach, thawed and drained
- 1 (8-ounce) package part-skim mozzarella cheese
- 2 (26- to 27-ounce) jars of light chunky spaghetti sauce
- 1 garlic clove, minced

Preheat oven to 350 degrees. Mix ricotta cheese, cottage cheese and spinach together. Set aside. In a 9 x 13-inch casserole dish coated with non-stick cooking spray, layer ingredients in the following order: spaghetti sauce, uncooked noodles, cheese and spinach mixture, spaghetti sauce and grated mozzarella. Repeat layers. Cover with foil. Bake for 30 minutes. Remove foil, and bake for 15 minutes. Let stand for 5-10 minutes before cutting to serve. Serves 6. Serving size: 1 slice

Amount Per Serving:

| Calories 464 | Saturated Fat 4 g | Sodium 1419 mg |
| Total Fat 9 g | Cholesterol 35 mg | |

Vegetable Lasagna Supreme

- 6 uncooked lasagna noodles
- 1 onion, chopped
- 1 cup (about 2 1/2 ounces) fresh mushrooms, thinly-sliced
- 3 garlic cloves, minced
- 2 Tablespoons water
- 1 cup low-fat, part-skim ricotta or cottage cheese
- 1/2 cup carrots, shredded
- 1 (9-ounce) package frozen, chopped spinach, thawed and squeezed dry
- 2 egg whites
- 1 (14-ounce) jar spaghetti sauce
- 3 ounces (3/4 cup) low-fat, part-skim mozzarella cheese, shredded
- 2 Tablespoons Parmesan cheese, grated

Preheat oven to 350 degrees. Cook lasagna noodles to desired doneness as directed on package. Drain and rinse with hot water. Coat medium, non-stick skillet with non-stick cooking spray. Heat over medium-high heat until hot. Add onion, mushrooms and garlic. Cook and stir for 1 minute. Add water. Cover and cook for 3 to 4 minutes until crisp and tender. In a small bowl, combine ricotta cheese, carrot, spinach and egg whites and mix well. In an ungreased 12 x 8-inch (2-quart) baking dish, layer half of cooked noodles, half of sauce, half of mushroom mixture and half of ricotta cheese mixture. Repeat layers. Sprinkle with mozzarella cheese and Parmesan cheese. Bake for 30 to 35 minutes until hot and bubbly. Let stand for 10 minutes before serving. Serves 8. Serving size: 1 cup

Amount Per Serving:

Calories 180	Saturated Fat 1 g	Sodium 230 mg
Total Fat 5 g	Cholesterol 16 mg	

Linguine with White Clam Sauce

- 12 ounces linguine
- 4 Tablespoons onion, chopped
- 2 garlic cloves, minced
- 1 Tablespoon olive oil
- 1 teaspoon lemon juice
- 4 Tablespoons dry white wine

- 1 teaspoon dried basil, crumbled
- 1 teaspoon dried thyme, crumbled
- 1/4 teaspoon black pepper
- 1 (6 1/2-ounce) can clams, chopped (do not drain)
- 2 Tablespoons fresh parsley, chopped

Prepare pasta according to package directions and rinse with cold water. Drain and set aside. In a medium saucepan, sauté the onion and garlic in olive oil. Add lemon juice, wine and spices, and heat slowly over low heat until onions are transparent. Add pasta to onion and garlic mixture. Toss well. Add clams with juice and heat on low, until the clam juice is absorbed. Sprinkle with parsley and serve. Serves 2. Serving size: 6 ounces

Amount Per Serving:

Calories 546	Saturated Fat 3 g	Sodium 100 mg
Total Fat 14 g	Cholesterol 209 mg	

Asparagus Linguine

- 1/2 pound dried linguine
- 1 onion, chopped
- 1 1/2 teaspoons garlic, minced
- 1/8 teaspoon dried thyme
- 3/4 pound fresh asparagus, trimmed and sliced
- 4 strips cooked turkey bacon, chopped
- 1 Tablespoon water
- 1 Tablespoon fresh lemon juice
- 2 Tablespoons Parmesan cheese, grated
- 2 Tablespoons pignolias, toasted
- salt and pepper to taste

Cook linguine in boiling water for 8-10 minutes and drain. Set aside. In a skillet coated with olive oil cooking spray, cook onion, garlic and thyme over medium heat. Cook until onion is transparent. (Add a little water if needed.) Add asparagus and turkey bacon, and cook about 2 minutes. Remove from heat. Add linguine, water, lemon juice, Parmesan cheese, pignolias, salt and pepper. Top with Parmesan cheese. Serves 4. Serving size: 1 cup

Amount Per Serving:

Calories 332	Saturated Fat 2 g	Sodium 281 mg
Total Fat 9 g	Cholesterol 11 mg	

Contributed by James Clary, Clary's American Grill in Springfield, Missouri.

Myth No. 37:
"Ozarkians believe eating food al dente means 'without dentures'."

Italian Linguine Bake

Prep Time: 20 minutes
Cooking Time: 20 minutes

- 1 pound linguine
- 1 Tablespoon olive oil
- 1/2 cup mushrooms, sliced
- 1/2 cup Spanish onion, julienned
- 1/2 cup bell pepper, julienned
- 5 ounces Canadian bacon, julienned
- 1 Tablespoon garlic, minced

- 2 Tablespoons basil leaves
- 1 1/2 teaspoons oregano leaves
- salt and pepper to taste
- 2 1/2 cups marinara sauce
- 1 cup mozzarella cheese, shredded
- 1/2 cup fat-free Parmesan cheese, grated
- 4 ounces pepperoni, sliced *

Preheat oven to 350 degrees. Cook pasta according to package directions. In olive oil, sauté mushrooms, onion, pepper and Canadian bacon. Add garlic, basil, oregano, salt and pepper. Cook 4-5 minutes and set aside. Lightly coat a 9 x 13-inch non-stick baking pan with non-stick cooking spray. When pasta is al dente, drain in colander; do not rinse. Place cooked linguine in baking dish, and spread out evenly. Place sautéed vegetable mixture over pasta, then add marinara sauce. Top casserole with mozzarella cheese, Parmesan cheese and pepperoni. Bake for 15-20 minutes. Let set for 5 minutes. Slice and serve immediately. Serves 8. Serving size: 1 cup

Amount Per Serving:

Calories 444	Saturated Fat 5 g	Sodium 1203 mg
Total Fat 15 g	Cholesterol 23 mg	

*Using 9 ounces of low-fat Canadian bacon instead of pepperoni reduces the total fat content to 10 grams.

Contributed by Chef Jesse Vegar, Pasta LaBella, manufactured by the American Italian Pasta Company in Excelsior Springs, Missouri.

Light Summer Pasta

Prep Time: 40 minutes
Cooking Time: 15-20 minutes

Sauce:

- 2 pounds ripe tomatoes, chopped
- 1/2 cup fresh basil, coarsely chopped
- 1/2 cup Italian or regular parsley, finely chopped
- 4 garlic cloves, minced
- 8 ounces part-skim mozzarella cheese
- 4 Tablespoons extra virgin olive oil
- 1/2 cup fresh Parmesan cheese, grated
- 1/2 teaspoon salt
- 1/4 teaspoon pepper

Pasta:

- 1 Tablespoon olive oil
- 1 teaspoon salt
- 1 pound linguine

In a large bowl, combine all ingredients for sauce except 1/4 cup Parmesan cheese and set aside. Add oil and salt to a large pot of boiling water. Add pasta and cook according to package directions. Drain well. Place pasta over sauce and toss to combine. Garnish with fresh basil leaves. Sprinkle with remaining Parmesan cheese. Serves 6.
Serving size: 1 cup

Amount Per Serving:

Calories 552	Saturated Fat 7 g	Sodium 531 mg
Total Fat 22 g	Cholesterol 28 mg	

Italian Chicken

- 2 pounds chicken breasts, boneless and skinless
- 1 (14.5-ounce) can tomato wedges, drained
- 1 (6-ounce) can whole mushrooms, drained
- 1 (6-ounce) can pitted ripe olives, drained
- 1 (14-ounce) can artichoke hearts, drained
- 1 (8-ounce) bottle fat-free Italian salad dressing
- 1/2 cup dry white wine
- 1 (1-ounce) envelope onion soup mix
- 8 ounces linguine, cooked according to package directions
- fat-free Parmesan cheese (optional)

Preheat oven to 350 degrees. Place chicken in a 3-quart baking dish that has been coated with non-stick cooking spray. Arrange tomatoes, mushrooms, olives and artichokes over the top. Combine salad dressing and wine. Pour over vegetables and chicken. Sprinkle soup mix on the top. Cover and bake for 1 hour. Serve over pasta. Sprinkle with fat-free Parmesan cheese before serving (optional). Serves 6. Serving size: 8 ounces

Amount Per Serving:

Calories 446	Saturated Fat 2 g	Sodium 1097 mg
Total Fat 11 g	Cholesterol 96 mg	

159

Stuffed Manicotti

- 12 uncooked manicotti shells
- 15 ounces fat-free ricotta cheese
- 8 ounces shredded, part-skim mozzarella cheese, divided
- 1/2 cup egg substitute
- 1/4 cup + 2 Tablespoons Parmesan cheese, grated
- 3/4 teaspoon dried Italian herb seasoning
- 1/4 teaspoon garlic powder
- 1/4 teaspoon salt
- 1/4 teaspoon pepper
- 3 cups prepared, low-fat spaghetti sauce

Preheat oven to 350 degrees. Cook manicotti per package directions and drain. Place in bowl of cold water to prevent sticking. In medium bowl, combine ricotta cheese, 1 1/2 cups mozzarella cheese, egg substitute, 1/4 cup Parmesan cheese and all other seasonings. Drain manicotti and pat dry. Fill shells with cheese mixture. Spread approximately half of the spaghetti sauce over bottom of shallow, 3-quart baking dish. Arrange filled manicotti over sauce and cover with remaining sauce. Sprinkle with remaining mozzarella and Parmesan cheeses. Cover dish loosely with foil. Bake about 40 minutes, until hot and bubbly. Serves 6. Serving size: 2 manicotti

Amount Per Serving:

Calories 413	Saturated Fat 5 g	Sodium 829 mg
Total Fat 11 g	Cholesterol 34 mg	

Pine Nut Stuffed Manicotti

- 10 manicotti shells
- 1-2 garlic cloves, minced
- 1 Tablespoon olive oil
- 1/2 cup fresh mushrooms, chopped*
- 1/4 cup green onion, chopped
- 1/2 cup canned artichoke hearts, chopped*
- 3/4 cup part-skim ricotta cheese
- 1/4 cup shredded low-fat mozzarella cheese
- 1/4 cup fat-free Parmesan cheese
- 2 Tablespoons pine nuts, chopped
- 1 Tablespoon parsley, chopped
- 1 teaspoon thyme
- 1/4 teaspoon salt
- 1/4 teaspoon pepper
- 2 cups fat-free marinara sauce
- 1/4 cup part-skim mozzarella cheese

Preheat oven to 350 degrees. Cook manicotti shells according to package directions. Sauté garlic in olive oil for 1 minute. Add mushrooms, and sauté for 1 minute more. Add onions, and sauté for another minute. Add artichoke hearts, and remove from heat. Mix next 8 ingredients into mixture. Use a spoon or pastry bag to fill manicotti with prepared mixture. Arrange stuffed manicotti in a 9 x 13-inch baking dish that has been coated with non-stick cooking spray. Top with marinara sauce. Cover with foil. Bake for 25-30 minutes or until it begins to bubble. Remove from heat, and sprinkle with grated mozzarella cheese. Return to oven uncovered until cheese is melted. Serves 5. Serving size: 2 manicotti shells

Amount Per Serving:

Calories 340	Saturated Fat 4 g	Sodium 637 mg
Total Fat 14 g	Cholesterol 22 mg	

*One cup of frozen spinach, thawed and drained, may be substituted for artichoke hearts and mushrooms.

Spinach and Chicken Mostaccioli Casserole

- 1 (10-ounce) package mostaccioli
- 1 (10-ounce) package frozen chopped spinach, thawed
- 3 (6-ounce) chicken breast halves, boneless and skinless, cut into 1-inch pieces
- 2/3 cup onion, chopped
- 2 large garlic cloves, minced
- 2 teaspoons vegetable oil
- 2 (14-ounce) cans whole tomatoes with juice, chopped
- 3 Tablespoons tomato paste
- 1 1/4 teaspoons dried basil
- 3/4 teaspoon oregano
- 1/4 teaspoon salt
- 1/2 cup fat-free Parmesan cheese, grated

Preheat oven to 350 degrees. Cook pasta according to directions on package. Squeeze excess liquid from spinach. Sauté chicken, onion and garlic in oil. Stir in tomatoes, tomato paste and spices. Simmer 5 minutes. Combine pasta, spinach, chicken mixture and 1/4 cup Parmesan cheese. Stir well. Spoon mixture into 13 x 9 x 2-inch pan. Sprinkle with remaining cheese. Bake for 20-30 minutes. Serves 12. Serving size: 1 cup

Amount Per Serving

Calories 182	Saturated Fat 0 g	Sodium 245 mg
Total Fat 2 g	Cholesterol 27 mg	

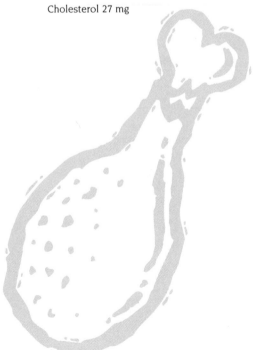

Pasta Prima Vera

Prep Time: 20 minutes
Cooking Time: 20 minutes

- 1 pound mostaccioli
- 1 1/3 cups broccoli (small flowerets)
- 1 1/3 cups zucchini, diced in 1/2-inch pieces
- 3/4 cup carrots, diced in 1/2-inch pieces
- 1/2 cup celery, diced in 1/2-inch pieces
- 1/2 cup yellow bell pepper, diced in 1/2-inch pieces
- 1 Tablespoon olive oil
- 3 large garlic cloves, minced
- 2 Tablespoons reduced calorie margarine
- 1 (2-ounce) can sliced mushrooms, drained
- 1 1/2 Tablespoons basil
- 1/2 teaspoon salt
- 1/4 teaspoon freshly-ground pepper
- 1/2 cup fresh, grated Parmesan cheese, optional
- fresh basil leaves (garnish)

Cook pasta according to package directions. Place vegetables (except mushrooms) in steamer basket, and steam for 5 minutes. Heat oil in small skillet and cook garlic for 2 minutes. Add margarine, mushrooms, basil, salt and pepper. Cook just until margarine is melted. Drain pasta. Add steamed vegetables and mushroom mixture to pasta. Toss until well combined. Stir in Parmesan cheese, if desired. Garnish with fresh basil leaves. Serves 8. Serving size: 2 cups

Amount Per Serving:

Calories 294	Saturated Fat 2 g	Sodium 336 mg
Total Fat 6 g	Cholesterol 5 mg	

If meat is desired, grilled and sliced chicken breast may be added.

Myth No. 55:
"Setting the table for an Ozark home-cooked meal involves pulling plasticware from the cellophane wrapper."

Spicy Party Pasta

Prep Time: 20 minutes
Cooking Time: 15 minutes
Chill Time: 1 hour

- 1 (12-ounce) package broad noodles
- 1/4 cup red pepper, chopped
- 2 cups raw broccoli flowerets
- 1 (15-ounce) can garbonzo beans
- 1 Tablespoon salt-free seasoning blend
- 1 (8-ounce) bottle light Italian salad dressing

Cook pasta according to package directions. Drain. In a large bowl, combine pasta and next 4 ingredients. Toss with salad dressing to coat evenly. Let chill for 1 hour before serving. Toss before serving. Serves 6. Serving size: 1 1/2 cup

Amount Per Serving:

Calories 303	Saturated Fat 0 g	Sodium 821 mg
Total Fat 3 g	Cholesterol 2 mg	

Pasta De Shazo

Prep Time: 10 minutes
Cooking Time: 30 minutes

- 3/4 cup chicken broth
- 3/4 teaspoon cornstarch
- 1 Tablespoon olive oil
- 1/8 teaspoon red pepper
- 1 Tablespoon garlic, chopped
- 1 teaspoon fresh parsley, chopped
- salt and pepper to taste
- 1 cup mixed vegetables, chopped (broccoli, tomatoes, yellow squash)
- 1/2 cup marinara sauce or tomato sauce
- 12 ounces cooked shell noodles
- 1/4 cup mozzarella cheese, cubed
- 1/4 cup Parmesan cheese, shredded

Mix chicken broth with cornstarch, and heat in a saucepan until thickened. In a medium skillet on high heat, saute olive oil, red pepper, garlic, parsley, salt and pepper for 3 to 4 minutes to bring out garlic flavor. Add mixed vegetables, and sauté until tender and crisp. Add chicken broth mixture and marinara sauce, and bring to a boil. Add noodles. Stir in mozzarella cheese cubes. Top with Parmesan cheese. Serve immediately on a warm plate. Serves 2. Serving size: 1 1/2 cup

Amount Per Serving:

Calories 477	Saturated Fat 5 g	Sodium 1067 mg
Total Fat 17 g	Cholesterol 16 mg	

Contributed by Doyle Simpson, Market Place Café, Springfield, Missouri.

164

Chicken Tetrazzini

Prep Time: 15 minutes
Cooking Time: 30 minutes

- 3 slices turkey bacon
- 2 cups onion, chopped
- 2 green peppers, chopped
- 4 celery stalks, chopped
- 1 (8-ounce) can mushrooms, drained

- 2 cans low-fat cream of mushroom soup
- 2 cups low-fat cheddar cheese, grated
- 4 cups chicken, cooked and cubed
- 5.25 ounces vermicelli, cooked according to package directions

Preheat oven to 400 degrees. Fry bacon until crisp. Drain grease, crumble bacon and set aside. Coat a large skillet with non-stick cooking spray. Cook onions, peppers and celery until soft. Add mushrooms and crumbled bacon. In a medium saucepan, heat soup and cheese. Add to skillet mixture. Add chicken and cooked vermicelli. Toss gently. Place mixture in a 9 x 13-inch baking dish. Bake for 20-25 minutes or until hot. Serves 8. Serving size: 2 cups

Amount Per Serving:

Calories 353

Total Fat 9 g

Saturated Fat 3 g

Cholesterol 79 mg

Sodium 622 mg

Pasta with Picante Black Bean Sauce

Prep Time: 15 minutes
Cooking Time: 25 minutes

- 1 medium onion, coarsely chopped
- 1 garlic clove, minced
- 1 Tablespoon canola oil
- 1 (15-ounce) can black beans, drained and rinsed
- 1 (16-ounce) can stewed tomatoes with juice
- 1 (8-ounce) can stewed tomatoes with juice
- 1/2 cup picante sauce
- 1 teaspoon chili powder
- 1 teaspoon ground cumin
- 1/4 teaspoon oregano, crushed
- 4 cups hot, cooked orzo or other favorite pasta
- 4 ounces low-fat cheese
- 1-2 Tablespoons parsley or cilantro, chopped

In a large skillet, cook onion and garlic in oil until onion is tender. Stir in remaining ingredients except pasta, cheese and parsley or cilantro. Bring to a boil. Reduce heat, cover and simmer 15 minutes, stirring occasionally. Uncover and cook over high heat until desired consistency. Serve bean mixture over pasta. Sprinkle with cheese and parsley or cilantro, if desired. Serve with additional picante sauce.
Serves 8. Serving size: 8 ounces

Amount Per Serving:

Calories 266	Saturated Fat 2 g	Sodium 428 mg
Total Fat 6 g	Cholesterol 10 mg	

Contributed by St. John's Nutrition Center, Springfield, Missouri.

Myth No. 170:
"Ozarkians believe exotic pasta varieties consist of dinosaurs, robots and ABC's."

Rigatoni Jardinere

Prep Time: 15 minutes
Cooking Time: 25 minutes

- 2 pounds rigatoni
- 2 cups carrot sticks
- 1 cup celery sticks
- 1 cup asparagus spears
- 1 cup cauliflower flowerets
- 1 cup broccoli flowerets
- 2 cups fat-free Italian salad dressing
- 1/2 cup olive oil
- 1/3 cup balsamic vinegar
- 1/2 cup Parmesan cheese
- 1 teaspoon garlic, minced
- 1 Tablespoon parsley, chopped
- salt and pepper to taste

Cook pasta al dente. Rinse, drain and set aside. In a separate pot, poach vegetables until tender, drain and set aside. In a mixing bowl, whisk together Italian salad dressing, olive oil, vinegar, Parmesan cheese and spices. Pour dressing mixture over pasta and vegetables in a large mixing bowl. Blend together well and serve. Serves 16.
Serving size: 8 ounces

Amount Per Serving:

Calories 440	Saturated Fat 4 g	Sodium 339 mg
Total Fat 23 g	Cholesterol 3 mg	

Contributed by Chef Jesse Vegar, Pasta LaBella, manufactured by American Italian Pasta Company in Excelsior Springs, Missouri

Egg Noodles

Prep Time: 45 minutes
Cooking Time: 20 minutes

- 1 cup egg substitute
- 1/3 teaspoon salt (optional)
- 2 2/3 cups flour

Slightly beat egg substitute and salt. Add flour, and mix with fork until completely moistened. Dough will be stiff. Knead and let stand 1/2 hour. Roll out 1/4-to 1/2-inch thick and cut into 1/2-inch strips. Drop into boiling water and cook approximately 20 minutes. Serves 8. Serving size: 8 ounces

Amount Per Serving:

Calories 174	Saturated Fat 0 g	Sodium 136 mg
Total Fat 1 g	Cholesterol 0 mg	

Pasta De Angela

- 1/2 cup chicken broth
- 1/2 teaspoon cornstarch
- 1 Tablespoon olive oil
- 1/8 teaspoon red pepper
- 1 Tablespoon garlic, chopped
- 1 teaspoon fresh parsley, chopped
- salt and pepper to taste
- 1/2 cup mushrooms, chopped
- 1/2 cup tomatoes, chopped
- 1/2 cup fresh spinach pieces
- 12 ounces cooked spaghetti
- 1/4 cup Parmesan cheese, shredded

Mix chicken broth with cornstarch, and heat in saucepan until thickened. In a medium skillet on high heat, sauté olive oil, red pepper, garlic, parsley, salt and pepper for 3 to 4 minutes to bring out the garlic flavor. Add mushrooms and tomatoes, and sauté until tender. Add chicken broth mixture, and bring to a boil. Add spinach pieces and cooked spaghetti. Mix and top with Parmesan cheese. Serves 2. Serving size: 1 1/2 cup

Amount Per Serving:

Calories 350	Saturated Fat 3 g	Sodium 704 mg
Total Fat 12 g	Cholesterol 8 g	

Contributed by Doyle Simpson, Market Place Café, Springfield, Missouri.

Basic Tomato Sauce

- 1 cup onion, chopped,
  or 1/8 teaspoon instant onion
- 2 garlic cloves, minced,
  or 1/8 teaspoon garlic powder
- 2 stalks celery, chopped,
  or 1/4 teaspoon celery seed
- 2 (28-ounce) cans whole tomatoes
- 1 (12-ounce) can tomato paste
- 2 Tablespoons dry parsley flakes
- 1 Tablespoon sugar
- 1 teaspoon basil
- 1/2 teaspoon oregano
- 1/4 teaspoon pepper
- 1 bay leaf
- 1/2 cup red wine (optional)
- 1/2 cup mushrooms, sliced

Stir all ingredients together in 3-quart casserole with lid. Cook in microwave on high for 15 minutes. Cook on medium for an additional 15 minutes. Serve with pasta, or use as a topping for chicken. Serves 16. Serving size: 1/2 cup

Amount Per Serving:

Calories 60	Saturated Fat 0 g	Sodium 390 mg
Total Fat 0 g	Cholesterol 0 mg	

Nonna's Ratatouille

- 2 Tablespoons extra virgin or flavorful olive oil
- 1 medium yellow onion, thinly sliced
- 1 green bell pepper, thinly sliced
- 3 cloves garlic, minced
- 1 large or 2 Japanese eggplants, peeled and cut into 1-inch cubes
- 1 medium zucchini squash, sliced in 1/2-inch rounds
- 1 medium yellow squash, sliced in 1/2-inch rounds

- 4 ounces mushrooms, sliced
- 1 jalapeño, seeded and diced (optional)
- 1/2 cup dry wine
- 2 Tablespoons fresh or 1 Tablespoon dry basil
- salt and pepper to taste
- 2 (16-ounce) cans diced tomatoes or the equivalent fresh Roma tomatoes, peeled and diced

Heat olive oil in large skillet, and sauté onion, pepper, garlic and eggplant. Add zucchini and yellow squash, mushrooms and jalapeño and continue to sauté 2-3 minutes. Add wine, basil, salt and pepper and tomatoes and serve over pasta of choice with freshly-grated Parmesan cheese. Serves 4. Serving size: 2 cups

Amount Per Serving:

Calories 214	Saturated Fat 1 g	Sodium 220 mg
Total Fat 8 g	Cholesterol 0 mg	

Best if made a day ahead of serving so flavors can mingle.
Can be served hot or cold as a side dish or as an entree.

Contributed by Nonna's Italian American Café, Springfield, Missouri.

Deliciously-Light Spaghetti Sauce

- 8 ounces pasta (any kind)
- 4 garlic cloves, minced
- 1 medium onion, minced
- 2 teaspoons olive oil
- 1 (14.5-ounce) can
  no-salt-added whole tomatoes,
  undrained and chopped
- 1 Tablespoon tomato paste

- 2 teaspoons sugar
- 2 teaspoons dried oregano
- 1 teaspoon dried basil
- 1/2 teaspoon salt
- 1/4 teaspoon pepper
- 1/4 cup grated Parmesan cheese
- 1/2 cup shredded part-skim
  mozzarella cheese, divided

Cook pasta according to package directions. Drain and set aside. Cook garlic and onion in olive oil over medium heat until tender. Add tomatoes and next 6 ingredients. Cook 5 minutes. Add Parmesan cheese and 1/4 cup mozzarella cheese. Stir until cheese melts. Serve over cooked pasta. Sprinkle with remaining mozzarella cheese.
Serves 4. Serving size: 1 cup

Amount Per Serving:

Calories 337	Saturated Fat 3 g	Sodium 519 mg
Total Fat 8 g	Cholesterol 13 mg	

Myth No. 100

"In the Ozarks garnishing more often conjures up visions
of lost wages than parsley and orange slices."

VEGETABLES & RICE

Myth No. 29:
"People from the Ozarks all smoke corncob pipes."

Fact:
"While we're famous for smoking turkeys, beef and ham,
we do not smoke corncob pipes. Most Junior League members
also report abstaining from smokeless tobacco."

VEGETABLES

RICE & COUSCOUS

Italian Baked Asparagus

Prep Time: 20 minutes
Cooking Time: 45 minutes

- 1 pound fresh asparagus
- 1/4 cup margarine spread
- 3 Tablespoons onion, minced
- 3 Tablespoons celery,
  finely chopped
- 2 Tablespoons
  Parmesan cheese, grated
- 2 Tablespoons bread crumbs,
  freshly grated

- 4 cans Italian tomatoes,
  drained and diced
- pinch of thyme
- pinch of oregano
- salt, to taste
- freshly-ground pepper, to taste

Preheat oven to 375 degrees. Break off tough ends of asparagus spears. Place margarine spread in a rectangular baking dish. Line bottom with asparagus. Sprinkle with onion, celery, cheese, bread crumbs and tomatoes, in that order. Season with thyme and oregano. Salt and pepper to taste. Cover and bake for 45 minutes or until asparagus is tender. Serves 4. Serving size: 8 ounces

Amount Per Serving:

Calories 87	Saturated Fat 1 g	Sodium 460 mg
Total Fat 2 g	Cholesterol 2 mg	

Red Cabbage with Apples & Wine

Prep Time: 15 minutes
Cooking Time: 20-25 minutes

- 1 medium red cabbage, thinly sliced
- 2 green apples, coarsely chopped
- 1 onion, chopped
- 1/2 cup white wine
- 1 Tablespoon vinegar

- 1 Tablespoon lemon juice
- 1 Tablespoon molasses
- 1/8 teaspoon pepper
- 1/4 teaspoon salt
- 1/4 teaspoon caraway seeds

Combine all ingredients in a saucepan. Cover and cook for 20-25 minutes. Serves 6. Serving size: 3/4 cup (6 ounces)

Amount Per Serving:

Calories 72	Saturated Fat 0 g	Sodium 101mg
Total Fat 0 g	Cholesterol 0 mg	

Glazed Carrots

Prep Time: 5 minutes
Cooking Time: 10 minutes

- 1 teaspoon margarine
- 1 cup carrots, slivered and blanched
- 1 teaspoon brown sugar
- 1/8 teaspoon powdered mustard
- Dash of salt
- Dash of hot pepper sauce (optional)

In a small skillet, heat margarine until bubbly. Add remaining ingredients and sauté. Stir occasionally until carrots are tender-crisp (about 5 minutes). Serves 2. Serving size: 6 ounces

Amount Per Serving:

Calories 82	Saturated Fat 0 g	Sodium 238 mg
Total Fat 2 g	Cholesterol 0 mg	

Fiesta Corn 'n Peppers

Prep Time: 15 minutes
Cooking Time: 10-15 minutes

- 1 medium onion, coarsely chopped
- 1 cup mixed red and green bell pepper, chopped
- 1 Tablespoon margarine
- 1 teaspoon ground cumin
- 1 (8-ounce) can whole kernel corn, drained or 1 cup cooked fresh corn
- 1 (8 3/4-ounce) can cream-style corn
- 1/2 cup picante sauce
- 1/4 teaspoon salt
- 1/2 cup baked tortilla chips, crushed
- cilantro, chopped (optional)

In a 10-inch skillet, saute onion and peppers in margarine until tender (about 4 minutes). Sprinkle with cumin. Stir in whole kernel corn, cream-style corn, picante sauce and salt. Cook until heated through (about 5 minutes), stir occasionally. Stir in chips; cook and stir until thickened. Sprinkle with cilantro, if desired. Serve with additional picante sauce. Serves 4. Serving size: 8 ounces

Amount Per Serving:

Calories 154	Saturated Fat 1 g	Sodium 712 mg
Total Fat 4 g	Cholesterol 0 mg	

Contributed by St. John's Nutrition Center, Springfield, Missouri.

Pineapple Carrots

Prep Time: 15 minutes
Cooking Time: 15 minutes

- 2 cups carrots, julienne
- 3/4 cup (6 ounces) unsweetened pineapple juice
- 3/4 teaspoon cinnamon
- 1/8 teaspoon nutmeg
- freshly-round black pepper, to taste

In a medium saucepan, combine all ingredients except carrots. Bring the mixture to a boil. Reduce heat, and add carrots. Cover and simmer for about 8 minutes or until carrots are tender-crisp. Serves 3. Serving size: 2/3 cup

Amount Per Serving:

Calories 94	Saturated Fat 0 g	Sodium 50 mg
Total Fat 0 g	Cholesterol 0 mg	

Spicy Lime Corn on the Cob

Prep Time: 15 minutes
Cooking Time: 35-40 minutes

- 4 ears fresh corn
- 4 Tablespoons fresh lime juice
- 3 teaspoons olive oil
- 1 teaspoon chili powder
- 3/4 teaspoon ground cumin
- 2 1/2 Tablespoons cilantro, chopped

Prepare outdoor grill for cooking, or preheat oven to 400 degrees. Tear off 4 sheets of heavy-duty aluminum foil. Remove husks and silks from corn. Place one ear of corn in center of each sheet of foil. In a cup, combine lime juice, olive oil, chili powder and cumin. Spoon over each ear of corn, turning corn to coat evenly. Sprinkle each ear with chopped cilantro. Bring edges of foil together, folding loosely to allow space for heat to circulate. Crimp ends to seal. Put on grill over medium-hot coals or in the oven. Cook for 40-45 minutes until tender. Serves 4. Serving size: 1 ear of corn

Amount Per Serving:

Calories 119	Saturated Fat 1 g	Sodium 12 mg
Total Fat 4 g	Cholesterol 0 mg	

Swiss Green Beans

- 1/2 cup onion, chopped
- 1 cup fresh mushrooms, sliced
- 3 Tablespoons margarine
- 1 pound fresh green beans,
  (cut into 1-inch pieces)
  or 2 (9-ounce) packages
  frozen green beans

- 1/2 teaspoon summer savory
  or 1 teaspoon parsley flakes
- 1/2 teaspoon salt
- 1/8 teaspoon pepper
- 1/2 cup (2 ounces) low-fat
  Swiss cheese, grated

In a 2-quart saucepan, sauté onions and mushrooms in margarine over medium heat until onions are transparent. Stir in beans and spices. Simmer covered, stirring occasionally until beans are tender (about 7 to 10 minutes). Sprinkle with cheese. Cover and cook an additional minute until cheese melts. Serves 6. Serving size: 4 ounces

Amount Per Serving:

| Calories 104 | Saturated Fat 2 g | Sodium 373 mg |
| Total Fat 7 g | Cholesterol 3 mg | |

Blazin' Black-Eyed Peas

Prep Time: 30 minutes
Cooking Time: 35 minutes

- 1/2 cup onion, chopped
- 1/2 cup green pepper, chopped
- 1 (15.8-ounce) can
  black-eyed peas, undrained
- 1 (14.5-ounce) can
  stewed tomatoes, undrained
- 1 teaspoon chili powder
- 1/2 teaspoon red pepper
- 1 Tablespoon soy sauce
- 1 teaspoon liquid smoke
- parsley to garnish

Coat a large skillet with non-stick cooking spray. Place over medium heat until hot. Add onion and green pepper. Sauté until vegetables are tender-crisp. Add peas and next 5 ingredients. Bring to a boil. Reduce heat. Simmer for 20 minutes, stirring often. Transfer to a hot dish. Sprinkle with parsley. Serves 6. Serving size: 3/4 cup (6 ounces)

Amount Per Serving:

Calories 146	Saturated Fat 0 g	Sodium 863 mg
Total Fat 1 g	Cholesterol 0 mg	

Myth No. 14:
"Ordering a la carte in the Ozarks may or may not include the employment of a mule."

Dilled New Potato Halves

- 8 small new potatoes
- 1/2 cup fat-free sour cream
- 1 Tablespoon prepared horseradish
- 1/8 teaspoon dried dillweed
- dried chives

Rinse potatoes and pat dry. Prick potatoes several times with a fork. Place in a ring on a paper towel in microwave oven. Microwave on high 6-7 minutes, turning over after 3 1/2 minutes. Let stand for 5 minutes. Cut potatoes in half lengthwise. Combine sour cream, horseradish and dillweed. Stir well. Spoon 1 teaspoon sour cream mixture onto each potato half. Sprinkle with chives. Serve at room temperature. Serves 4.
Serving size: 4 potato halves (6 ounces)

Amount Per Serving:

Calories 274	Saturated Fat 0 g	Sodium 75 mg
Total Fat 0 g	Cholesterol 0 mg	

Twice-Baked Potatoes

- 2 large baking potatoes
- 1/3 cup fat-free plain yogurt
- 3 Tablespoons green onion, chopped
- 3 Tablespoons Parmesan cheese

- 1 Tablespoon skim milk
- 1/2 teaspoon garlic powder
- 1/4 teaspoon white pepper
- 1/4 teaspoon paprika

Preheat oven to 375 degrees. Wash potatoes and coat with non-stick cooking spray. Bake for one hour or until done. Let cool to touch. Cut potatoes in half lengthwise. Scoop out pulp, leaving a 1/4 inch shell. Set shells aside. Combine potato pulp, yogurt, onions, Parmesan cheese, skim milk, garlic powder and white pepper. Mash until light and fluffy. Spoon into shells. Place on ungreased baking sheet. Sprinkle with paprika and bake uncovered for 10 minutes or until thoroughly heated. Serves 4.
Serving size: 1 half shell (6 ounces)

Amount Per Serving:

Calories 129	Saturated Fat 1g	Sodium 107 mg
Total Fat 2 g	Cholesterol 4 mg	

Parmesan Potatoes

- 6 large potatoes
- 1/4 cup flour
- 1/4 cup Parmesan cheese
- 3/4 teaspoon salt
- 1/4 teaspoon pepper
- 1/3 cup light margarine

Preheat oven to 375 degrees. Wash and peel potatoes. Cut into quarters or smaller. Combine flour, cheese, salt and pepper in a bag. Coat potatoes by shaking them in the bag. Melt margarine in 9 x 13-inch pan. Place potatoes in a single layer in the pan. Bake for 1 hour. Turn once during the baking. Serves 6. Serving size: 1 cup

Amount Per Serving:

Calories 298	Saturated Fat 2 g	Sodium 464 mg
Total Fat 6 g	Cholesterol 3 mg	

Myth No. 149:

"People from the Ozarks believe that 'Shirt and Shoes Required' is synonymous with 'Formal Attire'."

Broiled Fries

- 6 medium baking potatoes
- 1 Tablespoon lemon juice
- garlic salt, to taste

- seasoning salt, to taste
- pepper, to taste
- 1 Tablespoon Parmesan cheese, optional

Scrub potatoes, leave skin on, and cut into 3/4-inch wedges. Drop into a large pot of boiling water. Boil for 4-5 minutes and drain. Arrange potatoes on cookie sheet. Brush with lemon juice. Coat with non-stick cooking spray. Season with garlic salt, seasoning salt and pepper to taste. Sprinkle with Parmesan cheese, if desired. Broil 5-10 minutes. Turn and broil for another 5-10 minutes. Serves 6. Serving size: 8 ounces

Amount Per Serving:

Calories 243	Saturated Fat 1 g	Sodium 346 mg
Total Fat 2 g	Cholesterol 1 mg	

Herbed Potato Wedges

- 4 potatoes, scrubbed
  and cut into eighths, lengthwise
- 1/4 cup olive oil
- 4 Tablespoons Parmesan cheese
- freshly-ground pepper
- 1/2 teaspoon rosemary

- 1/2 teaspoon parsley flakes
- 1/2 teaspoon thyme
- seasoning salt
- 1/2 teaspoon Italian seasoning
- 2 Tablespoons chives
- 1 cup light sour cream

Preheat oven to 350 degrees. Coat large, shallow baking dish with 1/8 cup olive oil. Arrange potatoes in a single layer over the olive oil. Sprinkle with cheese and seasonings. Bake for 30 minutes. Take out of oven, and baste with remaining olive oil. Return to oven, and bake until tender (about 20-30 minutes). Mix chives with sour cream, and serve on the side. Serves 8. Serving size: 4 wedges (half of a potato)

Amount Per Serving:

Calories 181	Saturated Fat 2 g	Sodium 168 mg
Total Fat 10 g	Cholesterol 12 mg	

Spicy Baked Potatoes with Mushrooms

Prep Time: 15 minutes
Cooking Time: 15 minutes

- 4 medium baked potatoes
- 1 cup low-fat sour cream
- 1/2 teaspoon salt
- 1/8 teaspoon pepper
- 1/2 teaspoon cayenne pepper
- 1/2 teaspoon Beau monde
- 1 dash hot pepper sauce
- 1/4 cup skim milk

- 1 (8-ounce) can sliced mushrooms, drained
- 1 (15-ounce) can chicken broth
- 1/2 cup onion, diced
- 1 cup low-fat sharp cheddar cheese, grated
- Italian style bread crumbs

Bake potatoes in microwave until slightly soft. Cut potatoes in half lengthwise and scoop out pulp. Beat until smooth, while adding sour cream and seasonings. Heat milk on high for 1 minute, and gradually add to potato mixture. Sauté mushrooms, chicken broth and onions, and fold into potato mixture. Fold in cheese. Fill shells and sprinkle bread crumbs on top. Microwave or broil until heated through. These freeze well. Serves 8. Serving size: 1 half-shell (6 ounces)

Amount Per Serving:

Calories 169	Saturated Fat 1 g	Sodium 563 mg
Total Fat 4 g	Cholesterol 15 mg	

Myth No. 13:
"For tricky items like corn on the cob, Ozarkians prefer a matchbook over floss."

Herbed Mashed Potatoes

- 6 1/2 cups potatoes, peeled and cubed
- 2 garlic cloves, halved
- 1/2 cup low-fat milk
- 1/2 cup fat-free sour cream
- 2 Tablespoons parsley, minced
- 1 Tablespoon oregano
- 1 1/2 Tablespoons thyme
- 1 Tablespoon low-fat margarine
- 3/4 teaspoon salt
- 1/8 teaspoon pepper

Place potatoes and garlic in a large saucepan. Cover with water and bring to a boil. Cook 20 minutes or until very tender. Drain. Return potato mixture to pan. Add milk and remaining ingredients. Beat at medium speed with an electric mixer until smooth. Serves 6. Serving size: 1 cup

Amount Per Serving:

Calories 291	Saturated Fat 0 g	Sodium 324 mg
Total Fat 2 g	Cholesterol 0 mg	

Caribbean Medley

- 1 medium yellow squash
- 1 medium zucchini
- 1/2 Tablespoon low fat margarine
- 1/2 teaspoon garlic pepper
- 1/2 teaspoon dried thyme leaves
- 1 teaspoon Caribbean jerk seasoning

Cut squash and zucchini into 1/4-inch slices. Coat a 10-inch skillet with non-stick cooking spray. Melt margarine and add garlic pepper. Sauté squash and zucchini mixture in margarine. Sprinkle with thyme leaves and Caribbean jerk seasoning. Cook squash until tender-crisp. Adjust seasoning to taste. Serves 6. Serving size: 8 ounces

Amount Per Serving:

Calories 27	Saturated Fat 0 g	Sodium 60 mg
Total Fat 1 g	Cholesterol 0 mg	

Yellow Squash Casserole

- 2 pounds yellow squash, sliced
- 1/4 cup onion, chopped
- 1 (8-ounce) herb-season stuffing mix
- 1/2 cup butter, melted
- 1 cup carrots, shredded
- 1 cup fat-free sour cream
- 1 can fat-free cream of chicken soup

Preheat oven to 350 degrees. Cook squash and onion in water 5 minutes and drain. Combine stuffing and butter. Spread half of stuffing on bottom of 12 x 12-inch baking dish. Put squash, onions and carrots on stuffing. Combine sour cream and soup. Pour on top of vegetables. Top with remaining stuffing. Bake for 25-30 minutes. Serves 10. Serving size: 6 ounces

Amount Per Serving:

Calories 239	Saturated Fat 6 g	Sodium 748 mg
Total Fat 11 g	Cholesterol 29 mg	

Italian-Style Zucchini

- 1 medium zucchini, chopped
- 1 large tomato, chopped
- 1 small onion, thinly sliced
- 1/4 teaspoon garlic powder
- 1/4 teaspoon oregano
- 1/4 teaspoon basil
- 1 teaspoon olive oil

Add all ingredients to wok or small skillet coated with non-stick cooking spray. Simmer until vegetables are tender. Serves 4. Serving size: 8 ounces

Amount Per Serving:

Calories 44	Saturated Fat 0 g	Sodium 7 mg
Total Fat 1 g	Cholesterol 0 mg	

Easy Zucchini Bake

- 1 small can tomato sauce
- 1 medium zucchini, thinly sliced
- 2 Tablespoons seasoned bread crumbs
- 1 cup low-fat cheddar and Monterey Jack cheese combination, grated
- 1 Tablespoon Parmesan cheese

Preheat oven to 350 degrees. Coat a small baking dish with non-stick cooking spray. Layer the ingredients as follows: 1/4 of the can of tomato sauce, 1/2 of the zucchini slices, 1/2 of the bread crumbs, 1/2 of the cheese. Repeat the layers and top with the remaining 1/2 of the tomato sauce. Sprinkle the Parmesan cheese on top. Bake for 25 minutes. Serves 4. Serving size: 4 ounces

Amount Per Serving:

Calories 126	Saturated Fat 2 g	Sodium 461 mg
Total Fat 4 g	Cholesterol 11 mg	

Orange-Pineapple Couscous

- 1 (11-ounce) can mandarin oranges, drained (reserve liquid)
- 2 1/4 cups orange juice
- 1 1/2 teaspoons ground cumin
- 1 (10-ounce) box couscous
- 3 Tablespoons olive oil
- 1 Tablespoon reduced-sodium soy sauce
- 3 Tablespoons lime juice
- 1/4 cup fresh cilantro, chopped
- 2 Tablespoons fresh basil, chopped or 1 teaspoon of dried basil
- 3 Tablespoons green onions, chopped
- 1 1/2 teaspoons fresh ginger, grated
- 1 (15 1/4-ounce) can pineapple tidbits, drained
- 1/3 cup pine nuts, toasted

Add enough orange juice to the mandarin orange juice to make 2 1/4 cups liquid. Bring the orange juices and cumin to a boil in a saucepan. Remove from heat and add couscous. Cover and let stand for 5 minutes. Pour into a large bowl and let cool. Combine oil, soy sauce and lime juice. Stir into the couscous mixture. Stir in mandarin oranges, cilantro, basil, green onions, ginger and pineapple. Sprinkle with pine nuts. Serves 8-10. Serving size: 8 ounces

Amount Per Serving:

Calories 234	Saturated Fat 1 g	Sodium 67 mg
Total Fat 8 g	Cholesterol 0 mg	

Mexican Rice

Prep Time: 15 minutes
Cooking Time: 50 minutes

- 2/3 cup onion, chopped
- 1/3 cup green pepper, chopped
- 1/3 cup red bell pepper, chopped
- 1 Tablespoon margarine
- 4 cups cooked rice
- 2 cups fat-free sour cream
- 1 cup fat-free cottage cheese
- 1/2 teaspoon white pepper
- 3 (4.5-ounce) cans chopped
  green chilies, undrained
- 2 cups (8-ounce) low fat
  cheddar cheese, shredded

Preheat oven to 350 degrees. Sauté onion, green pepper and red bell pepper in margarine. Combine with cooked rice, sour cream, cottage cheese and pepper. Mix well. Coat an 11 x 13-inch baking dish with non-stick cooking spray. Pour 1/3 of the rice mixture in baking dish. Top with 1/2 of the chilies and 1/3 of the cheese. Spread another 1/3 of rice mixture over this layer. Repeat with the rest of the chilies and another 1/3 of the cheese. Spread the rest of rice over this. Bake uncovered for 45 minutes. Sprinkle the remaining cheese on top, and bake 5 more minutes. Serves 12. Serving size: 6 ounces

Amount Per Serving:

Calories 152	Saturated Fat 1 g	Sodium 235 mg
Total Fat 3 g	Cholesterol 7 mg	

Baked Rice

Prep Time: 10 minutes
Cooking Time: 1 hour and 15 minutes

- 2 cups long grain rice
- 1 small onion, chopped
- 1 can (10 1/2-ounces) beef bouillon
- 1 can (10 1/2-ounces) beef consommé
- 1 can (4-ounces) mushroom pieces
- 1/4 cup liquid Butter Buds

Preheat oven to 300 degrees. Mix together all ingredients. Place in a medium-size baking dish. Bake uncovered for 1 hour and 15 minutes. Stir twice. Serves 10. Serving size: 6 ounces

Amount Per Serving:

Calories 151	Saturated Fat 0 g	Sodium 338 mg
Total Fat 1 g	Cholesterol 0 mg	

Vegetarian Red Beans & Rice

- 2 Tablespoons olive oil
- 1 large onion, chopped
- 1 green pepper, chopped
- 3 stalks celery, chopped
- 1 garlic clove, minced
- 2 (8-ounce) cans tomato sauce

- 2 (15-ounce) cans red beans, thoroughly rinsed and drained
- 1 teaspoon salt
- 1 Tablespoon hot pepper sauce
- hot, cooked white rice

Heat olive oil in large saucepan over medium heat. Sauté onion, pepper, celery and garlic until tender. Add water to the sautéed vegetables if necessary, but use the oil initially to enhance the flavors. Add the tomato sauce, red beans, salt and hot pepper sauce. Simmer for 1/2 hour or more. Remove 1/2 cup of the beans and mash to paste. Add paste to bean mixture and stir until liquid is thickened. Serve hot over white rice. Serves 4. Serving size: 8 ounces

Amount Per Serving:

Calories 423	Saturated Fat 1 g	Sodium 1142 mg
Total Fat 8 g	Cholesterol 0 mg	

Myth No. 302:

"In the Ozarks twice-baked potatoes and refried beans
are more commonly referred to as leftovers."

DESSERTS

Myth No. 61:
"The manufacturing of ceramic pink flamingos is the
number-one industry in the Ozarks."

Fact:
"While some yards display this bright and interesting ornament,
the Junior League of Springfield does not endorse them for public
or private display. And we certainly do not recommend the
flamboyant fowl as a centerpiece."

Deep Dish Apple Pie

- 6 cups (Rome or Jonathan) apples, peeled and thinly sliced (about 2 pounds)
- 1/4 cup sugar
- 1 teaspoon cinnamon
- 1 Tablespoon cornstarch
- 1/8 teaspoon salt
- 3/4 cup flour
- 1/8 teaspoon nutmeg
- 3 Tablespoons margarine
- 3 Tablespoons cold water
- 1 Tablespoon skim milk

Preheat oven to 375 degrees. Coat a 10 x 6 x 2-inch baking dish with non-stick cooking spray. Place apples in dish. In a small mixing bowl, combine sugar and cinnamon. Set aside 1 teaspoon of mixture. Stir cornstarch and salt into remaining sugar mixture. Mix well. Sprinkle evenly over apples in dish. In a medium mixing bowl, stir together flour and nutmeg. Cut in margarine until mixture resembles coarse crumbs. Sprinkle 1 Tablespoon of water over part of the mixture and gently toss with fork. Push to the side of bowl. Repeat until all of mixture is moistened. Form into a ball. On a floured surface, roll dough into 12 x 8-rectangle. Cut decorative vents in pastry. Place over apples. Flute edges to side of dish. Brush pastry with milk and sprinkle with reserved sugar mixture. Bake 40 minutes or until apples are tender and crust is golden brown. Serves 8.
Serving size: 1 slice

Amount Per Serving:

Calories 156	Saturated Fat 0 g	Sodium 80 mg
Total Fat 3 g	Cholesterol 0 mg	

Key Lime Pie

- 1 (8-ounce) package fat-free cream cheese
- 1 (14-ounce) can fat-free sweetened condensed milk
- 1 teaspoon vanilla
- 1/3 cup key lime juice
- 1 prepared, low-fat graham cracker pie crust

Using an electric mixer, beat cream cheese until smooth. Slowly add condensed milk, vanilla and lime juice. Mix well. Filling will thicken after juice has been added. Pour into pie crust. Chill at least 1 hour before serving. Serves 8. Serving size: 1 slice

Amount Per Serving:

Calories 313	Saturated Fat 2 g	Sodium 390 mg
Total Fat 7 g	Cholesterol 10 mg	

Yogurt-Fruit Pie

Crust:
- 16 graham crackers, crushed (2 1/2-inch squares)
- 8 teaspoons margarine, softened

Topping:
- 30-40 seedless green grapes
- 2 small nectarines, pitted and sliced
- 1 cup strawberries, sliced

Filling:
- 1/4 cup frozen-concentrated orange juice (no sugar added), thawed
- 8 teaspoons sugar
- 1 envelope unflavored gelatin
- 2 cups plain, low-fat yogurt
- 1/2 cup canned, crushed pineapple, drained
- 1 teaspoon vanilla extract

Preheat oven to 350 degrees. Coat 9-inch glass pie plate with non-stick cooking spray and set aside. In a small bowl, combine cracker crumbs and margarine, mixing thoroughly. Using the back of a spoon, press crumb mixture over bottom and up the sides of the pie plate. Bake 8-10 minutes or until crust is crisp and brown. Remove to wire rack and let cool. To prepare filling, pour orange juice into small saucepan. Combine sugar and gelatin and sprinkle over juice. Let stand for 1 minute to soften. Cook over medium to low heat, stirring constantly, until sugar and gelatin are completely dissolved. Set aside. In a medium bowl, using a wire whisk, gently stir together yogurt and pineapple. Add gelatin mixture and vanilla; stir until completely blended. Pour mixture into cooled pie crust. Cover and refrigerate for 4 hours or until firm. Arrange fruit decoratively over filling. Serves 8. Serving size: 1 slice

Amount Per Serving:

Calories 202	Saturated Fat 2 g	Sodium 173 mg
Total Fat 6 g	Cholesterol 4 mg	

Pumpkin Pie

Crust:

- 1 cup all-purpose flour
- 1/8 teaspoon salt
- 1/4 cup margarine
- 4-5 Tablespoons ice water

Filling:

- 1 (1-lb.) can pumpkin
- 4 egg whites
- 1 cup sugar (white or brown)
- 1/2 teaspoon salt
- 1/2 teaspoon ginger
- 1/2 teaspoon nutmeg
- 2 teaspoons cinnamon
- 1 (12-ounce) can evaporated skim milk

Preheat oven to 350 degrees. In a large bowl, combine flour and salt. Cut margarine into flour mixture. Add water, a little at a time. Mix until pastry makes a ball. Cover and refrigerate at least one hour. On floured surface, roll ball into a circle. Place in pie pan. Trim and flute edges and prick the bottom lightly with a fork. For filling, combine pumpkin, egg whites, sugar, salt, ginger, nutmeg, cinnamon and milk. Mix well. Pour into pie crust. Bake for 50-60 minutes or until knife inserted in the center comes out clean. Refrigerate until ready to serve. Top with fat-free whipped topping before serving. Serves 8.
Serving size: 1 slice

Amount Per Serving:

Calories 185	Saturated Fat 1 g	Sodium 209 mg
Total Fat 6 g	Cholesterol 1 mg	

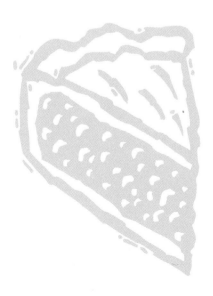

197

Easy Apple Pie

Prep Time: 45 minutes
Cooking Time: 15 minutes
Chill time: 3 hours

- 2 whole graham crackers, finely crushed
- 5 medium apples, peeled and chopped
- 2 cups water
- 1/2 teaspoon cinnamon
- 1/4 teaspoon nutmeg

- 1 package sugar-free lemon gelatin (4-serving size)
- 1 package sugar-free, cook-and-serve vanilla pudding
- 1/2 cup low-fat vanilla yogurt or light whipped topping

Coat a 9-inch pie plate with non-stick cooking spray and sprinkle with graham cracker crumbs, reserving 1 Tablespoon for garnish. Set aside. In a large saucepan, bring apples, water, cinnamon and nutmeg to a boil. Reduce heat to low, and simmer 5 minutes, stirring frequently. Stir in gelatin and pudding. Mix until well blended. Bring to full boil on high heat. Remove from heat, and let stand for 5 minutes. Spoon into pie plate, and sprinkle with remaining graham cracker crumbs. Refrigerate 3 hours or until firm. Garnish each serving with 1 Tablespoon vanilla yogurt or whipped topping. Serves 8. Serving size: 1 slice

Amount Per Serving:

Calories 74	Saturated Fat 0 g	Sodium 209 mg
Total Fat 1 g	Cholesterol 0 mg	

Angel Pie

Shell:
- 4 egg whites
- 1/4 teaspoon cream of tartar
- 3 Tablespoons sugar

Filling:
- 4 egg yolks
- 3 Tablespoons sugar
- 1 ounce baking chocolate, melted
- 1/8 teaspoon salt
- 1 cup light whipped topping
- chocolate shavings (optional)

Preheat oven to 275 degrees. Separate 4 eggs. Beat egg whites until frothy. Add cream of tartar and sugar and beat until stiff (meringue mixture). Line a 9-inch pie pan with meringue mixture. Bake 45 minutes. To make filling, beat egg yolks in top of a double boiler. Add sugar, chocolate and salt. Cook and stir until thick (about 10 minutes). Let cool. Fold in whipped topping. Pour into angel shell. Garnish with chocolate shavings and refrigerate. Serves 8. Serving size: 1 slice

Amount Per Serving:

Calories 101	Saturated Fat 2 g	Sodium 61 mg
Total Fat 5 g	Cholesterol 107 mg	

Chilled Blueberry Pie

- 4 cups blueberries, drained
- 2 Tablespoons cornstarch
- 2 Tablespoons water
- 1/2 cup light corn syrup
- 2 teaspoons lemon juice
- 1 (16-ounce) container light whipped topping
- 1 9-inch graham cracker crust
- fresh mint (optional)

Puree 1 cup blueberries in blender or food processor. Set aside. Combine cornstarch and water in a medium saucepan, stirring until blended. Add blueberry puree, corn syrup and lemon juice. Bring mixture to a boil over medium heat, stirring constantly. Cool 1 hour. Fold remaining 3 cups blueberries into blueberry mixture and set aside. Spread whipped topping onto the bottom and sides of graham cracker crust, forming a 1-inch shell. Spoon blueberry mixture into shell. Chill at least 4 hours. Serves 8. Serving size: 1 slice

Amount Per Serving:

Calories 337	Saturated Fat 2 g	Sodium 221 mg
Total Fat 15g	Cholesterol 1 mg	

Anita Bryant's Florida Citrus Cake

Cake:

- 1 package yellow cake mix
- 1 (3 1/4-ounce) package instant, lemon-flavored pudding mix
- 4 eggs
- 3/4 cup water
- 4 Tablespoons canola oil

Frosting:

- 1/2 pound powdered sugar
- 1/2 cup fat-free cream cheese
- 1 small can frozen, concentrated orange juice

Preheat oven to 325 degrees. Coat a 10-inch tube pan with non-stick cooking spray. In a large mixing bowl, combine all cake ingredients and mix well. Pour into prepared pan and bake for 50 minutes or until done. In a small bowl, combine all the ingredients for the frosting. Spread frosting over hot cake. Let cake cool in pan. Serves 10.
Serving size: 1 (2 x 4-inch) piece

Amount Per Serving:

Calories 472	Saturated Fat 2 g	Sodium 527 mg
Total Fat 13 g	Cholesterol 47 mg	

Contributed by Anita Bryant, the Anita Bryant Theatre in Branson, Missouri.

Myth No. 3:
"In the Ozarks gun racks are preferred to baker's racks 6 to 1."

"Died and Went to Heaven" Chocolate Cake

Cake:

- 1 3/4 cups flour
- 1 cup sugar
- 3/4 cup cocoa
- 1 1/2 teaspoons baking soda
- 1 1/2 teaspoons baking powder
- 1 teaspoon salt
- 1 1/4 cups buttermilk
- 1 cup packed brown sugar
- 2 large eggs, lightly beaten
- 1/4 cup canola oil
- 2 teaspoons vanilla
- 1 cup hot strong black coffee

Frosting:

- 1 cup powdered sugar
- 1/2 teaspoon vanilla
- 1-2 Tablespoons buttermilk
  or low-fat milk

Preheat oven to 350 degrees. Coat a 12-cup bundt pan with non-stick cooking spray. Dust pan with flour. In a large bowl, whisk together flour, sugar, cocoa, baking soda, baking powder and salt. Add buttermilk, brown sugar, eggs, oil and vanilla. With electric mixer, beat at medium speed 2 minutes. Whisk in the hot coffee. Batter will be thin. Pour the batter into the prepared pan. Bake 35 to 40 minutes or until toothpick inserted in center comes out clean. Avoid overbaking. Cool the cake in the pan on a rack for 10 minutes. Remove from pan and let cool completely. In a small bowl, whisk together powdered sugar, vanilla and enough buttermilk to make a thick but pourable frosting. Place the cake on a serving plate and drizzle the frosting on top. Serves 16. Serving size: 1 slice

Amount Per Serving:

Calories 316	Saturated Fat 1 g	Sodium 461 mg
Total Fat 6 g	Cholesterol 37mg	

Cinnamon-Carrot Bundt Cake

Cake:

- 3 1/2 cups flour
- 1/2 cup sugar
- 1 Tablespoon baking powder
- 2 teaspoons baking soda
- 2 teaspoons cinnamon
- 1 teaspoon ginger
- 3/4 teaspoon salt (optional)

- 1 cup firmly-packed brown sugar
- 1 (8-ounce) carton fat-free plain yogurt
- 1/3 cup vegetable oil
- 2 large eggs
- 2 large egg whites
- 1 teaspoon vanilla
- 1 pound carrots, shredded

Orange Glaze:

- 1 3/4 cups powdered sugar
- 2 Tablespoons orange juice

Preheat oven to 350 degrees. Coat a 10-cup bundt pan with non-stick cooking spray. In a medium-size bowl, combine flour, sugar, baking powder, baking soda, cinnamon, ginger and salt. In a large bowl, whisk together brown sugar, yogurt, oil, eggs, egg whites and vanilla until well blended. Stir in carrots and dry mixture until just blended. Pour batter into pan. Bake 50-55 minutes or until toothpick inserted in center of cake comes out clean. Cool in pan on wire rack for 10 minutes. Remove from pan and cool completely. To glaze, stir sugar and juice together until smooth. Drizzle glaze over cake. Serves 16. Serving size: 1 slice

Amount Per Serving:

Calories 308	Saturated Fat 1 g	Sodium 398 mg
Total Fat 6 g	Cholesterol 53 mg	

Golden Carrot-Pineapple Cake

Prep Time: 20 minute
Cooking Time: 40 minutes

- 2/3 cup fat-free, plain yogurt
- 1/2 cup egg substitute
- 2 teaspoons vanilla
- 1 (8-ounce) can pineapple, crushed
- 1 1/2 cups flour
- 1 cup whole wheat flour

- 2 teaspoons baking soda
- 2 teaspoons cinnamon
- 1/2 teaspoon salt
- 1 cup sugar
- 2-3 cups carrots, shredded
- 1/2 cup raisins

Preheat oven to 350 degrees. Beat together all wet ingredients. Combine all dry ingredients and add to wet mixture. Beat well. Stir in carrots and raisins. Bake for 30-40 minutes in a 13 x 9-inch pan or an 8 x 8-inch pan coated with non-stick cooking spray. Cake is done when it springs back when lightly touched. Cool completely before frosting cake.

Frosting:

- 2 Tablespoons light margarine
- 1 (8-ounce) package
  low-fat cream cheese
- 1 teaspoon vanilla

- Powdered sugar
  (Use until desired thickness is achieved, approximately 3 cups.)
- 1/2 cup pecans, chopped (optional)

Cream together margarine, cream cheese and vanilla. Add powdered sugar until desired thickness is achieved. Frost cake and sprinkle pecans on top. Serves 12. Serving size: 1 piece

Amount Per Serving:

Calories 412	Saturated Fat 3 g	Sodium 455 mg
Total Fat 8 g	Cholesterol 7 mg	

Contributed by St. John's Nutrition Center, Springfield, Missouri.

Raisin Spice Cake

Cake:

- 1 cup sugar
- 1 egg or 1/4 cup egg substitute
- 1/2 cup low-fat margarine
- 1 cup sour milk
  (add 1 Tablespoon lemon juice or
  vinegar to milk)
- 3 teaspoons cinnamon
- 1 teaspoon cloves
- 1 teaspoon nutmeg
- 1 teaspoon baking soda
- 2 cups flour
- 1 cup raisins, floured
  (Use part of the 2 cups
  of flour to flour raisins.)

Frosting:

- 2 Tablespoons low-fat margarine
- 1/2 -1 teaspoon vanilla
- 3 cups powdered sugar
  (approximate amount
  to make desired thickness)
- 1-2 Tablespoons milk
- 2 ounces bittersweet chocolate, melted

Preheat oven to 325 degrees. Beat together sugar, egg or egg substitute and margarine. Add sour milk and mix. Stir in spices, baking soda, flour and raisins. Pour batter in a loaf pan. Bake for 45 minutes. To make frosting, combine margarine, vanilla, powdered sugar and milk. Beat until smooth and desired thickness. Frost cooled cake. Drizzle melted chocolate over top of frosting. Serves 8. Serving size: 1 slice

Amount Per Serving:

Calories 564	Saturated Fat 3 g	Sodium 266 mg
Total Fat 11 g	Cholesterol 27 mg	

Contributed by St. John's Nutrition Center, Springfield, Missouri.

Lemon-Poppy Seed Cake

Cake:

- 1 package (97% fat-free) yellow cake mix
- 1/2 cup sugar
- 1/3 cup fat-free sour cream
- 1/4 cup water
- 1 cup plain fat-free yogurt
- 1 cup egg substitute
- 3 Tablespoons lemon juice
- 2 Tablespoons poppy seeds

Lemon Glaze:

- 1/2 cup powdered sugar, sifted
- 2 Tablespoons lemon juice

Preheat oven to 350 degrees. In a large mixing bowl, combine cake mix and sugar. Add sour cream, water, yogurt, egg substitute and lemon juice. Beat at medium speed for 5-6 minutes. Stir in poppy seeds by hand. Coat bundt pan with non-stick cooking spray. Pour in batter. Bake 40 minutes or until a toothpick inserted in center of cake comes out clean. Cool in pan for 10 minutes, then remove to a wire rack. Combine sifted powdered sugar and lemon juice to make glaze. Drizzle over warm cake. Serves 24. Serving size: 1-inch slice

Amount Per Serving:

Calories 141	Saturated Fat 1 g	Sodium 179 mg
Total Fat 3 g	Cholesterol 18 mg	

Myth No. 222:

"At Ozark weddings, couples traditionally place figurines of the bride and groom atop a seven-layer funnel cake."

Chocolate Eclair Cake

Prep Time: 25 minutes
Chill Time: 12 hours

- 1 (16-ounce) box low-fat honey graham crackers
- 2 (3 3/4 -ounce) packages fat-free, instant French vanilla pudding
- 3 cups plus 3 Tablespoons skim milk
- 1 (12-ounce) carton light whipped topping

- 1 1/2 cups powdered sugar, sifted
- 6 Tablespoons cocoa
- 2 Tablespoons low-fat margarine
- 2 teaspoons light corn syrup
- 1 teaspoon vanilla

Place a single layer of whole graham crackers on the bottom of a 9 x 13-inch pan. Combine pudding mix with 3 cups of the milk, stirring until thickened. Fold in whipped topping. Spread half the pudding on graham cracker layer. Add another layer of crackers. Cover this with remaining pudding. Top with third layer of crackers. In a small saucepan, combine remaining milk, sugar, cocoa, margarine, corn syrup and vanilla. Stir over low heat until liquefied. Pour over top layer of crackers. Refrigerate at least 12 hours. Serves 16. Serving size: 1 (2 x 3-inch) section

Amount Per Serving:

Calories 279	Saturated Fat 0 g	Sodium 315 mg
Total Fat 5 g	Cholesterol 1 mg	

Lemon Angel Food Cake with Berries

- 1 angel food cake mix (2 step)
- 1 (4-ounce) package vanilla pudding mix
- 16 ounces fat-free lemon yogurt
- 8 ounces light whipped topping
- fresh or frozen berries (blueberries, raspberries or strawberries)

Prepare cake according to package directions. Bake as directed in angel food cake pan. Cool upside down over a narrow-neck bottle. Blend dry pudding mix with lemon yogurt in a medium bowl, using a wire whisk. Fold in whipped topping. Remove cake from pan. Slice cake horizontally into 3 layers. Place bottom layer on serving plate and top with 1/3 lemon yogurt mixture. Repeat with remaining layers. Scatter berries across the top of cake. Refrigerate. Serves 12. Serving size: 1 slice

Amount Per Serving:

Calories 248	Saturated Fat 0 g	Sodium 264 mg
Total Fat 3 g	Cholesterol 2 mg	

Pumpkin Flan

- 1 1/2 cups sugar
- 4 eggs, beaten
- 1 (16-ounce) can pumpkin
- 1 (12-ounce) can evaporated skim milk
- 1 teaspoon cinnamon
- 1 teaspoon vanilla
- 1/2 teaspoon ginger
- 1/2 teaspoon nutmeg
- 1/4 teaspoon salt

Preheat oven to 350 degrees. In a large skillet, cook 1 cup of the sugar over medium-high heat until sugar begins to melt. Do not stir, just shake skillet occasionally. When sugar starts to melt, reduce heat to low, cook, stirring frequently until sugar is golden brown. Quickly pour sugar into a 10-inch pie pan. Tilt to evenly coat the bottom of pie pan. Place pie pan into a large roasting pan. Place on rack in oven. In a large mixing bowl, stir together remaining sugar, eggs, pumpkin, milk, cinnamon, vanilla, ginger, nutmeg and salt. Pour pumpkin mixture over sugar mixture in pie plate. Pour boiling water into roasting pan around pie plate to a depth of 1/2 inch. (You can do this while roasting pan is in oven to avoid spilling while carrying pan.) Bake for 50-55 minutes or until knife inserted in center of pie comes out clean. Cool, cover and refrigerate for 4 to 24 hours. To serve, loosen edges of flan with a knife. Serves 10. Serving slice: 1 slice

Amount Per Serving:

Calories 169	Saturated Fat 0 g	Sodium 120 mg
Total Fat 0 g	Cholesterol 1 mg	

Cheesecake a l'Orange

Crust:

- 1 cup graham cracker crumbs
- 1 Tablespoon walnuts, chopped
- 2 Tablespoons brown sugar
- 1 teaspoon cinnamon
- 1/3 cup low-fat margarine, melted

Cheesecake:

- 1 1/3 cups light sour cream
- 2 (8-ounce) package
  fat-free cream cheese, softened
- 2/3 cup sugar
- 1/2 teaspoon salt
- 2 teaspoons vanilla
- zest of one orange
- 2 eggs

Preheat oven to 375 degrees. Combine graham cracker crumbs, walnuts, sugar, cinnamon and margarine. Press into the bottom and half-way up the sides of a 9-inch springform pan. Bake crust 5-8 minutes. Cool crust while preparing cheesecake filling. In a food processor or electric mixer, combine sour cream, cream cheese, sugar, salt, vanilla, orange zest and eggs. Pour into crust and bake 50-60 minutes or until a knife inserted in center comes out clean. Cool for 2 hours, then refrigerate until chilled. Serves 12. Serving size: 1 slice

Amount Per Serving:

Calories 207	Saturated Fat 4 g	Sodium 458 mg
Total Fat 7 g	Cholesterol 59 mg	

Chocolate Mint Cheesecake

- 1/2 cup chocolate wafers, crushed (7-14)
- 1 cup low-fat cottage cheese
- 1 (8-ounce) package low-fat cream cheese
- 1 cup sugar
- 1/3 cup cocoa
- 3 Tablespoons creme de menthe liqueur
- 1 teaspoon vanilla
- 1/2 cup egg substitute
- 3 Tablespoons miniature semi-sweet chocolate chips

Preheat oven to 300 degrees. Sprinkle crushed wafers evenly in the bottom of an 8-inch springform pan and set aside. In food processor, blend cottage cheese until smooth. Add cream cheese, sugar, cocoa, liqueur and vanilla. The mixture will be thick, so scrape sides as necessary. Stir in egg substitute and chocolate chips. Pour into prepared pan. Bake for 35-40 minutes or until cheesecake appears set when shaken. Make sure center is done. Cool completely and chill several hours or overnight. Serves 12. Serving size: 1 slice

Amount Per Serving:

Calories 196	Saturated Fat 2 g	Sodium 223 mg
Total Fat 6 g	Cholesterol 9 mg	

Myth NO. 164:
"Ask Ozarkians if they like Cherries Jubilee
and chances are they'll say they love country music."

Chocolate Cookie Cheesecake

Prep Time: 30 minutes
Cooking Time: 1 hour
Chill Time: 2 hours

Cheesecake:

- 1 pound chocolate sandwich cookies
- 1/4 cup margarine
- 2 (8-ounce) packages fat-free cream cheese
- 2 eggs
- 3/4 cup sugar
- 1-2 teaspoons vanilla

Topping:

- 1 cup fat-free sour cream
- 1/4 cup sugar
- 1 teaspoon vanilla

Preheat oven to 350 degrees. In food processor or blender, crush cookies with 1/4 cup margarine. Set aside 2-3 Tablespoons of the crumbs. Coat bottom and sides of a 9-inch springform pan with non-stick cooking spray. Press crumb mixture onto bottom and 1 inch up the sides of springform pan. Beat together well the cream cheese, eggs, sugar and vanilla. Pour into prepared pan. Bake for 1 hour. To prepare the topping, beat together the sour cream, sugar and vanilla. Pour this over the top of cheesecake when it comes out of the oven. Sprinkle with the reserved cookie crumbs. Cool and refrigerate. Serves 8. Serving size: 1 slice

Amount Per Serving:

Calories 249	Saturated Fat 2 g	Sodium 392 mg
Total Fat 9 g	Cholesterol 31 mg	

Black Forest Cheesecake

- 3/4 cup chocolate
  graham cracker cookies, crushed
- 2 (12-ounce) packages
  fat-free cream cheese, softened
- 1 1/2 cups sugar
- 3/4 cup egg substitute
- 1 cup semi-sweet
  chocolate morsels, melted
- 1/4 cup cocoa
- 1 1/2 teaspoons vanilla
- 1 (8-ounce) carton
  fat-free sour cream
- 1 (21-ounce) can
  reduced calorie cherry pie filling
- 3/4 cup light whipped topping

Preheat oven to 350 degrees. Spread cookie crumbs on bottom of 9-inch springform pan, coated with non-stick cooking spray. Set aside. Beat cream cheese on high until fluffy. Gradually add sugar and egg substitute. Add melted chocolate, cocoa and vanilla. Stir in sour cream. Pour into prepared pan. Bake 1 hour and 40 minutes. Cover and chill at least 8 hours. Spread cherry pie filling over top and dollop with whipped topping. Serves 12. Serving size: 1 slice

Amount Per Serving:

Calories 356	Saturated Fat 1 g	Sodium 428 mg
Total Fat 7 g	Cholesterol 11 mg	

214

Stars and Stripes Cheesecake

Crust:
- 1 cup graham cracker crumbs
- 1/4 cup sugar
- 3 Tablespoons canola oil

Filling:
- 2 cups fat-free cottage cheese
- 1 (8-ounce) package
  fat-free cream cheese
- 1/2 cup egg substitute
- 1/2 cup sugar
- 2 teaspoons grated lemon peel
- 1 Tablespoon lemon juice
- 1/2 teaspoon vanilla
- 1/4 teaspoon salt

Sour Cream Topping:
- 1 cup fat-free sour cream
- 2 Tablespoons sugar
- 1 teaspoon vanilla

Fruit Glaze:
- 1/4 cup apple jelly
- 1 cup fresh or frozen raspberries
- 1 cup fresh or frozen blueberries

Preheat oven to 350 degrees. To make crust, combine graham cracker crumbs, sugar and oil. Press in bottom and up sides of a 13 x 9-inch oblong pan or a 9-inch springform pan. Bake crust for 5 minutes. Let cool while preparing filling. To make filling, blend cottage cheese in blender or food processor until completely smooth. Pour into large mixing bowl and add cream cheese and egg substitute. Blend 2 minutes at medium speed of electric mixer. Add sugar, lemon peel, lemon juice, vanilla and salt. Blend until smooth. Pour into prepared crust and bake for 30 minutes or until center is set. For topping, combine sour cream, sugar and vanilla. Spread over cheesecake and bake for an additional 5 to 10 minutes. Turn off oven, and allow cheesecake to cool in oven with door ajar for 30 minutes. Remove from oven and cool. Refrigerate at least 3 hours. For fruit glaze, melt jelly in microwave or saucepan. Combine half of the jelly with raspberries and half of the jelly with blueberries. Arrange berries as desired in a single layer over cheesecake. Refrigerate for 15 minutes before serving. Serves 10. Serving size: 1 slice

Amount Per Serving:

Calories 263	Saturated Fat 0 g	Sodium 409 mg
Total Fat 6 g	Cholesterol 6 mg	

Cream Puffs

Pastry Puff:

- 1 cup water
- 1/2 cup low-fat margarine
- 1 cup flour
- 4 eggs

Filling:

- 3/4 cup skim milk
- 1 (3-ounce) package French vanilla or chocolate cook-n-serve pudding
- 1 (4-ounce) container light whipped topping
- 2 Tablespoons powdered sugar

Preheat oven to 400 degrees. In medium saucepan, heat water and margarine to rolling boil. Add flour and stir vigorously over low heat for 1 minute. Remove from heat. Beat in eggs, all at one time. Continue beating until smooth. Drop 1/4- cup batter, 3 inches apart onto ungreased baking sheets. Bake 30 minutes or until puffed and golden. Cool. To prepare pudding, pour milk into saucepan and add pudding mix. Heat to boiling, stirring constantly. Remove from heat and cool. Refrigerate. When cold, fold in whipped topping. Cut pastries in half and fill with pudding. Replace tops. Dust with powdered sugar. Refrigerate. Serves 12. Serving size: 1 cream puff

Amount Per Serving:

Calories 160	Saturated Fat 2 g	Sodium 275 mg
Total Fat 9 g	Cholesterol 72 mg	

Chewy Cocoa Brownies

Prep Time: 25 minutes
Cooking Time: 25 minutes

- 4 egg whites
- 1/2 cup canola oil
- 1 1/2 teaspoons vanilla
- 1 1/3 cups sugar
- 1/2 cup cocoa
- 1 1/4 cups flour
- 1/8 teaspoon salt
- 1/2 cup walnuts, chopped

Preheat oven to 350 degrees. Coat bottom of a 9 x 9-inch pan with non-stick cooking spray. Set aside. Beat egg whites in a large bowl with a spoon until slightly frothy. Add oil and vanilla. Mix well. Stir in sugar and cocoa. Mix well. Stir in flour and salt until blended. Stir in walnuts. Pour into prepared pan. Bake 25-30 minutes. Avoid overbaking. Cool completely before cutting. Serves 30. Serving size: 1 brownie

Amount Per Serving:

Calories 129	Saturated Fat 1 g	Sodium 20 mg
Total Fat 7 g	Cholesterol 0 mg	

Caramel Bars

Prep Time: 25 minutes
Cooking Time: 25 minutes

Crust:

- 1 cup flour
- 3/4 cup oatmeal
- 1/4 teaspoon salt
- 1/2 cup brown sugar
- 1/2 cup margarine
- 1/4 teaspoon baking soda

Caramel Mixture:

- 1 (12-ounce) package light caramels
- 4 Tablespoons skim milk
- 1 cup milk chocolate morsels
- 1 cup walnuts, chopped

Preheat oven to 350 degrees. Mix together flour, oatmeal, salt, brown sugar, margarine and baking soda. Save one cup for topping. Pat the rest into the bottom of a 9 x 13-inch pan. Bake 10 minutes and cool. For the caramel mixture, melt caramels in milk. Cook until smooth. Sprinkle chocolate morsels and walnuts over the crust. Pour caramel mixture over it all, and sprinkle the remaining crumbs over the top. Bake 15 minutes. Serves 24. Serving size: 1 (2 x 2-inch) square

Amount Per Serving:

Calories 206	Saturated Fat 5 g	Sodium 115 mg
Total Fat 11 g	Cholesterol 10 mg	

Chocolate Chip Cookies

- 1 cup unsalted margarine
- 1 cup sugar
- 1/2 cup brown sugar, packed
- 1/2 teaspoon baking soda
- 1/4 teaspoon salt
- 2 egg whites

- 2 teaspoons vanilla
- 2 1/4 cups flour
- 1/3 cup oat bran
- 1/2 cup miniature semi-sweet chocolate morsels

Preheat oven to 375 degrees. In large mixing bowl, beat margarine at medium speed of an electric mixer for 30 seconds. Add sugar, brown sugar, baking soda and salt. Mix well. Add egg whites and vanilla. Beat until combined well. Beat in as much flour as possible. Stir in remaining flour and oat bran with a wooden spoon. Stir in chocolate morsels. Drop dough by rounded teaspoons (2 inches apart) onto an ungreased cookie sheet. Bake for 8 to 10 minutes or until edges are lightly browned. Remove cookies from cookie sheet and cool on a wire rack. Makes 50 cookies. Serves 50.

Serving size: 1 cookie

Amount Per Serving:

Calories 86	Saturated Fat 1 g	Sodium 23 mg
Total Fat 4 g	Cholesterol 0 mg	

Oatmeal Raisin Cookies

- 1/4 cup egg substitute
- 2 cups brown sugar
- 1/2 cup canola oil
- 1 cup applesauce, unsweetened
- 2 cups flour

- 1 teaspoon baking soda
- 2 teaspoons cinnamon
- 4 cups rolled oats
- 1 cup raisins

Preheat oven to 350 degrees. In a large bowl, combine egg substitute and brown sugar. Mix until creamy. Add oil and applesauce. In a medium bowl, blend together flour, baking soda and cinnamon. Add to egg and sugar mixture. Fold in rolled oats and raisins. Drop by teaspoonfuls onto a cookie sheet. Bake 12 to 15 minutes. Makes 9 dozen cookies. Serves 108. Serving size: 1 cookie

Amount Per Serving:

Calories 50	Saturated Fat 0 g	Sodium 15 mg
Total Fat 1 g	Cholesterol 0 mg	

Ginger Snaps

- 3/4 cup shortening
- 1 cup sugar
- 4 Tablespoons molasses
- 1 egg
- 2 cups flour

- 2 teaspoons baking soda
- 1 teaspoon cinnamon
- 1 teaspoon cloves
- 1 teaspoon ginger

Preheat oven to 350 degrees. Coat cookie sheets with non-stick cooking spray. Cream together shortening and sugar. Add molasses and egg. Beat well. Add sifted, dry ingredients. Beat until smooth. Roll into small balls. Roll in sugar and bake 2 inches apart on a cookie sheet. Bake 10 minutes. Makes 4 dozen cookies. Serves 48. Serving size: 1 cookie

Amount Per Serving

Calories 271	Saturated Fat 3 g	Sodium 217 mg
Total Fat 10 g	Cholesterol 18 mg	

Rocky Road Candy

Prep Time: 10 minutes
Chill Time: 3 hours

- 1 (340-gram) package low-fat, semi-sweet chocolate morsels
- 1 (14-ounce) can low-fat, sweetened condensed milk
- 1 cup peanuts
- 1/2 large package miniature marshmallows
- 1 teaspoon vanilla

Melt chocolate morsels with sweetened condensed milk in double-boiler or over low heat. When thoroughly melted, remove from heat. Add peanuts, marshmallows and vanilla. Pour into 11 3/4 x 7 1/2 x 1 3/4-inch baking dish, lined with waxed paper. Refrigerate approximately 3 hours or until hard. Cut into 40 squares. Serves 40. Serving size: 1 piece

Amount Per Serving:

Calories 106	Saturated Fat 0 g	Sodium 42 mg
Total Fat 4 g	Cholesterol 1 mg	

Candy Crackers

Prep Time: 25 minutes
Cooking Time: 5 minutes
Chill Time: Refrigerate until hard

- 40 low-sodium saltine crackers (2 x 2-inch)
- 1 cup brown sugar
- 1 cup margarine
- 1 (12-ounce) package milk chocolate morsels

Preheat oven to 350 degrees. Place saltines side by side on a foil covered cookie sheet. Bring sugar and margarine to a boil in a saucepan. Boil 3 minutes. Spread mixture over crackers. Bake 5 minutes. Sprinkle chocolate morsels over baked crackers. Let stand 5 minutes. Refrigerate until hard. Break into pieces. Serves 24. Serving size: 2 pieces

Amount Per Serving:

Calories 168	Saturated Fat 1 g	Sodium 121 mg
Total Fat 9 g	Cholesterol 2 mg	

Walnut Clusters

- 1/2 cup flour
- 1/4 teaspoon baking powder
- 1/8 cup margarine
- 1/4 cup canola oil
- 1/2 cup sugar
- 1/4 cup egg substitute

- 1 1/2 teaspoons vanilla
- 1 1/2 squares (1-ounce each) unsweetened chocolate, melted
- 1 1/2 cups walnut pieces
- 1 egg white
- 1 teaspoon water

Preheat oven to 350 degrees. Coat cookie sheets with non-stick cooking spray. In a medium size bowl, combine flour and baking powder. In a large bowl, beat together margarine, oil, sugar, egg substitute and vanilla until fluffy (about 3 minutes). Fold in flour mixture and melted chocolate. Fold in walnuts. Refrigerate dough for 15 minutes. Drop chilled dough by heaping teaspoonfuls, 2 inches apart on cookie sheets. Beat egg white with water in a small bowl. Brush over cookies. Bake 10-12 minutes or until firm. Makes 36 cookies. Serves 36. Serving size: 1 cookie

Amount Per Serving:

Calories 105	Saturated Fat 1 g	Sodium 17 mg
Total Fat 8 g	Cholesterol 0 mg	

Apple-Cranberry Crunch

- 3 cups Macintosh apples, unpeeled, chopped and cored
- 2 cups whole, fresh or frozen cranberries
- 3/4 cup sugar
- 1 1/2 cups old-fashioned oats
- 1/2 cup chopped pecans
- 1/2 cup packed brown sugar
- 1/3 cup whole wheat flour
- 1/4 cup canola oil

Preheat oven to 350 degrees. Mix together apples, cranberries and sugar. Place into a 6 x 12-inch ungreased pan. Set aside. In a medium bowl, combine oats, pecans, sugar, flour and oil. Pour over apple and cranberry mixture. Press down lightly. Bake for 45 minutes. Serves 12. Serving size: 1 (1-ounce) square

Amount Per Serving:

Calories 259	Saturated Fat 1 g	Sodium 5 mg
Total Fat 9 g	Cholesterol 0 mg	

Glorified Rice

- 2 cups cooked rice, cooled
- 1 (15-ounce) can pineapple tidbits, drained
- 1 cup miniature marshmallows (approximately 24)
- 1 cup apples, chopped
- 1/2 cup powdered sugar
- 16 maraschino cherries, halved
- 1/2 cup pecans, chopped (optional)
- 1 cup whipping cream

In a large bowl, combine rice, pineapple, marshmallows, apple, powdered sugar, cherries and pecans. In a medium bowl, whip cream to soft peaks. Fold into other mixture. Serves 10. Serving size: 6 ounces

Amount Per Serving:

Calories 159	Saturated Fat 0 g	Sodium 7 mg
Total Fat 5 g	Cholesterol 0 mg	

Creamy Cheese Triangles

- 1/4 cup margarine, softened
- 1/4 cup canola oil
- 1 1/2 cups flour
- 1/2 cup packed brown sugar
- 1/2 cup walnuts, finely chopped
- 2 (8-ounce) packages
  fat-free cream cheese, softened

- 1/3 cup sugar
- 2 Tablespoons orange peel, grated
- 1 teaspoon orange extract
- 1/4 cup egg substitute

Preheat oven to 350 degrees. Coat an 8 x 12-inch baking pan with non-stick cooking spray. In a small bowl, beat margarine, oil, flour and brown sugar at low speed until well blended. (Mixture will be crumbly.) Stir in walnuts. Reserve 1 1/4 cup crumb mixture. Evenly pat remaining mixture into bottom of prepared pan. Bake 20 minutes or until lightly browned. In a large bowl, beat together cream cheese, sugar, orange peel, orange extract and egg substitute at medium speed until well blended. Spread cream cheese mixture over baked layer in pan. Sprinkle with reserved crumb mixture. Bake 30 minutes or until golden. Refrigerate at least 2 hours. Cut into 48 triangles. Serves 48.
Serving size: 1 triangle

Amount Per Serving:

Calories 58	Saturated Fat 0 g	Sodium 71 mg
Total Fat 2 g	Cholesterol 2 mg	

Creamy Fruit Layer Dessert

Prep Time: 20 minutes
Chill Time: 1 hour

- 4 cups cold skim milk
- 2 (4-serving) packages fat-free, sugar-free, instant vanilla pudding
- 1 (12-ounce) package fat-free golden loaf cake, cubed
- 2 cups strawberries, sliced
- 1 cup blueberries

Pour milk into medium bowl and add pudding mixes. Beat with wire whisk for 1 minute. Let stand 5 minutes. Layer 1/2 of the cake cubes, fruit and pudding in a 3-quart serving bowl. Repeat layers. Garnish with fresh strawberries. Refrigerate for 1 hour before serving. Serves 12. Serving size: 1 cup

Amount Per Serving:

Calories 127	Saturated Fat 0 g	Sodium 235 mg
Total Fat 0 g	Cholesterol 1 mg	

Refreshing Fruit Cups

Prep Time: 25 minutes
Freeze Time: 2 hours

- 1 (12-ounce) can frozen orange juice, thawed
- 12-ounces water
- 1 (16-ounce) can crushed pineapple (Do not drain!)
- 1 (16-ounce) can apricots, diced and drained
- 6 bananas, diced
- 2 Tablespoons lemon juice

Mix together orange juice, water, pineapple, apricots, bananas and lemon juice. Pour into muffin tins lined with paper baking cups and freeze. Remove from paper liners and serve on lettuce leaves. Serves 32. Serving size: 4 ounces

Amount Per Serving:

Calories 55	Saturated Fat 0 g	Sodium 1 mg
Total Fat 0 g	Cholesterol 0 mg	

Orange Trifle

- 1 (12-ounce) package white angel food cake mix
- 1 package sugar-free, instant vanilla pudding (4-serving size)
- 2 cups skim milk
- 1 Tablespoon orange peel, grated
- 1 (4-ounce) container light whipped topping
- 6 Tablespoons orange juice
- 1/4 cup almonds, sliced

Preheat oven to 350 degrees. Prepare the cake mix as indicated on the package and divide between 2, ungreased 9 x 5 x 3-inch loaf pans. Bake until tops are deep golden brown and cracks feel dry (45-50 minutes). Do not overbake. Immediately invert pans. Cool completely. Remove from pans and freeze 1 loaf for future use. Cut remaining loaf into 1-inch cubes. Prepare pudding as directed on package, using skim milk. Fold orange peel and 1/2 of the whipped topping into the pudding. Place 1/3 of the cake cubes into a 2-quart serving bowl. Sprinkle with 2 Tablespoons orange juice. Spread 1/3 of the pudding over cake cubes. Repeat this twice. Spread remaining whipped topping over the top. Cover and refrigerate at least 3 hours. Sprinkle with almonds before serving. Serves 12. Serving size: 1 cup

Amount Per Serving:

| Calories 178 | Saturated Fat 0 g | Sodium 237 mg |
| Total Fat 4 g | Cholesterol 1 mg | |

Raspberry Whip

- 1 cup fresh or frozen raspberries
- 1 (3-ounce) package raspberry-flavored gelatin
- 1 cup boiling water
- 2/3 cup cold water
- 1 (8-ounce) carton low-fat vanilla yogurt

Thaw and drain raspberries if frozen. In small mixing bowl, dissolve gelatin in boiling water. Add cold water. Cover and chill for 40 minutes or until partially set. Add yogurt. Beat at medium speed for 1-2 minutes or until light and foamy. Chill mixture until it mounds when spooned. Divide half of the raspberries between 6 dessert dishes, or place half in bottom of serving dish. Spoon gelatin mixture on top. Garnish with remaining raspberries. Chill for 30 minutes or until firm. Serves 6. Serving size: 1 cup

Amount Per Serving:

Calories 30	Saturated Fat 0 g	Sodium 61 mg
Total Fat 0 g	Cholesterol 1 mg	

Peach Angel Dream

- 24 ounces frozen peaches
- 1 (16-ounce) angel food cake
- 2 (3 3/4-ounce) packages low-fat vanilla instant pudding
- 2 cups skim milk
- 2 (8-ounce) cartons fat-free peach yogurt
- 1 (12-ounce) carton light whipped topping

Allow peaches to thaw. Chop peaches into 1/2 to 1-inch pieces. Spread peaches evenly in bottom of serving bowl. Tear cake into bite-sized pieces and lay over fruit. Mix together pudding, milk and yogurt. Pour over cake layer. Top with layer of whipped topping. Refrigerate overnight. Garnish with fresh fruit. Serves 16. Serving size: 1 cup

Amount Per Serving:

Calories 231	Saturated Fat 0 g	Sodium 182 mg
Total Fat 3 g	Cholesterol 2 mg	

Strawberry Whip

- 3 1/2 cups strawberries, sliced
- 1/2 cup evaporated skim milk
- 1/2 teaspoon vanilla
- 2 egg whites
- 1/4 cup sugar
- 2 Tablespoons walnuts, finely chopped

Place strawberries in blender or food processor. Process until smooth. Cover and chill. Put milk in small bowl and freeze until ice crystals form. With chilled beaters, beat milk and vanilla at high speed until stiff peaks form. Fold into strawberries. In a small bowl, beat (room temperature) egg whites at high speed until foamy. Gradually add sugar, 1 Tablespoon at a time, beating until stiff peaks form. Fold into strawberry mixture. Serve immediately or freeze until firm. If frozen, let stand at room temperature for 10 minutes before serving. Sprinkle walnuts over each individual serving.
Serves 6. Serving size: 5 ounces

Amount Per Serving:

Calories 95	Saturated Fat 0 g	Sodium 44 mg
Total Fat 1 g	Cholesterol 1 mg	

Strawberry Trifle

- 1 (3-ounce) package fat-free, sugar-free strawberry jello
- 2 cups boiling water
- 20 ounces frozen strawberries in own juice
- 1 (1.5-ounce) package sugar-free, instant vanilla pudding
- 4 cups skim milk
- 1 round prepared angel food cake
- 1 (12-ounce) carton light whipped topping
- fresh strawberries (optional)

Dissolve jello in 2 cups boiling water. Add frozen strawberries and set aside to cool slightly. Prepare pudding according to directions, using skim milk. Slice cake into 3 layers. In a clear serving bowl, layer cake, jello mixture and whipped topping, repeating layers three times. Chill several hours or overnight. Garnish with fresh strawberries.
Serves 12. Serving size: 8 ounces

Amount Per Serving:

Calories 260	Saturated Fat 0 g	Sodium 287 mg
Total Fat 4 g	Cholesterol 2 mg	

Fresh Peach Freeze

- 4 medium peaches, peeled and sliced
- 1 (6-ounce) can frozen, concentrated orange juice
- 1/3 cup light corn syrup

In food processor or blender, blend peaches, orange juice and corn syrup until smooth. Place mixture into a 9-inch square metal pan. Cover and freeze until firm (at least 4 hours). Transfer to processor or blender and blend again until smooth. Spoon into serving bowls. Garnish with fresh fruit. Serves 6. Serving size: 1/2 cup

Amount Per Serving:

Calories 118	Saturated Fat 0 g	Sodium 13 mg
Total Fat 0 g	Cholesterol 0 mg	

Cranberry Ice

- 1 3/4 cups water
- 1 1/4 cups sugar
- 2 Tablespoons lemon juice
- 1 3/4 cups cranberry juice

Heat water, sugar and lemon juice until sugar is thoroughly dissolved. Cool. Add cranberry juice and freeze in ice cream freezer, or pour mixture into 8-inch square baking dish and place in freezer. After mixture has hardened, spoon into individual serving dishes. Serves 8. Serving size: 4 ounces

Amount Per Serving:

Calories 153	Saturated Fat 0 g	Sodium 2 mg
Total Fat 0 g	Cholesterol 0 mg	

Tiramisu

Prep Time: 40 minutes
Chill Time: 24 hours
Freeze Time: 2 hours

- 2/3 cup powdered sugar
- 1 (8-ounce) package
  fat-free cream cheese, softened
- 1 1/2 cups light whipped topping
- 1/2 cup plus 1 Tablespoon sugar
- 1/4 cup water
- 3 egg whites

- 1/2 cup hot water
- 1 Tablespoon instant espresso
  coffee granules
- 2 Tablespoons Kahlúa
  or other coffee-flavored liquor
- 20 lady fingers
- 1/2 teaspoon unsweetened cocoa

Combine powdered sugar and cream cheese in a large bowl. Beat at high speed of electric mixer until well blended. Gently fold 1 cup of whipped topping into cheese mixture. Dissolve 1/2 cup sugar in water in the top of a double boiler. Slowly stir this mixture into beaten egg whites. Beat at high speed until stiff peaks form. Gently stir 1/4 of egg white mixture into cheese mixture. Gently fold in remaining egg white mixture, and set aside. Combine hot water, sugar, espresso granules, and Kahlúa. Stir well. Split lady fingers in half lengthwise. Arrange 20 lady finger halves, cut side up, in the bottom of an 8-inch square baking dish. Drizzle half of the espresso mixture over the lady finger halves. Spread 1/2 of the cheese mixture over lady finger halves. Repeat procedure with remaining lady finger halves, espresso mixture and cheese mixture. Spread remaining 1/2 cup whipped topping evenly over cheese mixture. Sprinkle with cocoa. Place one toothpick in each corner and one in the center to prevent wrap from sticking to whipped topping. Cover with plastic wrap. Chill for 24 hours. Freeze 2 hours before serving, so it will cut cleanly. Serves 8. Serving size: 1 (8-ounce) square

Amount Per Serving:

Calories 241	Saturated Fat 1 g	Sodium 232 mg
Total Fat 3 g	Cholesterol 100 mg	

Strawberry-Rhubarb Slump

- 1 cup flour
- 1 cup plus 2 Tablespoons sugar
- 1 teaspoon baking powder
- 1/4 teaspoon baking soda
- 1/4 teaspoon salt
- 1/4 cup margarine,
  cut into small pieces
- 6 Tablespoons low-fat buttermilk
- 1/2 teaspoon almond extract
- 4 cups whole strawberries, hulled
- 4 cups rhubarb
- 1/2 cup water
- 1 Tablespoon cornstarch
- 2 Tablespoons apple juice or cider

In a large bowl, combine flour, 1/4 cup sugar, baking powder, baking soda and salt. Cut in margarine with pastry blender until mixture resembles coarse meal. Add buttermilk and almond extract, and toss with a fork until the dry ingredients are moistened. Set dough aside. In a 10-inch, oven-safe skillet, combine strawberries, rhubarb, 3/4 cup sugar and water. Cover and cook over medium heat for 10 minutes, stirring occasionally. In a small bowl, combine cornstarch and juice. Add to fruit mixture. Bring to a boil, and cook for 1 minute until thickened. Drop dough by heaping teaspoonfuls onto fruit mixture. Cover and cook over low heat for 10 minutes. Remove from heat, and sprinkle 2 Tablespoons of sugar over the dumplings and fruit. Broil for 3 minutes or until golden. Serves 8.
Serving size: 1 (8-ounce) slice

Amount Per Serving:

Calories 255	Saturated Fat 1 g	Sodium 97 mg
Total Fat 6 g	Cholesterol 0 mg	

A slump is similar to a cobbler but made on top of the stove, often in a cast iron skillet. The name originated because the dish "slumps" on the plate.

Myth No. 88:

"Ozarkians believe pie a la mode is best when served with ice cream."

JUST KIDDIN'

Myth No. 78:
"Ozark families have an average of 8.6 kids and end the evening with a
ceremonial 'good night, John Boy,' 'good night, Mary Ellen,' 'good night, Jim Bob'...
finishing just minutes before daylight."

Fact:
"Not true. We suggest dining less in front of the tv
and more often at the dinner table."

Special thanks to the Springfield Public School's Parents As Teachers professionals who provided many of the recipes and craft ideas suited especially for children.

We are proud that Missouri was first in the nation to offer this type of innovative early childhood education program and that Springfield offers one of the largest PAT programs in the state.

Some recipes are designated with a "Read the Book, Then Let's Cook!" logo.

Farmer's Pancakes

Prep Time: 30 minutes
Cooking Time: 15 minutes
Chill Time: overnight

- 1 cup old-fashioned oats
- 1 cup buttermilk
- 1/4 cup egg substitute
- 1/4 cup flour
- 2 Tablespoons sugar
- 1 Tablespoon baking powder
- 1/2 teaspoon baking soda
- 1/4 teaspoon cinnamon
- 1 Tablespoon margarine, melted

Combine oats and buttermilk in mixing bowl. Cover and refrigerate overnight. When ready to use, add egg substitute, flour, sugar, baking powder, baking soda, cinnamon and margarine, mixing thoroughly. Cook on preheated griddle coated with non-stick cooking spray. Serve hot with warm syrup and melted low-fat margarine if desired. Serves 4. Serving size: 2-3 pancakes

Amount Per Serving:

Calories 194	Saturated Fat 1 g	Sodium 589 mg
Total Fat 5 g	Cholesterol 2 mg	

Pancake, Pancake

by Eric Carle

READ THE BOOK THEN LET'S COOK!

Painted Toast

Prep Time: 5 minutes

- 4 Tablespoons low-fat milk
- food coloring (four different colors)
- 1 slice fortified white bread

Set up 4 small cups, and divide milk evenly between cups. Add a few drops of food coloring to make each cup a different color. Gently paint on bread slice, making designs or pictures. Be careful not to soak the bread with milk mixture! When creation is finished place in toaster on light setting. Enjoy with favorite topping. Serves 1. Serving size: 1 slice

Amount Per Serving:

Calories 69	Saturated Fat 0 g	Sodium 133 mg
Total Fat 1 g	Cholesterol 1 mg	

Hidden Treasure Muffins

- 1 cup all-purpose flour
- 1/2 cup quick oats (or wheat germ)
- 1/4 cup sugar
- 2 teaspoons baking powder
- 1/2 teaspoon salt
- 2 egg whites

- 2 Tablespoons vegetable oil
- 2 Tablespoons applesauce
- 3/4 cup skim milk
- 3/4 cup fresh or frozen (thawed) berries, chopped peaches, mashed bananas or fruit jam

Preheat oven to 400 degrees. Coat muffin tin with non-stick cooking spray. In a large mixing bowl, stir together flour, quick oats (or wheat germ), sugar, baking powder and salt. Make a well in the middle of mixture and set aside. In a smaller bowl, mix egg whites, vegetable oil, applesauce and milk. Add liquid to well in dry mixture, and stir until moistened, leaving mixture a little lumpy. Add one of the following:

- Fruit: 3/4 cup fruit to batter and fill muffin cups 3/4 full.

- Jam: Fill muffin cups halfway and drop on one teaspoon of jam. Top with a little more batter to cover jam.

- Fortune: Fill muffin cups halfway, then lay a fortune (written or typed on a small piece of paper) so that part of it sticks out. Add a little more batter to almost cover fortune.

Bake for 20-25 minutes. Serves 12. Serving size: 1 muffin

Amount Per Serving:

Calories 96	Saturated Fat 0 g	Sodium 173 mg
Total Fat 3 g	Cholesterol 0g	

Choco-Nana Muffins

- 1 1/4 cups all-purpose flour
- 1/2 cup sugar
- 1/4 cup brown sugar
- 1/4 cup cocoa
- 1 teaspoon baking powder
- 1/2 teaspoon baking soda
- 1/4 teaspoon salt
- 3 small, ripe bananas, mashed
- 1/2 cup egg substitute
- 2 Tablespoons vegetable oil
- 2 Tablespoons buttermilk
- 1 teaspoon vanilla extract

Preheat oven to 400 degrees. Coat muffin tin with non-stick cooking spray. Combine first 7 ingredients in a large bowl. Make a well in center of mixture, and set aside. Combine bananas and remaining ingredients. Add to dry ingredients, stirring just until moistened. Spoon into muffin tin, filling 2/3 full. Bake for 15 minutes. Cool in pans. Remove and serve warm or at room temperature. Yield: 12 muffins. Serves 12. Serving size: 1 muffin

Amount Per Serving:

Calories 159	Saturated Fat 0 g	Sodium 154 mg
Total Fat 3 g	Cholesterol 0 mg	

Punch in a Pail

For a fun gift idea, pack the following ingredients in a new, plastic beach or paint pail. Add a card with the recipe, fun straws, shredded tissue paper, tiny paper umbrellas and/or anything else festive!

- 1 (.17-ounce) package unsweetened, tropical punch flavored drink mix
- 1 (3-ounce) package cherry gelatin
- 1 cup sugar
- 1 (46-ounce) can unsweetened pineapple juice
- 1 (2-liter) bottle ginger ale

Combine drink mix, gelatin and sugar in a large plastic or metal bowl or in pail if it is large enough. Add 1 cup boiling water; stir until sugar dissolves. Stir in pineapple juice and 2 quarts cold water, and freeze mixture. Two hours before serving, remove mixture from freezer. Add ginger ale, and stir until slushy. Serves 15. Serving size: 7.5 ounces

Amount Per Serving:

Calories 165	Saturated Fat 0 g	Sodium 22 mg
Total Fat 0 g	Cholesterol 0 mg	

Halloween Swamp Muck Punch

- 1 (2-liter) bottle sugar-free lemon-lime soda
- 3 or 4 drops green food coloring
- 1 pint chocolate or chocolate- fudge frozen yogurt
- 1 ripe kiwi

Pour lemon lime soda into punch bowl. Add drops of green food coloring, and stir. Drop yogurt, by spoonfuls, to float on top of soda. "Swamp Muck" will start to bubble and foam. Wash kiwi, and cut into thin slices to float on top. You might want to add dry ice to add to the swamp effect. This looks disgustingly, wonderfully gross. Serves 8. Serving size: 10 ounces

Amount Per Serving:

Calories 63	Saturated Fat 1 g	Sodium 78 mg
Total Fat 2 g	Cholesterol 2 mg	

Purple Cow Shakes

Prep Time: 5 minutes

- 1 (6-ounce) can frozen grape juice concentrate
- 1 cup low-fat milk
- 2 cups vanilla frozen yogurt

Pour partially thawed juice concentrate and milk into blender. Add frozen yogurt. Cover and blend 30 seconds on high speed. Serves 4. Serving size: 6 ounces

Amount Per Serving:

Calories 241	Saturated Fat 3 g	Sodium 97 mg
Total Fat 5 g	Cholesterol 6 mg	

Cow in the Apple Orchard

Prep Time: 5 minutes

- 1 3/4 cups low-fat milk
- 1/3 cup frozen apple juice concentrate
- 1 cup vanilla frozen yogurt
- 1/2 teaspoon ground cinnamon

Pour partially thawed juice concentrate and milk into blender. Cover and blend well. Add frozen yogurt and cinnamon. Cover and blend until smooth. Serves 5. Serving size: 6 ounces

Amount Per Serving:

Calories 117	Saturated Fat 2 g	Sodium 72 mg
Total Fat 3 g	Cholesterol 7 mg	

When The Cows Come Home
by the Ozarks' own David Harrison

READ THE BOOK THEN LET'S COOK!

Jam-A-Rama Shake

Prep Time: 5 minutes

- 2 Tablespoons jam (any flavor)
- 1/4 cup cold low-fat milk
- 1 cup vanilla frozen yogurt

Place ingredients in blender. Blend until smooth. Serves 1. Serving size: 10 ounces

Amount Per Serving:

Calories 369	Saturated Fat 6 g	Sodium 160 mg
Total Fat 9 g	Cholesterol 7 mg	

Jam Berry

by Bruce Degan

Polka Dot Punch

Prep Time: 5 minutes

- 1 (46-ounce) can or carton of pineapple juice
- 1 (46-ounce) can or carton of fruit punch
- 1 (46-ounce) can or carton of orange juice
- 1 (2-liter) bottle of sugar-free, lemon-lime carbonated soft drink

Freeze pineapple juice, fruit punch and orange juice (or use any colorful juice you like) in separate ice cube trays. For each serving, pour chilled lemon-lime soft drink over different colored ice cubes. Serves 12. Serving size: 6 ounces

Amount Per Serving:

Calories 152	Saturated Fat 0 g	Sodium 54 mg
Total Fat 0 g	Cholesterol 0 mg	

Mighty Monster Mouths

Prep Time: 30 minutes

- 5 medium-size red apples
- 1/4 cup orange juice
- 1 cup creamy peanut butter
- 1 (10 1/2-ounce) package miniature marshmallows

Core and cut each apple into 14 (1/4-inch) wedges. Brush apple slices with orange juice, and spread 1 side of each wedge evenly with peanut butter. Press 4 marshmallows into peanut butter on half of the wedges. Top with remaining apple slices, peanut butter side down. Squeeze gently. Makes approximately 35. Serves 17. Serving size: 2 Monster Mouths

Amount Per Serving:

Calories 125	Saturated Fat 1 g	Sodium 43 mg
Total Fat 4 g	Cholesterol 0 mg	

Where the Wild Things Are
by Maurice Sendak

READ THE BOOK THEN LET'S COOK!

Fruit Freeze

- 2 (16-ounce) packages frozen strawberries
- 1 (6-ounce) can orange juice concentrate
- 1 (13-ounce) can sliced peaches, undrained
- 1 (8-ounce) can pineapple chunks, undrained
- 2 bananas, sliced and chunked

Thaw strawberries and orange juice concentrate. Mix all ingredients together. Pour into 9 x 13-inch pan, and freeze overnight. Remove from freezer five minutes before cutting. Serves 20. Serving size: 1/2 cup

Amount Per Serving:

Calories 110	Saturated Fat 0 g	Sodium 5 mg
Total Fat 0 g	Cholesterol 0 mg	

Homemade Caramel Applesauce

- 6 medium apples
- 3 Tablespoons margarine
- 1/3 cup brown sugar, packed
- 1/2 cup water
- 1/2 teaspoon cinnamon
- dash of nutmeg

Wash and peel apples. Cut into quarters, core and slice. Heat margarine and brown sugar over low heat until margarine melts. Remove pan from heat. Add apple slices, gently mixing until slices are coated with brown sugar mixture. Add water, cinnamon and nutmeg. (The apples will cook down, creating more liquid). Heat to boiling over medium-high heat, stirring occasionally. Reduce heat, cover and simmer about 20 minutes or until apples are fork-tender. Stir occasionally. Let apples cool, then mash with a fork or potato masher. Serves 6. Serving size: 6 ounces

Amount Per Serving:

Calories 178	Saturated Fat 1 g	Sodium 82 mg
Total Fat 6 g	Cholesterol 0 mg	

Alfalfa Sprouts

Prep Time: 5 minutes

- 1 Tablespoon alfalfa seeds
- quart jar
- cheese cloth
- rubber band or canning jar ring
- lukewarm water

Place alfalfa seeds in quart jar. Cover with cheese cloth, and fasten with a rubber band or the ring from a canning jar lid. Fill jar 2/3 full with lukewarm water. Shake one minute, and then, drain all water from jar. Lay jar on its side on kitchen countertop. Repeat this process once each morning and night for 6-7 days, until seeds are sprouted. Cover jar with a towel the first 2-3 days, then leave uncovered. When sprouted, rinse in colander. Store in refrigerator. Sprinkle on salads, stuffed celery, cheese or peanut butter sandwiches or crackers spread with cream cheese.

Munch 'n Crunch

Prep Time: 10 minutes
Cooking Time: 20 minutes

- 7 cups crispy corn cereal squares
- 1/2 cup dry-roasted peanuts
- 2 Tablespoons margarine, melted
- 3 Tablespoons honey
- 1/2 cup finely-chopped dried apricots (or other dried fruit)

Preheat oven to 300 degrees. Mix cereal and peanuts in a 13 x 9-inch pan. Mix margarine and honey. Drizzle over cereal mixture, and toss to coat. Bake for 10 minutes, stirring once. Add apricots, and bake another 10 minutes, stirring twice. Cool and store in airtight container. Yields: 6 cups. Serves 12. Serving size: 1/2 cup

Amount Per Serving:

Calories 141	Saturated Fat 1 g	Sodium 215 mg
Total Fat 5 g	Cholesterol 0 mg	

Green Goblin Veggies

- 1 green pepper
- 2 pimento-stuffed green olives
- 4 to 5 carrots
- 4 to 5 stalks celery

Cut top off green pepper, and scrape out seeds. Cut two, dime-size holes for "eyes" and another for a "nose". Cut out a funny "mouth", too. Place olives, pimento facing out, in the eye holes. Cut a whole carrot crosswise approximately 3 inches from the end, and place the pointed end of the carrot in nose hole. Fill spooky goblin with carrot and celery strips. Serve with salad dressing or dip. A fall variation of this recipe is tying bundles of julienned carrots together to make "corn stalks". Serves 4.

Amount Per Serving:

| Calories 45 | Saturated Fat 0 g | Sodium 99 mg |
| Total Fat 1 g | Cholesterol 0 mg | |

The Carrot Seed

by Ruth Krauss

READ THE BOOK

THEN LET'S COOK!

Tic-Tac-Toe-sted Sandwiches

Prep Time: 10 minutes
Cooking Time: 2 minutes

- 1 slice fat-free American cheese
- 1 slice whole wheat bread
- 1/2 ounce light Swiss cheese, cut into narrow strips
- 1/2 ounce extra-lean ham, cut into narrow strips
- 2 black olives, pitted and sliced

To make a sandwich, place American cheese slice on the bread slice. Arrange Swiss cheese strips to form a tic-tac-toe board. Make X's out of ham strips and O's out of olives. Grill under hot broiler until cheese bubbles.

Amount Per Serving:

Calories 207	Saturated Fat 3 g	Sodium 1037 mg
Total Fat 6 g	Cholesterol 31 mg	

Spooky Spider Sandwiches

- 2 slices of sandwich bread
- 2 teaspoons peanut butter
- 2 raisins
- 1 carrot (to make 8 carrot sticks)

To make a sandwich, cut circles out of 2 slices of bread. Spread peanut butter on one circle. Place 8 carrot sticks for "legs" on peanut butter. Top with other circle of bread. Add raisins for "eyes". Serves 1. Serving size: 1 sandwich

Amount Per Serving:

Calories 225	Saturated Fat 2 g	Sodium 391 mg
Total Fat 7 g	Cholesterol 0 mg	

The Very Busy Spider

by Eric Carle

READ THE BOOK THEN LET'S COOK!

Make-Your-Own Fish Sticks

- 1 pound white fish fillets
  (codfish, snapper or crappie)
- 3/4 cup dry bread crumbs
- 1/2 cup egg substitute
- 1/4 cup light margarine
- 2 Tablespoons pickle relish
- 1/4 cup fat-free mayonnaise
- 1 Tablespoon lemon juice

Preheat oven to 400 degrees. Coat a 9 x 13-inch baking dish with non-stick cooking spray. Wash and dry fish fillets, then cut each fillet into long pieces. Pour bread crumbs into shallow dish, and pour egg substitute into separate shallow dish. Dip each piece of fish in eggs and then in bread crumbs until thoroughly coated. Place fish sticks in baking dish. Melt margarine; pour over fish sticks, and sprinkle remaining bread crumbs over fish sticks. Bake 15 minutes. While fish is baking, mix pickle relish, mayonnaise and lemon juice for tartar sauce to serve with fish sticks. Serves 4. Serving size: 4 ounces

Amount Per Serving:

Calories 268	Saturated Fat 6 g	Sodium 609 mg
Total Fat 9 g	Cholesterol 40 mg	

Hot-Diggety Dogs

- 1/2 cup onion, chopped
- 1 (14-ounce) bottle of catsup
- 1/4 cup water
- 1/4 cup pickle relish
- 1 Tablespoon sugar
- 1 Tablespoon vinegar
- 1/4 teaspoon salt
- dash of pepper
- 10 (97% fat-free) hot dogs
- 10 hot dog buns

Coat a large skillet with non-stick cooking spray. Cook onion in skillet until tender. Add catsup, water, relish, sugar, vinegar, salt and pepper. Stir well. Add hot dogs, and simmer 15 minutes. Serve hot dogs in buns, and top with sauce mixture. Serves 10. Serving size: 1 hot dog

Amount Per Serving:

Calories 239	Saturated Fat 1 g	Sodium 1318 mg
Total Fat 4 g	Cholesterol 0 mg	

Chewy Whole Wheat Snickerdoodles

Prep Time: 30 minutes
Cooking Time: 10 minutes

Topping:

- 1 cup sugar
- 1/2 cup brown sugar, firmly packed
- 1 cup margarine, softened
- 1/3 cup egg substitute
- 1 1/2 cups whole wheat flour
- 1 1/4 cups all-purpose flour
- 1 teaspoon baking soda
- 1/4 teaspoon salt

- 2 Tablespoons cinnamon
- 2 Tablespoons sugar

Preheat oven to 400 degrees. In a mixing bowl, cream sugars and margarine until fluffy. Add egg substitute and beat well. Combine dry ingredients, add to creamed mixture and beat well. In a small bowl, combine topping ingredients. Shape dough into quarter-sized balls, and roll in cinnamon sugar. Place 2 inches apart on ungreased cookie sheet. Bake for 8-10 minutes. Cookies will puff up and flatten as they bake. Yield: 2 dozen. Serves 12. Serving size: 2 cookies

Amount Per Serving:

Calories 174	Saturated Fat 1 g	Sodium 185 mg
Total Fat 8 g	Cholesterol 0 mg	

If You Give A Mouse A Cookie

by Laura Joffe Numeroff

Ozark Haystacks

Prep Time: 5 minutes
Cooking Time: 10 minutes

- 3 Tablespoons butter
- 1 (10-ounce) package marshmallows
- 1 (6-ounce) package Chinese noodles

Melt butter and marshmallows over low heat, stirring constantly. Place noodles in a large bowl and add butter and marshmallow mixture. Mix well. On wax paper, divide into 12 haystacks. Serves 12. Serving size: 1 haystack

Amount Per Serving:

Calories 183	Saturated Fat 3 g	Sodium 111 mg
Total Fat 8 g	Cholesterol 10 mg	

Best-Tasting Fingerpaint Ever

Prep Time: 5 minutes

- 1 (3.9-ounce) package fat-free/sugar-free instant pudding mix
- 2 cups low-fat milk

Combine pudding and milk. Place 2 Tablespoons of mixture on wax paper or fingerpaint paper. Paint, and lick fingers as you go. You'll have a delicious time! Serves 8. Serving size: 2 Tablespoons

Amount Per Serving:

Calories 73	Saturated Fat 1g	Sodium 177 mg
Total Fat 1g	Cholesterol 5 mg	

Rock & Roll Ice Cream

You will need:

- 6 baby food jars
- 1 (3-pound) coffee can
- crushed ice
  (enough to fill 3-pound coffee can)
- rock salt
- 1 package fat-free, sugar-free,
  instant pudding mix
- 1/3 (14-ounce) can low-fat sweetened,
  condensed milk
- 2 cups low-fat milk

Mix pudding mix and milk together. Spoon into clean baby food jars. Put the lids on tightly and place one jar in coffee can. Fill coffee can with ice and salt, around the jar. Put lid on coffee can and roll from child to child. Continue with each jar. Serves 6.
Serving size: 1 jar

Amount Per Serving:

Calories 167

Total Fat 2 g

Saturated Fat 1 g

Cholesterol 9 mg

Sodium 847 mg

Hairy Potato People

- 1 large raw potato
- dirt
- grass seed

Slice off one end of the potato so it will stand upright. Scoop a hollow in the top. Fill hollow about 3/4 full with dirt. Sprinkle grass seed on dirt. Cover with dirt and pack lightly. Keep watered, and place in a sunny location. Potato will grow green hair in a few days. Give potato a face. Anything stuck into the potato will work great.

Volcanoes

* 12 ounces modeling clay (e.g. Play Dough)
* 1 heaping teaspoon baking soda
* 3-4 drops of red food coloring
* 3-4 drops of yellow food coloring
* 3-4 drops liquid dish soap
* 1 Tablespoon vinegar

Form clay into a volcano shape, hollowing out the center. Keep model on a plate or tray to catch the mess. Put baking soda, food coloring and dish soap into hollow. Add vinegar. The eruption will start immediately. Repeat, adding vinegar two to three more times until "lava" doesn't flow well any longer. Volcano can be reactivated by adding more baking soda and vinegar. The hardened clay volcano can be used several times.

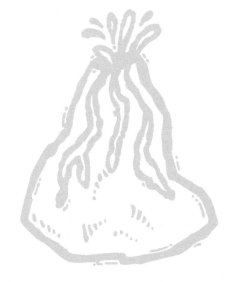

Ooey Gooey

Prep Time:10 minutes

- 4 ounces white glue
- 1 1/2 cups water
- 1 teaspoon Borax
- drops of food coloring, as desired

Pour glue in a jar. Add 1/2 cup water, and stir. Mix Borax and 1 cup water in a disposable container. Carefully stir glue mixture into Borax mixture. Add food coloring if desired. Drain off excess liquid, and knead until smooth. Store in plastic bag.

Salty Crawling Crystals

Prep Time: 15 minutes

- 1/3 cup Epsom salt
- 1/3 cup water
- 1 1/4 teaspoons food coloring (do not use yellow)

Heat Epsom salt and water in a saucepan until salt dissolves. Remove from heat, and add food coloring. Divide mixture between 3 or 4 small containers such as custard cups, mini pie tins or inverted jar lids. (Mixture might stain pottery or plastic containers.) These slow-growing crystals will take on a variety of forms, depending on the container size and shape. It will take several days for the crystals to stop changing and growing. Crystal mixture can also be used as a paint before it begins to harden.

Bubble Recipe

Prep Time: 5 minutes

- 2 cups liquid dish soap
- 6 cups water
- 3/4 cup white syrup or sugar

Mix ingredients together. Let sit for 4 hours before using. Will last 2-4 days (longer if refrigerated).

Handy-Dandy Salt Dough

Prep Time: 15 minutes

- 4 cups flour
- 1 cup salt
- 1 1/2 cups water
- 3-4 drops oil
- Food coloring (Add to water to color dough, if desired.)

Mix all ingredients together, and knead until smooth. This may be kept in a cool spot in a covered bowl or plastic bag for a long time. Dough can be used again and again.

Fruit-Scented Playdough

Prep Time: 30 minutes

- 2 (.17-ounce) packages unsweetened fruit drink mix
- 2 1/2 cups flour
- 1 cup salt
- 2 teaspoons cooking oil
- 2 cups boiling water

Mix dry ingredients. Add oil and water. Knead until smooth. Store in air-tight container. Will keep for at least a month.

Homemade Playdough

Prep Time: 20 minutes

- 1 cup flour
- 1/2 cup salt
- 2 teaspoons cream of tartar
- 1 cup water
- 2 Tablespoons salad oil
- food coloring

Mix flour, salt and cream of tartar together in a large saucepan. Add the water, salad oil and food coloring (until desired color is obtained). Cook and stir over medium heat until dough forms into a ball and leaves the sides of the pan. Roll dough out onto counter and knead until smooth. Keep dough in airtight container. Will last for a month or longer.

Candied Cookie Cutter Ornaments

Prep Time: 1 hour

- 1/4 cup margarine, softened
- 1/3 cup light corn syrup
- 1 teaspoon vanilla
- 1 (16-ounce) package powdered sugar, sifted

- food coloring (optional)
- decorative frostings and/or candies

Mix margarine, corn syrup and vanilla in a large bowl at medium speed. Gradually add half of the sugar, and beat until smooth. Stir in remaining sugar to make a stiff dough. Knead until smooth. Divide dough, and add food coloring as desired. Roll on a surface sprinkled with powdered sugar until 1/8-inch thick. Cut into desired shapes with cookie cutters. Make a hole in tops with a straw, and decorate with frosting and candy. Let stand at least 4 hours, and transfer to wire racks. Let dry for 24 hours. Add ribbons and tie for hanging. Makes 16-24 ornaments depending on size of cookie cutters.

Apple-Cinnamon Christmas Ornaments

Prep Time: 30 minutes

- 1 cup applesauce
- 1 (4.12-ounce) container of ground cinnamon

Mix applesauce and cinnamon until a thick dough forms. Roll out on wax paper to 1/4-inch thick. Cut shapes with cookie cutters. With a straw, make a hole for a ribbon. Let dry on rack for a week to 10 days, flipping often. When dry, tie with ribbon and hang.

Bath Salts

- 1 cup epsom salt
- 1/2 teaspoon food coloring
- perfume oil (any scent; optional)

Stir epsom salt, food coloring and perfume oil in large bowl. Store in a jar or plastic bag. Use a handful in your next bath. Layer several colors in a clear container. Makes a wonderful gift.

Soap Crayons

- 2 Tablespoons water
- soap flakes (approximately 1 cup)
- food coloring

Pour water into 1-cup measuring cup. Finish filling cup with soap flakes. Mix water and soap flakes together with a spoon until mixture becomes thick, soapy paste without any big lumps. Add about 30-40 drops of food coloring, and stir well until soap mixture has color. Spoon into cube space of an ice-cube tray, and press down until cube space is full. Continue filling tray until all soap mixture is used. Dry cubes in a warm, dry place for 1-2 days until soap paste gets hard. Soap crayons will pop out of tray. Great bath fun!

Note: If you can't find soap flakes in the store, you can grate a bar of soap in a food processor or on a hand grater. (Soap flakes are used in this recipe and the two following recipes.)

Clean-As-You-Go Fingerpaint

Prep Time: 5 minutes

- 1 cup soap flakes
- 1/2 cup water

Beat soap flakes and water on high speed for one minute or until fluffy. Fingerpaint on formica counter top, in the sink or all around the tub.

Fingerpaint

Prep Time: 15 minutes

- 1 Tablespoon cornstarch
- 1 Tablespoon soap flakes
- 4 Tablespoons water
- 1 teaspoon hand lotion (Fruit scent is a nice touch.)
- 10 drops of food coloring (Example: Use 5 drops of yellow and 5 drops of red if you want to make your fingerpaint orange.)

Heat cornstarch, soap flakes and water in small saucepan, stirring constantly. When mixture thickens and becomes foamy, remove from heat. Stir in hand lotion and food coloring. Store in a container with a tight-fitting lid or in a small, pump-topped container for easy use. Paint will remain fresh for months.

The Big Orange Splot

by Daniel Manus Pinkwater

READ THE BOOK THEN LET'S COOK!

Juli Moseley
Julia Moulder
Ginny Muetzel
Mary Lynne Mullins
Stacy Mummert
Kathy Munsey
Amy Murray
Faye Murray
Connie Myers
Sharon Nahon
Margot Neale
Marcia Nelson
Sara Newton
Carla Nibert
Clare Nixon
Cynthia Nixon
Carol Lynn Noble
Andrea Norton
Ruth Norton
Carolyn Nunn
Kathy Nunn
Lou Ann Nye
Pam O'Reilly
Lisa Officer
Fay Ollis
Judy Ollis
Karen E. Ollis
Teresa A. Ollis
Nancy Onstot
Dena Oscar
Sara Owen
Ann Owens
Peggy Owens
DiDi Park
Dianna Parker
Jane Parker
Jackie Parthe
Phyllis Patterson
Nancy Paul
Judith Payton
Peggy Pearl
Cindy Pearson
Debbie Jean Penn

Lee Penninger
Jennifer W. Penny
Vickie Peterson
Becky Petteway
Alison Pettit
Sue Phillips
Martha J. Pickering
Teresa Pierpont
Tracy Pigott
Angie Pinegar
Carol Pinegar
Sandy Pinkerton
Laurie Pokorny
Cathy Potts
Cathy Powell
Harriet Powell
Judi A. Powell
Susan Powell
Marie Prater
Patty Preston
Kathy Price
Barbara L. Pruett
Dee Putnam
Josie Raborar
Amy Raff
Beth Raidel
Linda Rankin
Darlene W. Rea
Jeanne Redfern
Pris Reed
Kim Reese
Lisa Revelle
Jill Reynolds
Teet Reynolds
Mary Rhodes
Elizabeth Rice
Karen Rice
Lisa Rice
Phoebe Rice
Mary Ann Ringenberg
Bev Roberts
Jeanne B. Roberts
Carol J. Robinson

Linda Rogers
Theresa Rogers
Rosalie Roper
Mary Kay Ross
Ann Rossiter
Sandy Russell
Holly A. Ryan
Gaylene Rykowski
Abba Salisbury
Anne Sallee-Mason
Erin Sanders
Lynelle Sanders
Katie Sapp
Peggy A. Sauer
Heather Jane Schaefer
Sally Scheid
Jane Schneider
Kristin Schneider
Teresa Schwab
Deb Scott
Pamela Scott-Garton
Bonnie M. Shackter
Karen E. Shannon
Cynthia Sharp
Kathy Sheppard
Jacquie Sherman
Yoko Shimoda-Williams
Julie Shipley-Hoos
Shanne Shipman
Julie Short
Crista Shuler
Jo Ellen Simkins
Judy Sipe
Juliann Slone
Kelly Smalling
Ali Smith
Carla Smith
Deanie Smith
Donna Ann Smith
Henley Smith
Kathy Smith
Mary Lilly Smith
Debbie Snellen

Nancy Southworth
Mary Jane Sponenberg
Bobbi Springer
Sharill Springston
Chris Squibb
Amy Squires
Anna Squires
Julie Squires
Katie Squires
Kelly Squires
Neanie Squires
Patty Squires
Mary Nell Stamatis
Jobeth E. Stanton
Sherry Stark
Kathy Steinberg
Beverly Stenger
Lezah Stenger
Diane L. Stephens
Krissie Stewart
Sara Still
Tina Stillwell
Debbi Stinnett
Kristin Stock
Wendy Stone
Jane Straus
Janet Strube
Leslie Sullivan
Shannon Swanson
Karen Sweeney
Barbara Sweet
Terry Tacke
Becky Taggart
Lisa A. Tait
Lisa Tanner
Teresa Tarrasch
Maura Taylor
Stacey Taylor
Lori Tedrick
Angela Teters
Nancy L. Teters
Linda K. Thomas
Lora Thomas

Donna E. Thompson
Joanie Thompson
Bettie Tipsword
Jeanne Toombs
Sara Toombs
Valerie Toombs
Mary Lou Toth
Cathy Tracy
Dottie Trau
Joni Tregnago
Heather Trinca
Tammy Tumy
Ann Turner
Connie Tyndall
Katy Tynes
Pam Tynes
Mary Vanderhoff
Karen VanHooser
Letty Van-Kleeck
Cathy VanLanduyt
Cathy Vaughn-Tracy
Ann L. Vincel
April L. Vincel
Angie Vincent
Ann Vogel
Susan Von Willer
Becky Voss
Christina J. Waggoner
Mary Waggoner
Cindy Waites
Linda L. Walker
Mary Walker
Pat Walker
Sandy Walker
Sharman Walker
Pat Wallis
Virginia Walsh
Debbie Walter
Vickie Wand
Sally Wantuck
Cynthia Watkins
Jean Watson
Susan Waxman

Stacy Webb
Janet Weber
Annie Webster
Julie Webster
Erica Weingarten
Marcie Wentzel
Terri West
Diane Westbrooke
Sheri Weter
Louise Whall
Dara White
Nancy White
Terry White
Charlene Whitlock
Jackie Whitlock
Kay Whitlock
Barb Williams
Sally Williams
Shirley Williams
Shirley J. Williams
Carol L. Williamson
Beth Wilson
Janice Wilson
Betsy Wise
Louise Ann Wissbaum
Vicki Wong
Elaine Wooddell
Ann Woody
Terri Woody
Rosalie Wooten
Barbara Wright
Barbara T. Wright
Martha H. Wright
Wendy Wright
Courtney Wymore
Cindy Wyrsch
Doris A. Wyrsch
Sandie Yaktine
Jennifer A. Yarbrough
Anita Young
Beverly Young
Amy Zabek
Pat Haas, Secretary
Cathy Leiboult, Exec. Administrator

INDEX

On A Healthy Note

The Nutrition Center at St. John's is proud to be a part of *Women Who Can Dish It Out*. Registered Dieticians at the Nutrition Center have completed nutrition analysis for each recipe and have worked with the Junior League of Springfield to modify recipes so they are delicious and healthy.

I know you will use *Women Who Can Dish It Out* simply for the wonderful recipes. The great thing is that you and your family will be eating healthy, and no one will ever know it.

Lynn Langenberg, R.D.
Director, The Nutrition Center at St. John's

JUNIOR LEAGUE of
SPRINGFIELD, MO

2574 E. Bennett
Springfield, MO
65804

Phone Orders:
417-887-9422
or
Fax Orders:
417-887-7705

Please Ship To:

Name:

Street Address:

City / State / Zip:

Daytime Phone:

Please Circle Payment Form: *Charge To:*

Check / Money Order / Credit Card   MC / Visa

Account Number: Expiration Date: /   /

Name As It Appears On Card:

Signature:

Cookbook:	Qty:	Total:
Sassafras!: $17.95 each		
Women Who Can Dish It Out: $19.95 each		
Subtotal:		
Shipping & Handling: $3.95 each		
Gift Wrap: $1.50 Each		
Total Amount		

Make Checks Payable To:
JLS Cookbooks

JUNIOR LEAGUE of
SPRINGFIELD, MO

2574 E. Bennett
Springfield, MO
65804

Phone Orders:
417-887-9422
or
Fax Orders:
417-887-7705

Please Ship To:

Name:

Street Address:

City / State / Zip:

Daytime Phone:

Please Circle Payment Form: *Charge To:*

Check / Money Order / Credit Card   MC / Visa

Account Number: Expiration Date: /   /

Name As It Appears On Card:

Signature:

Cookbook:	Qty:	Total:
Sassafras!: $17.95 each		
Women Who Can Dish It Out: $19.95 each		
Subtotal:		
Shipping & Handling: $3.95 each		
Gift Wrap: $1.50 Each		
Total Amount		

Make Checks Payable To:
JLS Cookbooks

JUNIOR LEAGUE of
SPRINGFIELD, MO

2574 E. Bennett
Springfield, MO
65804

Phone Orders:
417-887-9422
or
Fax Orders:
417-887-7705

Please Ship To:

Name:

Street Address:

City / State / Zip:

Daytime Phone:

Please Circle Payment Form: *Charge To:*

Check / Money Order / Credit Card   MC / Visa

Account Number: Expiration Date: /   /

Name As It Appears On Card:

Signature:

Cookbook:	Qty:	Total:
Sassafras!: $17.95 each		
Women Who Can Dish It Out: $19.95 each		
Subtotal:		
Shipping & Handling: $3.95 each		
Gift Wrap: $1.50 Each		
Total Amount		

Make Checks Payable To:
JLS Cookbooks

JUNIOR LEAGUE *of*
SPRINGFIELD, MO

2574 E. Bennet
Springfield, MO
65804

JUNIOR LEAGUE *of*
SPRINGFIELD, MO

2574 E. Bennet
Springfield, MO
65804

JUNIOR LEAGUE *of*
SPRINGFIELD, MO

2574 E. Bennet
Springfield, MO
65804